STRATEGIES FOR COMMUNITY POLICING

Elizabeth M. Watson

Former Chief of Police,
Austin and Houston, Texas

Alfred R. Stone

Texas Dept. of Public Safety (Retired)

Stuart M. DeLuca

Library of Congress Cataloging-in-Publication Data

Watson, Elizabeth M.,
    Strategies for community policing / Elizabeth M. Watson, Alfred R. Stone, Stuart M. DeLuca.
        p.   cm.
    Includes bibliographical references and index.
    ISBN 0-13-441197-8
    1. Police—United States.   2. Community policing—United States. I. Stone, Alfred R.
II. Deluca, Stuart M.   III. Title
HV8141.W37   1998
363.2'0973—dc21   97-25534
                                                                          CIP

Acquisitions Editor: *Neil Marquardt*
Production Editor and Interior Designer: *Robin J. Lucas*
Managing Editor: *Mary Carnis*
Director of Manufacturing and Production: *Bruce Johnson*
Manufacturing Buyer: *Ed O'Dougherty*
Editorial Assistant: *Jean Auman*
Marketing Manager: *Frank Mortimer, Jr.*
Formatting/page make-up: *Robin J. Lucas*
Printer/Binder: *R. R. Donnelley & Sons, Harrisonburg, VA*
Cover Design: *Miguel Ortiz*

©1998 by Prentice-Hall, Inc.
Simon & Schuster / A Viacom Company
Upper Saddle River, New Jersey 07458

Printed in the United States of America

10   9   8   7   6   5   4   3   2   1

ISBN 0-13-441197-8

Prentice-Hall International (UK) Limited, *London*
Prentice-Hall of Australia Pty. Limited, *Sydney*
Prentice-Hall Canada Inc., *Toronto*
Prentice-Hall Hispanoamericana, S.A., *Mexico*
Prentice-Hall of India Private Limited, *New Delhi*
Prentice-Hall of Japan, Inc., *Tokyo*
Simon & Schuster Asia Pte. Ltd., *Singapore*
Editora Prentice-Hall do Brasil, Ltda., *Rio de Janeiro*

We are especially grateful to Dana C. DeWitt, Chadron State College; John Riley, University of Maine at Presque Isle; and Richard H. Martin, Elgin Community College, who reviewed the manuscript at various stages, and whose many helpful comments and criticisms have informed our efforts. We also wish to thank Robin Baliszewski and Neil Marquardt, our editors at Prentice Hall, for their relentless encouragement.

Elizabeth M. Watson
Alfred R. Stone
Stuart M. DeLuca
Austin, Texas

That the whole should protect all of its parts, and that each part should pay obedience to the will of the whole: or in other words, that the community should guard the rights of each individual member and that (in return for this protection) each individual should submit to the laws of the community; without which submission of all it was impossible that protection could be extended to any.

—William Blackstone,
Commentary on Common Law,
explaining the origins of laws

CONTENTS

PREFACE   **vii**

CHAPTER 1 BEGINNING AT THE BEGINNING   **1**

What Laws Are Made Of   1

Agreeing to be Social   3

Who Makes the Laws   4

Law Enforcers   8

Forces for Change   18

Reinventing Policing   25

American Law Enforcement Today   29

**CHAPTER 2 DEFINING COMMUNITY
AND COMMUNITY POLICING**   **35**

Community as a Place   35

What Communities Do   38

Crime and Community   43

Histories in Concrete   44

"New and Improved"?   47

Myths and Misconceptions
About Community Policing   54

CHAPTER 3 UNDERSTANDING COMMUNITY NEEDS   **61**

Police Services   62

Order Maintenance   64

Community and Neighborhood Characteristics   66
Giving the Customers What They Want   73

CHAPTER 4   DEVELOPING A PLAN   **82**
Dealing with Change   82
Analyzing and Interpreting the Assessment   85
Making a Statement   88
Establishing Priorities   91
Setting Goals and Objectives   95
Going Public   97

CHAPTER 5   MANAGING CHANGE: STRUCTURES AND SYSTEMS   **100**
Aligning the Organization and Its Goals   100
Organization and Community   104
Case in Point: Austin   110
Making the System Work   112

CHAPTER 6   MANAGING CHANGE: HUMAN RESOURCES   **119**
Obstacles, Roadblocks, and Brick Walls   119
Roles and Jobs   122
Some Implications   125
Leadership and Discipline   134

**CHAPTER 7   ADDRESSING THE ISSUES: THE QUALITY
OF COMMUNITY LIFE**   **140**
The Quality of Life   141
Managing Neighborhoods   141
Establishing Community Knowledge   142
Neighborhood-Oriented Patrol   145
Crime-Reduction Strategies   147
Developing Police-Community Partnerships   151
Sharing Information   157

**CHAPTER 8   EVALUATING COMMUNITY POLICING
IMPLEMENTATIONS**   **161**
Evaluating Community Policing   161
Criteria for Evaluating a Community Policing Agency   163
Evaluating Agency Performance   167
Indirect Methods of Evaluation   172

Bibliography   178
Index   181

PREFACE

The good of the people is the chief law.
—Cicero, De Legibus, III

Once upon a time, everyone knew what police were for. They kept watch over the people in their assigned neighborhood; if they saw something suspicious, or someone misbehaving, they stepped in to preserve order, keep the peace, and uphold the law.

That was a long, long time ago.

More than a century ago, ideas about what the police were for began to change. In particular, the experts on law enforcement persuaded the public that the police needed to be technicians and specialists, highly trained and disciplined. In a word, the police needed to become "professionals" whose goal was to prevent crime through the application of scientific methods, applied objectively and dispassionately.

Police historian Samuel Walker wrote in the mid-1970s,

> The history of the police . . . becomes intelligible when we think of it in terms of its halting progress along the scale of professionalism.[*]

Ironically, even as Walker wrote those words, the entire concept of professionalism in law enforcement was being challenged. The tumultuous decade of the 1960s, ten years of civil demonstrations, assassinations, and riots, had brought the performance of the American

---

[*]Samuel Walker, *A Critical History of Police Reform* (Lexington, Mass.: Lexington Books, 1977), p. 4.

police into serious question. At the same time, new ideas were being generated about what the police are for. These new ideas came to be collected under the general heading of *community policing*.

There are hardly any two people in American law enforcement, much less among the public, who can agree on a precise definition of community policing. This in itself is not surprising: There was never any universal consensus on precisely what "police professionalism" meant, either. Nevertheless, the very idea of community policing seems to have broad popular appeal, and thus it has come to be embraced by an entire generation of police administrators—even those who are skeptical or downright critical of what they perceive to be its main features.

It is particularly important to understand that community policing is, by its very nature, a continual "work in progress." One of the core ideas of community policing is that the practices and techniques of law enforcement must be subject to continuous criticism and improvement. There should never be a day when everyone says, "Okay, this is community policing, now and forevermore."

The lead co-author of this book, Elizabeth Watson, never expected to be caught up in some sort of reform movement when she became a cop in Houston in 1972. Over a period of fifteen years, she rose through the ranks in a career that was distinguished but not unlike that of many other outstanding officers.

In 1987, a new chief of police, Lee P. Brown, appointed her to the position of deputy chief in charge of the West Patrol Bureau, serving one fourth of the city. At the time, the Houston Police Department generally was regarded as staunchly traditional.

Brown brought to Houston his own ideas about what the police are for. Those ideas—combined with ideas from within the department and from the community at large—came to be called Neighborhood Oriented Policing, a variant of community policing. The southwest quadrant of the city, Deputy Chief Watson's command, was selected as the test bed for this new concept.

In 1990, Brown abruptly left Houston and Elizabeth Watson was selected by the mayor to head the police department. Two years later, the mayor was defeated for reelection in a bitter campaign. Chief Watson was replaced. A few months later, she was offered the position of chief of police in Austin, a city about one-third the size of Houston and with a somewhat less volatile political climate.

In coming to Austin, Chief Watson brought not only the concept of community policing but also the extraordinary experience she had gained in Houston. She has become one of the nation's best known authorities, a frequent speaker at seminars and conferences on the development of community-oriented law enforcement, and a contributor to numerous journals and symposia. This book is based to a great extent on her personal experiences and observations. Most of this material appears for the first time in this book; it has not been published elsewhere.

In January 1997, just as this book was going into production, Ms. Watson resigned from the position of chief of police in order to devote full time to the development of leadership training programs and materials for community policing.

Of course, we have not ignored the great quantity of information that has been published in journals, books, monographs, research reports, and elsewhere. The sources we cite in the text should not be taken as exhaustive, but rather as a sampling of the material we found most useful. The Selected bibliography at the end of the text represents a broader survey of the literature for those who wish to pursue specific topics.

This book is intended first of all for students of law enforcement, to provide them with some insight into the current thinking about community policing; second, for police administrators and municipal officials who are contemplating, or have already begun, the challenging task of implementing community policing in an existing police department; and third, for all interested citizens who have seen or heard the term and want to know what all the fuss is about.

We begin with a chapter of general background on the origins of American law enforcement and its evolution up to the recent past. Much of this material should be very familiar to students, but perhaps less so to the general reader. In either case, we have approached the history of American law enforcement from a particular perspective. Our intention is to demonstrate that the core concept of community policing—a working partnership between the professional police agency and the citizenry—has always been implicit in the American approach to criminal justice. In some sense, community policing is not a revolutionary new idea at all; it is a return to a tradition that was inadvertently submerged in the laudable effort to instill a high standard of professionalism.

In Chapter 2, we offer our own definitions of two critical terms: community and community policing. Even a cursory review of the police literature of the past two decades indicates a surprising degree of confusion and ambiguity over these terms. Our definition of community goes well beyond the simple identification of a group of people with a certain geographic area. We bring into the discussion some of the ideas and insights of sociologists and political scientists whose studies of communities ought to be more familiar to law enforcement personnel than they are. We conclude the chapter with our working definition of community policing, and a cautionary note about some of the misconceptions that have arisen about this approach to law enforcement.

In Chapter 3, we begin to establish a working model of community policing and of the process by which it can be established in a police agency. We start by considering what precisely is meant by "police services," how different communities value those services, and how the characteristics of different communities impact the ability of the police to deliver various services. Next we propose specific steps that can be taken by a police executive to establish a baseline of information, an assessment of what his or her clientele expects and wants from the police agency.

From Chapter 4 onward, we assume that what the community wants is, to some degree, what we mean by community policing, and that the police executive is committed to the implementation of community policing in an established, presumably traditional police agency. We examine the steps that must be taken in preparation for what is likely to be a difficult transition.

Chapter 5 presents the first tangible steps in that transition: redefining the expectations of agency personnel at every level, from rookie officer to top-level administrator. We consider the impact that the transformation process must have on training, on management, on the maintenance of discipline, and on the agency's relationship with the community as a whole.

Chapter 6 focuses on some of the structural and organizational issues that are implicit in community policing. We discuss methods of managing the police service workload so that public expectations of police service are not compromised. We also consider the effects of community policing on the internal structure of a police agency and the relationships (both formal and informal) among the various elements of a traditional department.

Chapter 7 turns our attention to the police-community relationship, which is ultimately the axis around which community policing revolves. We offer specific methods to broaden and deepen the base of community knowledge within the police ranks, to attack the particular problems of crime and disorder that most concern the community, and to develop a continuing partnership between the police and the people they serve.

Finally, in Chapter 8, we consider both the need and the difficulty in evaluating a community-oriented police agency. We review both the methods that can be used to evaluate a police department and the criteria that, we propose, ought to be used in a department that claims to adhere to the community policing philosophy.

Elizabeth M. Watson
Alfred R. Stone
Stuart M. DeLuca
Austin, Texas

CHAPTER 1

BEGINNING AT THE BEGINNING

WHAT LAWS ARE MADE OF

Laws are the formal expression of the collective judgment of a society as to the acceptable behavior of its members.

Philosophers, political scientists, sociologists, and social psychologists (among others) have offered numerous theories about how laws are generated and what purposes they serve. We do not intend to review all those theories, much less attempt to determine which of them may be valid and useful. For our purposes, the definition given above—admittedly rough and imprecise—is sufficient.

From our point of view, the most significant fact about laws is that they represent, however imperfectly, the collective judgment of a group of people. Even though a law may be promulgated by an autocratic king or emperor, history shows that unpopular laws—those that fail to reflect the people's consensus—quickly become unenforceable, and may lead to the removal of the tyrant from his or her throne.

The conventional wisdom in American law enforcement has been that police officers, and even administrators, should not be overly concerned with the origins and content of the laws. Their duty is to enforce whatever laws are promulgated by the appropriate legislative body. If their opinions are asked in advance, they are free to comment; otherwise, where laws come from and why should not be their concern.

Community policing does not diminish the duty of the police to enforce the law. However, if police officers are to become partners with the community in maintaining social order, we think that they need to have a deeper understanding of the nature and sources of laws.

So Many Laws, So Little Time

Some 3,500 years ago, King Hammurabi of Babylonia ordered a stone pillar to be inscribed with all of the laws of his empire. The pillar was placed in the courtyard outside his palace, so that his subjects would know what was required and what was prohibited.

Hammurabi's law consisted of twenty-eight paragraphs, each of which concerned several specific issues. There was no provision for enforcement by a police agency. A citizen who claimed to be the victim of a violation of the law was expected to bring the offender to court. The role of the court, then, was to mediate between the accuser and the accused.[1]

One Hundred and Five Offenses

More than 3,000 years later, the Common Council of New York City appointed a committee to investigate the city's law enforcement system. The committee submitted its report in 1844. One of the committee's complaints was that there were too many laws for the police to enforce.

The committee's report obligingly contains a list of all of the criminal laws of New York State at the time. There are approximately 105 offenses in the list. Most of them are familiar: murder and arson were capital offenses. So was treason. "Compulsory marriage" was a felony. Three degrees of burglary and four degrees of forgery were specified. Dueling was a felony if fought to the death. Apparently, dueling was not an offense if no one was killed.

According to the report, New York City at the time had "two principal Departments of Criminal Police and Health Police [sic]; the object of the former, being to prevent, detect, arrest, and punish crime; that of the latter, to preserve the public health. . . ."[2]

The report also describes in detail the organization of the criminal police. The mayor and the sheriff, both of whom were elected, were responsible for supervising an unspecified number of marshals, who also were individually elected. The sheriff had fourteen deputies, most of whom were assigned as jailers. Thirty-four constables were individually elected but were nominally under the authority of the mayor. The mayor also hired and supervised a night watch of some 1,100 men, a day watch of 16 men, a Sunday watch of approximately 110 men, and 12 dock masters.[3]

The committee proposed to replace this organizational mess with a united, streamlined force of police officers "in due subordination to each other"[4] along the general lines of the London Metropolitan Police, which had been reorganized in 1829 by Sir Robert Peel, the Home Secretary.[5]

The New York City version of Peel's system involved combining the three watches, the marshals, and the constables into a single police force under the supervision of a commissioner. Police officers would be assigned to patrol the streets, prevent crime, and arrest offenders on sight. They would be divided into a number of precincts, each of which would be under the command of a captain, who was given the authority to hire patrol officers.[6] A separate Detective Division was not added until 1857.[7]

Implementation began in 1845. New York thus became the first large American city to adopt a modified form of the Peel system, which quickly became the standard of police organization and administration in this country. However, nothing was done to reduce the number of laws that the police were expected to enforce.

The Texas criminal code listed more than six hundred separate offenses (not including traffic laws or other regulatory laws) before the state legislature enacted a new criminal code in 1995. Now the code contains only about five hundred offenses. Dueling is not among them, but computer crime is.[8]

The New York City Council committee was neither the first nor the last to complain that there are too many laws. Yet the number of criminal offenses continues to grow. Why are there so many laws?

The short answer is that *the people make the laws; the legislature merely writes them down*. For a more complete answer, we must look to the social scientists.

AGREEING TO BE SOCIAL

In 1690, the English philosopher, John Locke, published an essay, *The Second Treatise of Civil Government*. According to Locke, in ancient times humans lived in a "state of nature," in splendid isolation, proud, independent, and free of restraint. The only "laws" were those of nature itself. Unfortunately, this way of life imposed various rigors and dangers. People came to realize that they could reduce some of the disadvantages of their natural way of life by forming cooperative social groups. In time, people organized governments to regulate these social groups. By implication, then, people gave up some of their autonomy and freedom, in exchange for the protection and other benefits that society offered.

This theory was further elaborated by a French musician, novelist, and sometime philosopher, Jean Jacques Rousseau, in his essay, *The Social Contract*, published in 1762.[9]

Rousseau's vision of a social contract merged with Locke's idea of a *limited* grant of power from individuals to their social group. These ideas permeate the *Declaration of Independence* ("We hold these truths to be self-evident, that all men are...endowed by their Creator with certain unalienable Rights....That to secure these rights, Governments are instituted among Men, deriving their just powers from the consent of the governed . . .") and the *Constitution of the United States* ("We the People of the United States . . . do ordain and establish this Constitution . . ."), as well as the writings of the Founding Fathers.

Laws, according to this perspective, are simply the tangible and explicit expression of the agreements that people make by joining in the social contract.

But that still does not answer the question: Why are there so darned *many* of them?

Norms, Morals, and Laws

What is crime? "[C]rime is a *legal* concept: what makes some conduct criminal, and other conduct not, is the fact that some, but not others, are 'against the law.'"[10]

In any small, *homogeneous* social group (that is, one in which all the members are similar in background and social characteristics), usually it is not difficult to obtain agreement about what kinds of behavior are acceptable. Behaviors that the members consider favorable to the group's success (or mere survival) are encouraged, mostly through informal rewards such as praise; behaviors that the members consider unfavorable or threatening are discouraged, again through informal punishments such as criticism. As long as the members feel a strong commitment to the group, such *sanctions* (rewards and punishments) are sufficient to enforce the group's norms.[11]

The system of required and prohibited behaviors, with associated sanctions, comprise a social group's *mores*: the code, mostly implicit, that defines moral behavior.

Mores tend to become more explicit as a society becomes larger and *heterogeneous* (that is, composed of diverse people with varying backgrounds and characteristics). Behaviors that are either required or prohibited are specified, and so are the sanctions associated with these laws.[12]

That is why Hammurabi "published" his code of laws. He had conquered an empire similar in size and shape to that of California, containing a dozen or so cities (each with a population of a few thousand) and numerous villages. It was a population made up of many small tribes, varying in ethnicity and culture. Governing this motley collection of humanity required the establishment of some uniform standard of behavior: what was acceptable and what was not, what was required and what was prohibited, and what would happen to those who violated the standard.

People's ideas about what is acceptable and unacceptable behavior change, and laws must accommodate those changes (though usually with some lag). Blasphemy and heresy were capital offenses in some of the American colonies in the late seventeenth and early eighteenth centuries.[13] Neither offense is included in the 1844 list of New York criminal statutes. We could cite countless similar instances of laws that were rigidly enforced at one time, but gradually faded away into nonenforcement and, eventually, repeal. We could also cite any number of criminal laws currently on the books that did not exist as recently as a generation ago.

Laws change not only because people change their minds but also because social conditions change. One would hardly expect to find ordinances to regulate automobile traffic in, say, 1850: The automobile had not yet been invented. In fact, most cities and states did not begin to enact traffic laws until the early part of the twentieth century, when automobiles not only existed but were rapidly becoming a major hazard to public health and safety.

WHO MAKES THE LAWS

Laws generally become more explicit and more rigid as a society becomes larger and more complex; that is, as an increasingly heterogeneous population cannot agree on what standards of behavior should be observed. Increasingly, the standard embodied in the law becomes the behaviors that are accepted by the dominant members of a society, the people who, through their economic, social, and political power, control the lawmaking process.[14]

What, then, becomes of Locke's idea, expressed in the *Declaration of Independence* as the "consent of the governed"?

Of course, those who disagree with their government or its policies may be able to bring about change through political activity of one sort or another. Citizens who do not necessarily agree with everything their government does may still "consent" to the authority of their government. But neither Rousseau nor Locke offered a convincing solution to the citizen who, for whatever reasons, decides *not* to consent to his or her government.

Dissent of the Governed

History shows that people who do not consent to their government have three choices: to submit, to rebel, or to leave. History also shows that all three choices involve considerable cost to individuals. Submission may mean giving up personal freedom; in extreme cases, it can mean sacrificing one's life. But rebellion and flight often involve such extraordinary costs—including the lives of the rebels or "departers"—that these solutions are sought only in extreme desperation.

If, as we said earlier, "people make the laws, the legislature merely writes them down," it is also evident that *people make laws for other people to obey*. This tendency can be observed even in small social groups; it seems to be a feature of human nature. Most people consider their own behavior beyond reproach, but the behavior of others could stand improvement.[15]

The city of San Francisco enacted an ordinance in 1876 that prohibited the operation of a laundry in a wooden building except with the approval of the Board of Supervisors (the city's governing agency, roughly equivalent to a city council). Laundries operating in a brick or stone building, which were extremely rare, were exempt. Over the following decade, the supervisors approved only a few laundries in wooden buildings; all were owned by Caucasians. Finally, in 1886, a Chinese laundry operator persuaded the U.S. Supreme Court that the ordinance was unconstitutional because it denied Chinese equal protection. Of course, that was indeed the intent of the law: to drive Chinese launderers out of business.[16] The laundry ordinance was one of several enacted in San Francisco, Oakland, and other California cities to "control" the Chinese population, which had come to be a despised minority.

Laws aimed at "those people" are not always as subtle as the laundry ordinance. In the southern states, after the Civil War, laws were enacted to keep the newly freed slave population "in their place." The underlying premise of these laws was endorsed by the U.S. Supreme Court in 1890, in *Plessy v. Ferguson*, which concerned a Louisiana statute requiring railway carriages to be segregated. The Court found that there was nothing unconstitutional about state laws requiring "equal but separate" public accommodations.[17] Later, this notorious phrase was reversed to "separate but equal."

After 1890, the southern states freely enacted scores of "Jim Crow laws" that did not begin to be discarded until the 1950s, after the landmark decision in *Brown v. Board of Education*, in which the Supreme Court decided in 1954 that the segregated schools of Topeka, Kansas, were "inherently unequal."[18]

If it is "only natural" for people to make laws that other people are expected to obey, it is just as natural for the targets of those laws to feel oppressed and resentful. If it is also true that laws are made by the dominant element in society, then several consequences are likely to follow. In no particular order, some of these consequences are:

- Most laws, especially criminal laws, are intended to apply primarily to minority groups* in the population.
- Unless there is one large group that is completely dominant, there will be continual competition among the various groups for dominance.
- Groups that have little chance of gaining dominance, because of their size or lack of economic or political power, may become increasingly alienated; they are likely to feel little reason to support the larger society that oppresses them.

In short, groups that feel oppressed and alienated may "opt out" of the social contract in whatever ways they can.[19] Open rebellion is only a last resort. Covert rebellion, such as flouting the law, is, at least in the short run and for some individuals, a safer and more profitable outlet for rebellion.

We must point out that alienation and rebellion are not inevitable. Whether a particular group is "oppressed" and is justified in being alienated or in dissenting depends as much on the *perception* of the group's members as it does on its objective relationship to the dominant element of society.

We can see some of these processes at work in the history of American law enforcement.

Rebellion I: The Workers

Throughout the nineteenth century, the production of manufactured goods shifted from small craft shops to factories owned by wealthy stockholders who took no direct part in management. The managers, hired by the stockholders, were under great pressure to hire labor as cheaply as possible and drive the workers to produce as much as possible. The result was some of the most appalling work environments imaginable.

By 1820, several American guilds had become trade unions, associations of workers who demanded the right to negotiate collectively with their employers over wages and working conditions. The factory managers and their bosses, the investors, perhaps understandably took a dim view of these developments. They persuaded state legislatures to enact laws prohibiting "conspiracy to raise wages."

In 1842, a Massachusetts court decided that such laws were unconstitutional, and that workers could organize strikes and use other bargaining tactics. The decision was not legally binding on other states, but it did encourage unionists to continue organizing.

The response of legislatures was to outlaw the unions altogether, and to enact laws prohibiting strikes as a disruption of commerce. Many of these laws enjoyed widespread support not only among the capitalists and their hired managers but also among the middle-class public who valued an orderly society of respectable citizens, not the violent behavior of vulgar mobs.

After the Civil War, in city after city, union efforts to pressure management into collective bargaining ended in strikes. Since strikes were illegal in most states, the

---

*Let us be very clear here. In this discussion, "minority group" does not necessarily mean the particular ethnic or "racial" groups that are usually identified as "minorities," such as African-Americans or Hispanic Americans. Rather, we mean any identifiable group that is not dominant, that does not have sufficient power to make and enforce rules for others to follow.

police were called upon to arrest the striking workers. The predictable result was a riot, which did little to endear the unionists to the larger public.[20]

One response of the unions was to seek redress of their grievances through the political process. Workers, after all, usually could vote, and there were potentially more voters among the working classes than among the propertied class. Union leaders encouraged their members to register and urged them to vote for friendly candidates. Illinois' legislature responded in 1893 by enacting a law protecting the right of workers to form unions.[21] Similar laws were passed in other states that had large numbers of industrial workers, between 1890 and 1920. In 1917, the federal government finally recognized the legitimacy of the union movement; Congress approved the establishment of a Department of Labor in the administration.

For more than a century, industrial workers had sought the right to join organizations to negotiate with their employers. The employers had used their power to influence legislators to discourage the workers' efforts. The workers, in turn, had ignored and violated the laws that were intended to keep them at an economic disadvantage. Eventually, the workers achieved a sufficient level of political power themselves that they could overturn the unfavorable laws and enact new laws, protecting their right to organize and, in a series of federal and state laws passed between 1915 and 1930, prohibiting employers from some of the more odious practices of industrial capitalism.

Rebellion II: The Drinkers

Another example: Since colonial days, American society has wrestled with the problem of controlling the use of intoxicating beverages. The mechanization of industry and the rapid growth of the cities in the early nineteenth century made alcohol abuse a growing concern: As Lawrence Friedman puts it, "a drunken farmer was one thing, a drunken factory hand another."[22]

In 1846, Maine enacted a law prohibiting the manufacture, sale, and use of alcoholic beverages. Three other New England states passed similar laws in 1852. Many other states enacted, or reinforced existing laws that stopped short of outright prohibition but regulated the production and consumption of alcohol. Most states had laws making public drunkenness a criminal offense (usually a misdemeanor). Since the development of Peel-style police agencies around mid-century, arrests for drunkenness have outnumbered arrests for all other criminal offenses in the United States—whether or not alcohol was prohibited.

After the Civil War, campaigns against alcohol grew in number, size, and sophistication. A national Prohibition Party was formed in 1869; it still nominates a candidate for president every four years. The Women's Christian Temperance Union was organized in 1874, the Anti-Saloon League in 1895. All three organizations lobbied Congress and state legislatures, with varying effects, to outlaw the use of alcohol. Between 1880 and 1900, prohibition was enacted by four midwestern states. Eight southern states outlawed booze between 1900 and 1915, and were joined by four western states in 1914. Four more states joined the parade in 1916.

Finally, in 1918, Congress passed the Eighteenth Amendment to the Constitution, prohibiting the manufacture and sale of alcoholic beverages in interstate commerce. Three fourths of the states ratified the amendment in 1919, and it went into effect a year later. The Volstead Act of 1919 provided for the enforcement of Prohibition by the federal government. Since the amendment and the law applied only to interstate commerce, supportive state laws were still necessary; such laws were quickly adopted.

Prohibition is generally regarded as the most disastrous social experiment in American history. Not only was the law widely flouted, but the refusal of a large segment of the public to accept Prohibition created an enormous, and enormously profitable, market for organized crime.

One segment of American society, possibly for the best of reasons, succeeded in imposing its will by outlawing the use of alcoholic beverages. Another segment of society, those who wished to drink, responded by ignoring the law. Yet another segment of society responded by organizing the manufacture and distribution of the illegal beverages. The battle among these three segments was not just over alcohol, but over control of the machinery of social order. It was a battle fought not only in the halls of Congress and state capitols, but in the streets and alleys, with bullets and bombs.

In the end, the victor was the segment that simply wanted to drink. In 1933, Congress adopted the Twenty-first Amendment, repealing Prohibition; it was ratified by the states in about ten months. A number of states, mostly in the South and Midwest, continued to prohibit the manufacture and sale of alcoholic beverages within their borders, but most of the states were satisfied with less extreme regulation. Mississippi was the last state to completely abandon prohibition, in 1966.

Once again, we see an issue of social order—this one more clearly connected to questions of morality and acceptable behavior—over which factions of society have battled for decades. It would be misleading to suggest that the changes in the laws are solely due to changes in public attitudes about the abuse of alcohol, or specifically about the complete prohibition of alcohol, although those attitudes undoubtedly have changed over time.

When the Millenium Arrives

Perhaps it is possible to imagine that, sometime in the distant future, American society will become so homogeneous that there is universal agreement on what behaviors are acceptable, which ones are required, and which ones are prohibited. Or, if that is too much to hope for, perhaps the writing of criminal laws will be turned over to some entirely rational, mechanical system, computers with artificial intelligence that is not perturbed by emotion, superstitition, prejudice, ambiguity, or inconsistency.

Until then, we should expect the body of criminal law to remain a patchwork quilt, made up of conflicting values and ideas about social order, sewn together through compromise and sometimes subterfuge, representing at best the implied agreement of those who are most strongly committed to the social contract.[23]

LAW ENFORCERS

The subject of this book is law enforcement, not lawmaking. We have begun by examining how and why criminal laws are made because it seems certain to us that the law enforcers of the future—the very *near* future—will need a much better understanding of these matters than they probably needed in the past. People whose job is to maintain social order in conjunction with the community they serve, rather than to impose social order on the community to which they are assigned, should know what the criminal law means to that community and what part the community has had in making the law.

If American criminal law has changed drastically over the past two hundred years or so, one would expect at least some of those changes to be reflected in the practice of American law enforcement. In fact, the changes in law enforcement have been even more drastic and far-reaching.

Land Without Cops

Two hundred years ago, there simply was no law enforcement in America, at least not anything remotely resembling the police agencies of today.

During the colonial period, the traditional English system of law enforcement was followed.[24] That system consisted principally of three elements: *magistrates*, a *sheriff*, and *constables*. All were local officers, appointed by the local nobleman, and all had various duties that were unrelated to criminal law enforcement (insofar as there was a clear distinction between the criminal law and other types of law). In the British colonies, these officials were appointed by the colonial governor.

The constable's job was to patrol the town, or some portion of it, and maintain public order. Mostly he enforced the law by warning the disreputable, by sending the disorderly home to sober up, and, when necessary, by intervening in a brawl or loud argument.

The magistrate's job was to hear complaints, determine whether the accused was guilty of an offense, and dispense justice. He could perform whatever investigation he felt was warranted, including interrogating suspects or witnesses, or applying the "trials by ordeal" that were popularly considered useful.[25]

Some of the traditional English practices were modified in the colonies, but the basic system remained intact: It was the responsibility of the *victim* of a crime to identify, locate, and (possibly with the help of the constable or sheriff) arrest the offender. Until the middle of the eighteenth century, most of the colonies did not have public prosecutors; the victim presented his or her complaint to the magistrate.

If the accused was not already in custody, the magistrate would send the sheriff or constable to make an arrest. Once the accused was in custody, he or she would be "examined" (that is, interrogated) by the magistrate, who would then decide whether there was sufficient evidence to justify a trial. The trial often was held immediately, or at most within a few days. If a jury was needed, the sheriff rounded up half a dozen or so men who, at least for the moment, were not otherwise occupied. If some of the jurors knew the victim or the defendant, or knew something about the alleged crime, all the better: They could render a verdict based on the truth as they knew it.

Neither the victim nor the accused was entitled to representation by an attorney until the office of district or county attorney was established, around the middle of the eighteenth century in most of the colonies. Even after that, the defendant not only had no legal right to an attorney, but was not permitted to be represented in court (except in capital cases, in some colonies). The magistrate usually set punishment, except that in some colonies the jury decided the penalty in capital cases. Either way, the sentence would be carried out as soon as the trial ended—or, in capital cases, as soon as the gallows could be erected.

After the Revolution

By the time the colonies gained their independence, some aspects of this system already had begun to change. The prosecution of offenders became the duty of a specially appointed officer, usually one trained in the law. The use of juries chosen for their objectivity also became more common, and the role of the magistrate shifted from that of inquisitor to that of impartial judge, at least in the more formal courts where the more serious cases were heard.

Sheriffs and constables continued to be the primary law enforcement officers; both became elective offices in the new republic. In some of the young states, judges were appointed by the legislature or by the governor; in other states, judges were also elected.

In the larger cities, the constables were supplemented by a *night watch*, originally composed of individuals—usually merchants and business owners—who rotated the duty among themselves. When this practice became inconvenient, the merchants and business owners began to hire nightwatchmen, usually unemployed laborers and pensioners. By about 1820, the night watches were taken over by the city government in the larger cities. Some cities added a day watch, usually much smaller than the night watch. The system described to the New York Common Council, in 1844, was broadly typical of what law enforcement existed in most of the larger cities of New England and the Atlantic seaboard, as far south as Charleston. In principle, the sheriff was responsible for law enforcement only outside of the city limits. Within the city, *marshals*, sometimes elected but more often appointed by the mayor, served as another agency of law enforcement.

If this "system" seems hopelessly confused and contradictory, that is exactly the case. The authority to investigate complaints from victims, to arrest accused offenders, to hold the accused in custody, to gather and present evidence in court, and to carry out the court's sentence after a conviction, was fragmented, duplicated, and compromised. It was never clear just who was responsible for what. Most of the actors in this "system" were amateurs; some were unpaid volunteers, others were paid only a pittance. Many were elected or appointed without previous training or any other qualifications. There was little if any provision for management and supervision at any level.[26]

The transition from the colonial system to the beginnings of a professional law enforcement system, early in the nineteenth century, had developed without any rational plan, indeed without any serious thought being given to what was wanted and needed.

In the villages and small towns of colonial America, society was highly homogeneous: Everyone understood, and generally agreed about, what kinds of behavior were acceptable and unacceptable. But as the cities grew larger and more heterogeneous, their populations swollen with new immigrants and displaced farm workers, merely making the system somewhat more formal made matters worse instead of better.[27]

Order in the City

The Peel reforms, which seemed to be very successful in England, promised to bring order and rationality to American law enforcement. The duties of patrol officers (as they were to be called, since the office of constable had a different meaning in New York than it had in London) were to be clearly defined, and they were to be organized and supervised to an unprecedented degree.[28]

No one seems to have recognized that the conditions of society in England and in America had become very different. England remained mostly a very homogeneous society, built on a rigid but stable class structure. Members of the various classes might not agree on what constituted acceptable and unacceptable behavior, but at least they generally kept their unacceptable behaviors to themselves.

America, on the other hand, had rapidly become an extremely heterogeneous society, and an extremely mobile one. Mobility in America meant not only the ability to move about from place to place with few restraints—and that in a country with a practically limitless western frontier—but also the ability to move from class to class. Americans could rise from poverty to wealth, not in a generation but in a year or even a month—and they could go from wealth to poverty just as quickly. Furthermore, the republican and democratic ideals of young America consciously blurred the lines between classes; there was a nearly universal intention to eliminate class distinctions as far as possible.[29]

At least the Peel-style reforms adopted in New York in 1845, and in other American cities over the next two decades, imposed some sort of order on law enforcement. The actual practices of the police were not very different from those of the predecessor day- and nightwatches, except that the city police officer had a specific power of arrest and was expected to use it.

The New York Common Council, in adopting the Peel system, made one fatal error. In Peel's London police, the constables were hired and trained by the central administration; most were young men from rural areas, newly arrived in the city. In New York, the patrol officers were hired by the precinct captains, almost always from the very neighborhoods that they were to patrol.

One might suppose that hiring patrol officers and assigning them to patrol their own neighborhoods could be a very good idea. After all, who would know the community better than someone who had grown up in it, whose family and friends lived in it? Who would know better which of the neighbors were honest, respectable citizens, and which were petty thieves or worse?

The problem, of course, is that enforcing the law with any reasonable degree of equity and objectivity might require an officer to haul his brother or his best friend off to jail. That is a lot to ask of someone who is paid a meager salary to work long hours (patrol officers commonly worked eighteen-hour shifts), with little training and not a great deal of supervision.

But if the patrol officers carried out their duties with a bit of favoritism now and then, that was only to be expected. A far worse problem stemmed from the political structure of the larger American cities in the mid-eighteenth century.

A Spoiled System

That political structure was highly partisan. In each city there were two or more political parties who engaged in biennial wars for control of the city government and the lucrative contracts for road and bridge construction, supplies, and so forth that a growing city needed to award. The parties were virtually identical in organization: a small corps of well-known leading citizens, usually successful businessmen, supported by legions of local functionaries, some full-time and paid, most part-time and unpaid (at least, not paid a legitimate salary). The key functionaries were the ward bosses, one for each precinct; it was their duty to ensure that voters loyal to their party turned out in force at each election.

Loyalty was "earned" by rewards, and one of the easiest rewards to give a loyal follower was a job—for the voter or his ne'er-do-well brother-in-law. One city job that required little in the way of qualifications and that demanded less than most forms of employment was that of police officer.

In short, by the time the Civil War broke out, the law enforcement system in New York and virtually all other larger cities evolved into a "spoils system." The city council and its political leader, the mayor, appointed the precinct captains, who were actually designated by the ward bosses. The precinct captains, in turn, hired the sergeants and patrol officers, each of whom had been approved by the ward boss. Promotions, favorable assignments, and other perquisites were likewise subject to political favoritism. In some cities, a policeman's job could be bought and sold through "campaign contributions" or outright bribes placed with precinct captains or ward bosses. In addition, the police officers naturally were expected to do their utmost to keep their jobs by ensuring that their bosses stayed in office.[30]

Whenever the city government changed hands, one result was the complete replacement of the police personnel. The party assuming power naturally preferred to staff the police department with its own loyal followers.

By the end of the Civil War in 1865, law enforcement in America's small towns and rural areas had changed very little from the system that existed at the beginning of the century. Elected sheriffs and constables, and appointed marshals in most towns, were responsible for arresting lawbreakers and bringing them to court, but usually only when the victim asked for help or public order was disturbed.

In the larger cities, the Peel system was in full flower. In lower-class and working-class neighborhoods, the cop on the beat was almost always a neighbor, someone from the community. The public generally understood that favoritism and politics drove the police department and that, likely as not, most of the cops were willing if not eager to accept bribes and gifts. Nevertheless, an honest citizen who caused no problems had little to fear from the police, and those whose activities skirted the law but did not cause a public scandal could count on the friendly cop to look the other way.

In middle-class neighborhoods, the police in general were regarded with contempt, not just for their corruption but for their ineffectuality. The neighborhood patrol officer in most cases came from another part of town. As long as he made some effort to be helpful and to maintain public order, his presence was welcome.

The police were mostly absent from upper-class neighborhoods, except when they were summoned. When a crime occurred, a servant would be sent to the precinct station to bring the police to the scene. No doubt most wealthy citizens were well aware of the political corruption of the police, but as long as their interests were not affected, they were not concerned.[31]

Making America "Perfect"

America was founded in part by people seeking to escape religious persecution and oppression in Europe. Oddly enough, this historical fact did not mean that Americans were imbued with a deep-seated tolerance for religious diversity. Throughout the nation's history, Americans have struggled with the urge to impose their own religious beliefs on others, especially where those beliefs concern morality.

As we mentioned earlier, heresy and blasphemy were capital offenses in some of the colonies. So were adultery (sexual activity involving a married person and someone other than his or her spouse), fornication (sexual activity between two persons who are not married), and homosexuality.[32] After America gained independence, most of the states enacted new laws to protect public morality. Sexual crimes remained felonies, but no longer were capital offenses. Gambling, prostitution, and public drunkenness were treated as misdemeanors.

By mid-century, some states had reduced the severity of the sexual morality laws even further. Michigan's law in 1846 made fornication an offense if it was carried on "lewdly and lasciviously" or if people behaved in "open and gross lewdness." Similarly, California's penal code of 1872 prohibited adultery only if it was "open and notorious." [33] Increasingly, sexual misbehavior was viewed as a social problem— and thus as a criminal offense—only if it occurred in public, or became so widely known as to constitute a scandal.

In effect, the job of the police (and the rest of the criminal justice system) had been redefined. In colonial days, the law existed to protect people from their own evil behavior. In the nineteenth century, the purpose of the law was to protect the general public from being exposed to the immoral behavior of the few.

Attitudes changed again after the Civil War. The outcome of the war included abolishing the great and terrible evil of slavery; why not finish the job by eliminating all of the evils in American life? As we have already mentioned, groups were organized in the late 1860s to promote temperance and prohibit the use of alcoholic beverages. But alcoholism was not the only evil that became the target of moral crusaders during the postwar period.

For the most part, the laws against private sexual behavior, such as adultery and fornication, remained unchanged; if anything, they were relaxed in some states. The reformers were more concerned with the commercialization of sex. New, stringent laws against prostitution, public lewdness, and obscenity (both in print and in public performances) were passed in many states. Similarly, tough new laws were enacted to suppress gambling and to control the use of certain drugs.[**]

The moral crusaders were well aware that merely passing new laws would make little difference unless the laws were enforced. In fact, in many states the laws already on the books were adequate; it was the lack of vigorous enforcement that permitted prostitutes, gambling books, and burlesque houses to operate openly in many

---

[**]Some of these laws may have had purposes other than protecting public morality. For example, California adopted laws against the possession and sale of opium, but these laws were intended at least partly to "control" the Chinese minority. See Friedman, *Crime and Punishment*, p. 137.

cities. Therefore, concurrently with putting pressure on the legislatures, the moral reformers began pressuring city governments and police officials to "do their duty."

For the police, these new laws created a serious dilemma, especially at the precinct level. Arresting a neighbor for robbing, assaulting, or murdering another neighbor was one thing; at least there was no doubt that the arrest was necessary to preserve an acceptable degree of public order. Arresting a friend or relative for gambling or for indulging in the "pleasures of the flesh" was quite another matter.

Of course, the public morality laws were not aimed at the wealthy, nor at the upper-middle class. The people in those strata of society were perfectly capable of keeping their sins, whatever they might be, from public notice. Nor were the new laws aimed primarily at the middle class, the members of which were, for the most part, deeply concerned with maintaining the appearance of respectability and decency. Rather, the laws were aimed squarely at "those people," the working poor, newcomers with strange accents and even stranger attitudes. In fact, this was the same segment of society that provided most of the rank-and-file police officers.

By the last quarter of the nineteenth century, the police in most of the larger cities had arrived at an arrangement that worked wonderfully well. Instead of enforcing all the new vice laws indiscriminately, they used the laws to *license* crime. For a price, they would do as they had always done: They would look the other way.

Indeed, if the price was high enough, the police would protect the prostitutes, gamblers, liquor dealers, and other petty criminals, not only from the "interference" of arrest and punishment, but also from the more serious forms of mayhem that are invariably associated with illicit behavior. A streetwalker or bookie or heroin seller who made regular payments to the precinct could count on swift and effective help if a customer got rough. On the other hand, failing to make the requisite payment, or carrying on one's illegal business in a way that attracted too much public notice, guaranteed police reprisal.[34]

The extent of police corruption at the end of the nineteenth century is uncertain, since it appears that at least some of the "investigations" that purported to uncover massive corruption were carried out more for political purposes than in an honest effort at reform.[35]

Platform for Reform

Nevertheless, the idea of reform, not just in the police but in all areas of government, had immense popular appeal. The federal government led the way by adopting the *Civil Service Reform Act of 1883*, also known as the Pendleton Act. President Chester A. Arthur, whose support ensured passage of the law by Congress, certainly knew as much as anyone about political corruption: He previously had been the administrator of the spoils system for the Republican Party in New York.

The Pendleton Act established a federal bureaucracy that was supposed to be free of political influence and favoritism. Workers were to be hired on the basis of objective tests of their knowledge and competence (the so-called merit system); they were prohibited from most forms of political activity, except for voting, and were theoretically protected from political interference.

Between 1885 and 1900, virtually all major cities and several states adopted their own versions of the Pendleton Act. By the end of the century, the reformers could claim almost complete victory in eradicating the spoils system. Police chiefs in most of the larger cities and many smaller ones saw the handwriting on the wall; the days of the spoils system were numbered. In 1893, several hundred law enforcement administrators formed the National Police Chiefs Union. It was an unfortunate choice of titles, in an era when the public generally regarded "union" as an epithet; in 1901, the name was changed to the International Association of Chiefs of Police (IACP).[36]

The IACP provided a forum for reform-minded officials. Over a period of several years, the members worked out a common agenda, a definition of the kind of policing they thought America needed. They wanted law enforcement to become a *profession*; they wanted police officers at every level to be individuals of unquestioned integrity and ability; they wanted new recruits to be thoroughly trained before they were given a badge; they wanted policing to be completely insulated from political interference. Corruption would no longer be tolerated.[37]

Another part of the widely accepted definition of "police professionalism" proved to be a source of future problems. As the leadership of the IACP saw it, the primary job of the police was not merely to arrest offenders, but to *prevent crime* by patrolling. Thus, in a sense, arresting a criminal represented a *failure* of policing; the failure to prevent the crime from occurring in the first place.

August Vollmer

Many people in law enforcement contributed to the development of the idea of police professionalism, but few contributed as much as August Vollmer. In 1905, Vollmer, a veteran of the Spanish-American War, was elected town marshal in Berkeley, California. Before his four-year term expired, he had persuaded the city council to rewrite the city charter, creating the appointed position of police chief—to which he was appointed in 1909.

About 1910, Vollmer established a training program for recruits in the Berkeley Police Department; in 1916, he moved the training program to the campus of the University of California, where he began teaching courses in criminology and criminal justice (while continuing as Berkeley police chief).[38]

Vollmer took a year's leave of absence from Berkeley in 1923 to help reorganize the Los Angeles Police Department. After a year of studying the agency's problems and needs, he submitted a report to the Los Angeles City Council. The document, recently reprinted, gives a good idea of the range of concerns and the vision of this remarkable man.

Vollmer began by explaining to the city fathers, "A fundamental rule in police administration is to decentralize the force as far as possible . . . for the reason that commanding officers must be intimately acquainted with and responsible for crime and vice conditions existing within their district." [39] He therefore called for the reorganization of the patrol force, adding seven divisions and three "neighborhood stations." He also asked for a new central headquarters and an "industrial farm . . . for our prisoners."[40] He wanted a system of "signal and alarm devices" similar to what he had installed in Berkeley, with a teletype terminal in every police station.

Naturally, Vollmer insisted on the implementation of a merit system: "Through a system of rewards, interest in the practical and scientific principles related to police work will be encouraged," he promised. New recruits would be subject to "rigid examination" and "intensive" training.[41]

In fact, Vollmer strongly urged the city to require all new recruits to be college graduates! This is a remarkable idea, coming at a time when less than one percent of the adult population had as much as a high school diploma, much less a college degree.[42]

Another of Vollmer's recommendations reflects his view of what policing was all about. "It has been found," he wrote, "that specialization is necessary in modern police organizations." He therefore proposed to reorganize the department into eleven "functional divisions": general patrol, vice, reserves, and eight specialized investigative divisions. Once an officer had been assigned to one of the specialized divisions, "no transfer is permissable [sic]." Vollmer intended his officers to devote their entire careers to a specific area of crime control, and through intensive training and on-the-job experience to become experts in their specialties.[43]

Before returning to Berkeley in 1924, Vollmer saw most of his proposals implemented in Los Angeles: New precincts were established and new stations were opened; the telegraphic callbox system was ordered; and changes were made in the agency's organizational structure that effectively divided the agency into two parts: patrol and investigation. The idea of hiring only college graduates was rejected, of course, since it was wholly impractical, and the rule prohibiting transfer among the investigative divisions was not adopted.

For more than two decades, Vollmer served as a consultant on police agency organization and administration for the San Diego, Detroit, Chicago, Kansas City, and several other metropolitan police departments. He was one of the principal leaders of the IACP.

Vollmer continued as police chief in Berkeley until 1932, when he "retired"; he continued his career as a college professor, first at the University of Chicago and then back at the University of California. Among his students were many of the major leaders of the police reform movement in America. Those who did not study under his tutelage were almost always graduates of schools of criminal justice modeled after his programs at Chicago and Berkeley.

Like most visionaries, Vollmer had his blind spots. Lacking a high school diploma, he was mostly self-educated; he developed an extreme faith in the value of formal education. He idolized scientists and technologists, and in this regard he was very much a man of his times. His proposals are peppered with the words "scientific" and "science." In 1921, one of his Berkeley crime lab officers, John A. Larson, developed a crude polygraph. Vollmer believed that it would put an end forever to false testimony.[44] In 1919, he experimented with radio receivers in patrol cars to receive broadcasts from the central headquarters, but the equipment was too fragile to be practical.[45]

What Vollmer advocated was a corps of technicians. The patrol force would use the best modern technologies to prevent and to detect crimes. They in turn would be supported by a legion of technical specialists, equipped with scientific devices to investigate crimes, identify offenders, and prepare evidence.

The irony is that almost everything Vollmer proposed and accomplished was based not on the scientific methods of empirical observation, hypothesizing, and experimentation, but on the traditional means: intuition, casual observation, and "common-sense" conclusions. There is no question that Vollmer and his followers accomplished a great deal to improve American law enforcement, but it would be decades before anything approaching the methodology of science would be applied to the practice of policing.

Between Wars

The "scientific" approach of Vollmer and the "professionalization" doctrine of the IACP blended into a new idea of policing. The police no longer would be merely a friendly face in the neighborhood; they would be specialists, hired and trained to fight the scourge of social disorder. They would be incorruptible—and closely supervised to make sure that they stayed that way. They would be impartial, enforcing the law "without fear or favor." They would be, somewhat like Peel's bobbies, respectful of the rights and dignity of citizens, but implacable in the face of "the criminal element."

By the end of World War I, these new "professional" police had been installed in all of the major urban police agencies. In smaller towns, where resources were more limited, the goal was to come as close as one could to the professional model.

American law enforcement faced an overwhelming challenge immediately after World War I. The advent of national Prohibition gave organized crime, which had existed in some form for generations, unparalleled prosperity. Young police officers, many of them having barely survived the war against the Kaiser, were pressed into service in a new and, by previous standards, extraordinarily violent war against criminals.

The Volstead Act was enforced by federal agents, not local police. However, all forty-eight states had similar laws on their books, some of them predating the Eighteenth Amendment. State and local law enforcement agencies thus occupied a peculiar position: They were legally responsible for enforcing state laws and local ordinances, but offenses under those laws usually were also federal crimes subject to enforcement by the Federal Bureau of Investigation and other agencies. Despite the difficulties and the public resistance to the law, the police generally did their duty as best they could; they certainly made their share of arrests for liquor-law offenses![46]

Unfortunately, with as much money flying around as bullets, the "incorruptible" police proclaimed by the IACP proved all too easy to corrupt in many cities. In several major cities, the police who proved to be most susceptible to corruption were those assigned to the highly touted vice squads.[47]

The end of Prohibition in 1934 did not mean the end of organized crime; it meant that the gangs had to find new "markets" to exploit. They did not have to look very far.

A few states had enacted laws against opium and heroin as early as the 1870s. Early in the new century, most states prohibited the sale and use of these drugs and cocaine. Marijuana remained legal until the late 1930s. Congress passed the Marijuana Tax Act in 1937, which in effect prohibited the commercialization of pot; state laws quickly followed.

The antidrug laws had only marginal effect at first, mostly because only a marginal segment of the population used the proscribed substances. Opiates and coca derivatives had first become popular in the United States in medicines, both prescription and patent, and the antidrug laws generally were obeyed by the legitimate pharmaceutical manufacturers. No one knows how many people became opiate addicts by following their doctors' advice or by believing the extravagant advertisements for over-the-counter nostrums. However, those unfortunates, if they were sufficiently wealthy, presumably could circumvent the drug laws with relative impunity. Those who were caught up in the crackdown were mostly members of the underclass: the poor, despised minorities, the disreputable.[48]

During the 1930s, the Great Depression probably did more to suppress drug abuse and other vices than any set of laws or law enforcement practices. At the same time, the horrendous financial condition of many cities caused massive layoffs of police personnel.

The onset of World War II virtually coincided with the end of the Depression. More than 16 million men and women served in the U.S. military between 1941 and the end of 1946, out of a total population of about 135 million.[49] Of course, not all served in combat overseas. Nevertheless, the very scope of the war effort dwarfed every other aspect of American life. No one had much concern for law enforcement except insofar as it affected the war effort.

After World War II

After the war, America discovered that it was suddenly, almost inexplicably, prosperous. The national economy expanded at an explosive rate as factories shifted from making bombs and tanks to making home appliances and automobiles. Hundreds of thousands of military enlistees, many of them young with no other career experience, competed for a limited number of jobs. Many of them found law enforcement to be an attractive career option. At the same time, cities were scrambling to catch up with a rising population, rising prosperity, and most of all rising expectations about what government could and should do for its citizens. Enlarging and modernizing the police force became a major concern.[50]

During the postwar period, from roughly 1945 through the 1950s, there were few significant structural changes in American law enforcement. The drive for "professionalization" along the lines set down by the IACP and the turn-of-the-century reformers continued. The automobile, equipped with a two-way radio, became the principal technology used in crime prevention; by the end of the 1950s, foot patrols had been eliminated in most American cities.

FORCES FOR CHANGE

Three developments in the postwar period had a great impact on policing. The first was the "Red Scare"; the second was the series of Supreme Court decisions that directly affected the way the police carried out their duties. The third development was the African-American migration to the north and the concurrent civil rights movement.

Looking Under Beds: The Red Scare

It is difficult for young people today to comprehend the significance of postwar anticommunist sentiment in America. The sentiment itself was not entirely new. When Karl Marx and Friedrich Engels published their *Communist Manifesto* in 1848, predicting the eventual triumph of socialism over capitalism, the initial response among America's capitalists was more one of feeling insulted than feeling threatened. By the end of the century, however, many middle-class Americans had concluded that European socialism was antithetical to the free enterprise system and the liberty that the system supported. Communists and anarchists were condemned not only in Wall Street boardrooms, as one might expect, but also from the pulpits of neighborhood churches. Many people from all strata of society regarded those foreign ideologies as a menace to everything that Americans held sacred.

The fact that socialism seemed to have growing popularity among the working class and some segments of the intelligentsia only made its threat to the Establishment more potent. In 1900, a socialist union organizer and former member of the Indiana state legislature, Eugene V. Debs, ran for the presidency as the candidate of the Social Democratic Party and drew nearly 100,000 votes (out of about 14 million), enough to worry some members of Congress. Debs ran for the presidency again in 1904, 1908, and 1912, each time with less success.

Socialism, communism, anarchism, and miscellaneous other "isms" remained only potential threats until the Russian revolution of 1917-1918. Europe already was consumed with World War I; the United States had been drawn in despite considerable public opposition.

In March 1917, a coalition of rebels forced Russia's Czar Nicholas to abdicate. A moderate socialist government was formed, but it quickly splintered into competing factions. The Bolshevik Party, led by V. I. Lenin, took control; by 1918, Lenin was the head of Communist Russia. In 1924, Josef Stalin succeeded the late Lenin and instituted a brutally dictatorial regime, marked by periodic purges of dissidents and backsliders.

The United States and the USSR were nominal allies in World War II, along with Great Britain and the French government-in-exile. It was, of course, a desperate alliance whose only reason for existence was the overwhelming menace of German Nazism (which also claimed to be a form of socialism). When the war ended, the alliance split at the seams.

Stalin, claiming to fear encroachment by Western Europe, established a barrier by invading and taking over a string of Eastern European countries, all of which were devastated in the war. Stalin's actions (not to mention his past history) convinced British and American politicians that the Soviet Union intended to bring Marx's communist utopia into being through military conquest or, failing that, through subversion. The fear reached nearly hysterical proportions in 1948 when a former minor official of the U.S. Department of State, Alger Hiss, was convicted of passing secret documents to an acknowledged spy for the Soviets.

Two events, both in 1949, seemed to reinforce these fears. In September, the USSR announced the successful test of an atomic bomb similar to the bombs used by the United States to bring Japan to its knees three years earlier. Barely a month later, Mao Tse-tung's Communist army succeeded in driving the nationalist forces, which had been supported by the United States, out of China.

American military officials and scientists had insisted that the Soviets did not have the intellectual or industrial capability to design a workable atomic weapon. Therefore, the politicians concluded, someone must have given them the secret. Two years later, someone was found guilty: Julius and Ethel Rosenberg, who were arrested on charges of espionage in 1950, convicted in March 1951, and executed three months later.

Similarly, the politicians claimed, someone must have been responsible for "losing China." No one was ever found guilty, but inflammatory rhetoric on the subject ruined the careers of a number of diplomats and administration officials.

A television series, *I Led Three Lives*, was successfully produced and syndicated (sold to individual stations, not to one of the major networks) from 1953 to 1956. The series, in the form of half-hour dramatic episodes, purported to tell the "true-life" tale of an FBI counterespionage agent who infiltrated and exposed communist "cells" bent on subversion in the United States. The series never was among the top ratings leaders, but its fictionalized, pseudo-documentary form (not unlike the more popular *Dragnet* police drama series) seemed to tell the public just how the communists were destroying the American way of life.[51]

Anticommunist hysteria reached its apex in the shabby career of Joseph McCarthy, Republican senator from Wisconsin, who succeeded in commanding the attention of the American public for most of a year by claiming, without any real evidence, that communists had already infiltrated both the State Department and the U.S. Army. McCarthy, brandishing "lists" that he never actually made public, conducted hearings in 1954 into the influence of communism on the military. The hearings were televised, giving the public a close look at the man. As the hearings ended, television journalist Edward R. Murrow publicly accused McCarthy of demagoguery. The senator was later chastised by the Senate for abuse of its rules.[52]

Communist subversion presumably was a national problem, not a local matter. Indeed, few states had criminal laws that even mentioned the subject. The FBI had the primary enforcement responsibility, and its director, J. Edgar Hoover, was perhaps the most resolute communist fighter of all.

Nevertheless, it was popularly believed that the communist subversion was composed of thousands of mysterious "cells," each consisting of a handful of members who somehow received instructions by devious means from their foreign overseers. Furthermore, the subversives were thought to be encouraged and supported by legions of sympathizers and apologists, many of whom, no doubt, would stand side-by-side with the insurrectionists when the inevitable open war ensued.

The subversive "cells" were supposed to be small and scattered throughout the population. Thus they could be said to operate on the local level. If nothing else, local law enforcement officials ought to be aware of them and should report their existence and activities to the national authorities. Therefore, it was suddenly the responsibility of the ten thousand or so local police agencies in the United States to spy on their citizens.

There is no way of knowing how many local police agencies did in fact engage in counterespionage activities. Whatever "intelligence reports" on the activities of presumed subversive citizens may have been generated never saw the light of day, and most surely were destroyed long ago. However, most of the major urban police agencies did establish intelligence units whose responsibilities included gathering information about organized crime, patterns of criminal activity, and not incidentally evidence of subversion. Whether smaller agencies engaged in this sort of activity probably depended on the political attitudes of the agencies' executives, and on prevailing community sentiment. Judging by such indirect evidence as headlines and editorials in local newspapers, it does appear that the public expected their local police to protect them not just from street crime, but from political activities that were deemed subversive.[53]

Anticommunist fervor continued even after McCarthy fell into disgrace. The U.S. House of Representatives' Un-American Activities Committee published a frequently updated list of organizations that were deemed subversive. Anyone who was or ever had been a member of any of those organizations, or who might be related to someone who was a member, could be denied the security clearance required for employment in any company that held a supply contract with the military. The committee held frequent, highly publicized "hearings" to investigate subversion in one industry or another.

In 1947, President Harry S. Truman, under pressure from Congress, had required all federal employees to sign an oath of loyalty.[54] As late as 1990, college students and faculty members in some states were required to sign similar loyalty oaths before they could receive their paychecks, grants, scholarships, or fellowships.

Again, it is important to understand that most local police departments probably never took an active role in the anticommunist hysteria. Nevertheless, a climate of hostility, suspicion, and mistrust permeated American life for much of two decades, from the mid-1940s to the mid-1960s. People *expected* the police to spy on them, whether or not the police actually did so.

Changing the Rules: The Supreme Court Decisions

While Congress was busy hunting for and suppressing subversives, another branch of the federal government pursued a very different course. This was the second major development affecting American law enforcement after World War II.

Earl Warren served as governor of California from 1942 to 1953, when President Dwight D. Eisenhower appointed the moderate Republican to the office of Chief Justice. Warren, who had once served as district attorney in Alameda County (Oakland and Berkeley), California, was expected to maintain the tenuous conservative majority on the Supreme Court.

The Court had decided in 1914 that evidence that had been improperly obtained (contrary to the Fourth Amendment) could not be presented against the accused, no matter how compelling the evidence might be. This "exclusionary rule" applied only to federal criminal cases, however; in 1949, the Court ruled that the states were not bound by the same rule. Nevertheless, in 1961, under Warren, the Court reversed itself (*Mapp* v. *Ohio*), and thereby launched a series of decisions that shook the very foundations of American law enforcement.

In *Gideon* v. *Wainwright* (1963), the Court ruled that *every* defendant in a criminal case was entitled to the services of an attorney, and that the states must provide that assistance if the defendant could not afford to hire one. In *Griffin* v. *California* (1965), the Court ruled that the prosecution could not call the jury's attention to the fact that the defendant had not testified in his own behalf. In *Miranda* v. *Arizona* (1966), the Court ruled that the police could not question a suspect until he had been advised about his constitutional rights.[55]

These decisions did not materialize out of thin air; they were not lightning strikes from a clear blue sky. In fact, all of these decisions merely extended to the states the same rules that had previously applied to federal criminal cases. Nevertheless, the cries of alarm that arose from politicians, police officials, and street cops gave the impression that the Warren Court was making up the rules as they went along, and that they had embarked on a deliberate course of undermining law and order in America.

In 1969, President Richard M. Nixon appointed Warren Burger, a federal judge from Minnesota, to replace the retired Earl Warren. Some conservative politicians expected the Burger Court to reverse the "anti-law-enforcement" decisions of the previous decade, but that did not happen. Eventually, the police adapted their policies and procedures to accommodate the new rules, but a residue of bitterness remained.

Sharing the Dream: Black Aspirations

The Supreme Court also played a significant role in the third development that changed forever not just the landscape of law enforcement, but of American society.

Before and during the Civil War, a trickle of slaves and black freedmen managed to escape from the brutal oppression of the Southern plantations. They made their way north, sometimes all the way to Canada. After the war ended and slavery was abolished, the trickle became a steady stream, motivated in no small part by the Jim Crow laws, lynch mobs, and Ku Klux Klan terrorism that swept over the former Confederate states.

After World War I, the stream of black migration became a flood: Hundreds of thousands of African Americans fled from the poverty and oppression of the rural South, seeking greater freedom and economic opportunity in New York, Philadelphia, Detroit, Cleveland, Chicago, and the other northern metropolises.

Many of the migrants were disappointed. They lacked the education and skills to compete for all but the most menial jobs at starvation wages. Furthermore, the northern states had few laws to enforce racial segregation, but racist attitudes supplied what the laws lacked. Blacks were systematically excluded from housing outside of tenements, from schools except those in inner-city ghettos, from union apprenticeships that were required for well-paying industrial jobs. Blacks could not obtain bank loans to buy homes or start businesses, and they were not welcome to apply for public employment as police officers, firefighters, or bureaucrats.

Still they came north, finding jobs as bus drivers and garbage collectors, janitors and dishwashers. Those with talent found a few doors open in fields such as entertainment and the arts. Black writers found publishers; African-American entertainers appeared in movies and radio programs, and later television programs. The roles they played were often stereotyped and implicitly racist, but even so, by their very presence they denied the reality of an all-white America.

African-American soldiers had fought for the Union in the Civil War, fought in the Indian Wars on the western plains, and fought alongside Teddy Roosevelt in Cuba during the Spanish-American War. African-American troops fought in Europe in

World War I and in North Africa, Europe, and the Pacific in World War II. In all cases, blacks fought in segregated companies, usually commanded by white officers.

President Truman issued an executive order in July 1948, requiring all branches of the armed forces to integrate their black and white units.[56] The order stunned Congress and the Defense Department, but Truman refused to back down. A year earlier, he urged Congress to enact a series of laws to protect the civil rights of African-Americans and other minorities, but outraged southern Democrats and conservative Republicans refused to consider his proposals. By integrating the military, Truman gained credibility with black leaders and liberals, and encouraged further agitation for an end to racial segregation throughout the country.

The Korean War and the festering anticommunism preoccupied the country in the first half of the 1950s. Truman left office in 1952, succeeded by Dwight D. Eisenhower, war hero and conservative Republican. The prospects for improvement in the civil rights of minorities seemed dim.[57]

Unexpectedly, the Supreme Court, in one of the first major decisions of the Warren Era, brought the question off the back burner. The case involved African-American children in Topeka, Kansas, whose parents believed that the segregated school system was inherently unfair. To the surprise of almost everyone, the Supreme Court agreed, ruling that the Fourteenth Amendment prohibits "separate but equal" public facilities. Furthermore, the Court ordered the Topeka public schools—and by implication *every segregated school system in the country*—to be integrated "with all deliberate speed" (*Brown* v. *Board of Education*, issued May 17, 1954).[58]

Reaction in the South was swift and venomous. White Citizens' Councils sprang up, vowing to resist school desegregation at all costs. One county in Virginia closed its public schools altogether rather than submit to desegregation. President Eisenhower, despite his conservative personal views, ordered federal marshals and, when necessary, National Guard troops to enforce the Court's rulings in Little Rock, Arkansas (1957), and other southern cities.

Meanwhile, the Supreme Court issued a series of rulings in cases brought to it by the National Association for the Advancement of Colored People (NAACP) and other African-American organizations. The Court struck down one Jim Crow law after another. Even the laws against "miscegenation" (interracial marriage) were overturned.[59]

On December 1, 1955, an African-American woman, Rosa Parks, refused to give up her seat to a white man on a crowded Montgomery, Alabama, city bus. Mrs. Parks was forcibly ejected from the bus and arrested for violating the city's segregation law. A young Baptist minister, Martin Luther King, Jr., called for a boycott of the city bus system. The boycott began the following week and lasted until the following September, when the Supreme Court ruled the ordinance unconstitutional.[60]

The Montgomery bus boycott marked a turning point in the struggle for civil rights for minorities. Previously, African-American leaders had pursued their cause through the courts and, when they found a sympathetic ear, through the efforts of white politicians like President Truman. But King proved that a different approach could work even in the most diehard Southern community. He advocated *civil disobedience*, the deliberate refusal to obey laws that were blatantly unjust. His model was the great Indian pacifist rebel, Mahatma Gandhi, who had used nonviolent protest to stunning effect against British colonialism between 1920 and 1947.

America Comes Unglued

King and a number of like-minded African-American leaders formed the Southern Christian Leadership Conference which, with its associated Student National Coordinating Committee (also known as the Student Nonviolent Coordinating Committee), organized a series of public protests and demonstrations against segregationist laws and practices.

Meanwhile, other events were disturbing social order in America.

President Eisenhower was succeeded in 1960 by President John F. Kennedy, who continued Eisenhower's policy of supporting pro-Western groups in Southeast Asia. In that land with a tortured past, nationalists, communists, and opportunists of various stripes were intent on overthrowing the remaining European colonial powers. Since the end of World War II, American policy had been to encourage *gradual* independence, preferably along democratic lines.

Criticism of this policy began long before American troops were dispatched to "advise" the pro-Western government of South Vietnam, but large-scale antiwar protests did not occur until a few years later. After Kennedy was assassinated in 1963, President Lyndon B. Johnson decided that a greater American presence in Vietnam was necessary. On August 2, 1964, he asked Congress for the authority to send American troops to the area, presumably to protect American interests and to further assist the beleaguered South Vietnamese. On August 7, Congress gave him the authorization he requested. Two years later, nearly half a million American military personnel were in Vietnam, Cambodia, and Thailand.

Protests against the war increased as rapidly as the troop deployment. By 1965, between civil rights marches and demonstrations and the antiwar protests, along with miscellaneous demonstrations on behalf of students' rights, women's liberation, and various other causes, there seemed to be at least one major civil disturbance somewhere in America every other day.

And the police were caught in the middle of it all.

In the South, the police were expected not only to preserve the peace but also to preserve a way of life that the federal courts had found to be intolerable. In the North and Midwest and West, the police were called upon to protect "the right of the people peaceably to assemble" (as stated in the First Amendment) even when the "assembly" was a noisy protest that threatened to turn into a riot. Many of the demonstrations were accompanied by counterdemonstrations—people who were opposed to desegregation, people in favor of pursuing the war in Southeast Asia, people who for whatever reasons despised college students with long hair and unruly attitudes. The police often were *literally* caught in the middle between rock-throwing mobs and demonstrators chanting obscene slogans.

Needless to say, most American law enforcement agencies were ill-prepared for this kind of work. By far the vast majority of the demonstrations, for whatever cause, began and ended peacefully, giving vent to the demonstrators' strong convictions without substantial harm to public order or property. But that was not always the case. Nor was it always clear that the police acted only as neutral protectors of legitimate authority.

In August 1965, a protest against alleged police brutality turned into a riot in the Watts section of Los Angeles, a predominantly African-American neighborhood. Thirty-five people died before order was restored. In July 1967, riots in the black ghetto of Newark, New Jersey, and Detroit left 66 dead and thousands homeless. In August 1968, antiwar demonstrations near the Democratic National Convention in Chicago turned ugly; some demonstrators threw excrement at the police, who retaliated in what some observers characterized as a "police riot." In May 1970, an antiwar demonstration at Kent State University in Ohio ended when National Guard troops opened fire on the demonstrators, killing four students.

These incidents were infrequent, and each involved factors that were unique. After each violent episode, Washington politicians sought to allay the public's fears and avoid future explosions by appointing investigative committees. One after another, these committees concluded that *the police were, at least in part, to blame* for failing to maintain law and order.

Police officers, after all, do not represent a cross section of the population. In the 1960s, the vast majority of police officers were white European-American men from middle-class families with, at best, a high school education. What was true of rank-and-file officers was equally true of their superiors, virtually all of whom had risen through the ranks without the benefit of any more training or education than they had received thirty or more years earlier. For many of these men, their duty to uphold the law neatly coincided with their strong belief in protecting the established social order.

Restoring Order

The Civil Rights Act of 1964, the Voting Rights Act of 1965 (which extended the Voting Rights Act of 1957), and subsequent laws dealing with equality of employment opportunity and fair housing resolved the main issues of the civil rights movement. *Legal* segregation came to an end, although the struggle to eradicate racial discrimination and extralegal segregation continues to the present day.[61]

Richard M. Nixon won election to the presidency in 1968 by promising to end the war in Southeast Asia "honorably" and to restore order on America's streets by waging a "war on crime." Congress reacted to his election by passing the Omnibus Safe Streets and Crime Control Act of 1968, before President Nixon took office. The act established a Law Enforcement Assistance Administration (LEAA) in the Department of Justice and authorized LEAA to award grants to local and state police agencies. Several billion dollars were allocated for the "war on crime" in subsequent years.

Ending the Southeast Asian war took longer. The scale of U.S. military involvement began to be reduced in 1971, but the official end of the war did not come until April 1973, in Vietnam, and all U.S. military activity in the region ended by the following August. By then, President Nixon's administration was in disarray over the Watergate scandal and other disasters.

REINVENTING POLICING

President Jimmy Carter drastically reduced funding for LEAA in 1978. Most of the grant programs simply disappeared, and the LEAA bureaucracy was absorbed back into the Department of Justice. Nevertheless, in its relatively brief history, LEAA had an enormous impact on American law enforcement. For the first time, scholarly and scientific attention was devoted to some of the key questions about American policing.

New Money, New Ideas

In 1972, the Ford Foundation sponsored the establishment of the Police Foundation, a consortium supported by the IACP and several other police professional associations, and with additional funding from LEAA. The Police Foundation was to be the mechanism for distributing federal and private foundation money for research projects in the broad field of criminal justice.

One of the first Police Foundation grants went to the Kansas City, Missouri, police department for a series of experiments to determine which of several possible methods of organizing preventive patrol would prove to be the most effective and efficient. The initial report on the experiment was published in 1974 and caused an immediate uproar in police circles. According to the report, *none* of the varying methods had proven to be significantly more effective than having no preventive patrols at all.[62] Both the experimental methods and the conclusions drawn in the Kansas City project have been questioned, but the immediate impact was to cast doubt on the most fundamental tenet of American law enforcement: that randomly patrolling officers in motor vehicles will prevent crime.[63]

At about the same time, another LEAA-funded project was studying the other half of the standard American police agency. A research team at the RAND Corporation of Santa Monica, California, was given a grant to study the organization and methods of criminal investigators. A preliminary version of their report was published by RAND in 1976; a somewhat fuller version was published a year later.[64]

Very briefly, the RAND report concluded that most police detectives do little if any real investigation, and that hardly any crimes are "solved" unless the criminal is known to the victim or falls into the detective's lap. Once again, the basic structure of American law enforcement apparently was found to be ineffectual.

It would be misleading to overstate the effect of these two studies. To the best of our knowledge, not one single American police department disbanded its patrol force or its investigative units. Instead, the Kansas City and RAND studies stimulated police administrators, professional organizations, and scholars to reexamine the techniques used in patrol and investigation. Before long, even fundamental assumptions about crime and law enforcement practices were open to question and serious reevaluation.[65]

One effect of the LEAA funding was the establishment of dozens of criminal justice educational programs in universities, some offering graduate degrees. Graduate degrees typically require the completion of a research project reported in a thesis or dissertation. Consequently, by the mid-1970s, hundreds of erstwhile graduate students were looking for, and easily finding, topics for research into law enforcement practices and procedures. Meanwhile, professors of criminal justice were busily producing textbooks and journal articles reporting not just their opinions (which had filled the journals for decades), but, for the first time, the results of legitimate, reasonably credible research.

New ideas about what the police should do and how they should do it blossomed. Money was available from LEAA, the Police Foundation, and various other sources to try almost anything. In retrospect, some of the experiments seem a bit suspect, not to say harebrained, but it is often difficult to tell whether an idea has merit until it is put into effect; there can be positive surprises as well as negative ones.[66]

Team Policing

Not only were there experiments in policing techniques, but new and far-reaching theories about policing also surfaced. One of the first was the idea that police officers, whether on patrol or in investigation, should collaborate more closely with one another, sharing information and jointly seeking solutions to crime problems. This idea led in turn to a variety of experiments in what came to be called *team policing*.

In some cases, a "team" consisting entirely of patrol officers was assigned joint responsibility for patrolling a large area that ordinarily would have been subdivided into individual beats. In other cases, a "team" consisted of several patrol officers plus one or more investigators; the patrol officers were given increased responsibility for investigating crimes on their beats, with the investigators available to provide expert advice or additional help on complicated cases. One early experiment involved placing two patrol officers, a detective, and a social worker in each patrol vehicle, so that the entire "team" could respond to each call. That experiment did not last long.[67]

In fact, many of the team policing experiments did not survive simply because they did not prove to be more effective or efficient than the practices they replaced.[68]

However, the failures of team policing did not discourage more new ideas and approaches. Throughout the 1970s and the decade that followed, even long after the LEAA had faded away, virtually every aspect of policing was subjected to vigorous examination and experimentation.

Police and the Community

One of the concerns raised by the series of investigative commissions in the 1960s was the fundamental relationship between the police, as an agency of government, and the community. It was a relationship that had been marked by tension and strain for at least a generation.[69]

James Q. Wilson and George L. Kelling co-authored an article in *The Atlantic Monthly*, published in March 1982, that attracted a great deal of attention. The article, entitled, "Broken Windows," suggested that police professionalism had taken a wrong turn in emphasizing the "objective" enforcement of discrete laws, when what the public really wants is the maintenance of an *orderly* society. The symbolism of the title is apparent: A broken window is not a violation of the law, and therefore it is ignored by the "professional" police officer. However, it is an indicator of social disintegration, and therefore deserves the attention of the *community-oriented* cop.[70]

At about the same time, an experiment was being conducted in Flint, Michigan, with the support of criminologist Robert J. Trojanowicz and his students at Michigan State University. The experiment involved assigning patrol officers to patrol *on foot* in neighborhoods that had experienced a high crime rate. Trojanowicz reported some positive results in 1982; crime did not disappear, but public confidence in the police rose and public fear of "street crime" declined markedly.[71] Within a few years, dozens of other cities followed Flint's example; in many cases, foot patrols that had been abandoned only a few years before were reintroduced.

The Michigan experiment was not the first attempt to revive foot patrols, of course. The New York City Police Department had experimented with variations on foot patrolling as early as 1954, and again in 1966, but the results had been ambiguous and, no matter how promising the experiments, the financially pressed city was not inclined to increase police manpower sufficiently to implement widespread foot patrols.[72]

Dealing with Problems

In 1979, Wisconsin law professor Herman Goldstein published an essay on a different idea about policing, a *problem-oriented* approach.[73] Goldstein suggested that law enforcement might be made more effective if the police, instead of randomly patrolling neighborhoods, concentrated on specific crime problems. The problems to be targeted could be identified from crime incident reports and other conventional sources of police intelligence, but Goldstein also advocated getting the community involved in deciding what problems deserved the most attention.

Crime targeting was not an entirely new idea; several major metropolitan police departments had used tactical patrols for just that purpose, with generally good results. However, in most tactical patrol systems, the selection of targets was based mainly on incident reports, as analyzed by an agency's intelligence or research division.[74] Sometimes choosing a target was based on little more than the intuition of managers. Goldstein's idea of involving the community in choosing the targets was new, and it struck a responsive chord.

The Newport News, Virginia, police department took up Goldstein's approach in 1984. First, the agency spent two years analyzing criminal incident patterns, soliciting community input, and proposing possible crime targets. More than two dozen potential targets were offered; from those, three were selected for immediate attention: burglaries in a large apartment complex, prostitution-related robberies in the central business district, and thefts from vehicles in a parking lot near the city's famed shipyards. Specific tactics were adopted—again with community input—to address all three types of crime. The projects were launched and, with the assistance of the Police Executive Research Forum (PERF), the results were evaluated.[75]

The thefts from vehicles were reduced over a one-year period by about 55 percent; robberies in the downtown area were reduced by 40 percent; and burglaries in the targeted apartment complex were reduced by 35 percent. The latter figure, though impressive by most standards, was considered unacceptable to the community, so tenants were relocated and the apartment complex was razed.[76]

As the Newport News projects demonstrate, Goldstein's approach differed from conventional tactical patrol concepts and from the team policing concept in one crucial respect: Problem-oriented policing is intrinsically *research based*. Identifying a target problem depends on research using whatever information resources are available, explicitly including community perceptions and preferences. Once research has identified potential crime targets, an experimental design is developed and carried out; the results are then analyzed to determine whether the experiment worked as expected. If not, a new design can be developed, implemented, and evaluated.

Goldstein's ideas were presented more fully in his 1990 book, *Problem-Oriented Policing.*[77] By then, many of his ideas were already familiar to most law enforcement practitioners.

Meanwhile, a somewhat different set of approaches to policing had arisen.

Community-Oriented Policing

The San Diego police began a *community-oriented policing* program in the early 1970s. Patrol officers were trained and instructed to become thoroughly familiar with their beats through a process of "beat profiling." Each patrol officer was required to compile information about the population, condition of housing and other structures, and patterns of criminal incidents on his or her beat. Officers then were taught how to design specific patrol strategies to deal with the types of crime problems that were experienced in their assigned areas.[78]

Baltimore County, Maryland, initiated a Citizen-Oriented Police Enforcement (COPE) program in the early 1980s, in which a special problem-targeting and -solving unit was established. Newark, New Jersey, implemented a community-oriented program based on increased use of foot patrols; so did New York City. Madison, Wisconsin, police designated an "experimental patrol district" in which various forms of community policing could be tested.[79]

In 1982, Lee P. Brown was hired as chief of police in Houston, Texas. Brown came from Atlanta, where he had attempted a variety of new ideas in police organization and management. He wasted no time in Houston, one of the largest and most traditional police forces in the country. He initiated a "Directed-Area Response Team" (DART), a tactical patrol program, and he authorized several other experimental projects suggested by his staff. Within two years, there were some fifty or sixty different experiments in progress.

Next, Brown assembled a committee of police officers from all ranks and divisions within his department, plus a panel of community leaders, to study the results of the various experiments. The committee chose those elements of the more successful experiments, as well as ideas gathered from other community-oriented projects around the country, and welded them together into a single new concept, which they called "Neighborhood-Oriented Policing." One sector of the department (amounting to roughly one fourth of the city's area and population) was chosen as a test bed for Neighborhood-Oriented Policing, beginning in 1986.

Brown left Houston abruptly in 1990 to become commissioner of police in New York City. Elizabeth M. Watson, a co-author of this text, had been commander of the sector involved in the neighborhood-oriented policing project. She was promoted to chief of police by then-mayor Kathy Whitmire. By the time Chief Watson left office in 1992, neighborhood-oriented policing had been partially implemented throughout the agency. Watson's successor, under political pressure, discontinued the formal neighborhood-oriented policing program, but elements of the program have been retained.[80]

AMERICAN LAW ENFORCEMENT TODAY

Perhaps the single most significant feature of America's criminal justice system is not its underlying philosophy, but rather its fragmented, localized structure.

The Constitution adopted in 1787 leaves the criminal justice system almost entirely to the states. Before the creation of the LEAA in 1978, the federal government had almost nothing to do with the way the states discharged that responsibility. Each state made and enforced its own criminal laws, and in most states, the actual enforcement of the criminal laws (supplemented by local municipal ordinances) fell to the municipal governments and county sheriffs.

There are presently more than thirteen thousand law enforcement agencies in the United States; they employ approximately six hundred thousand commissioned officers, or fewer than fifty officers per agency. Approximately half of the county and municipal police agencies have fewer than ten officers.

Every state has a state police agency. Usually it is combined with a state highway patrol whose principal duty is traffic law enforcement. Most of the state police agencies provide consultative and coordinative services to the local police departments; the latter are the primary source of all criminal law enforcement services in their communities.

The federal government itself enforces criminal laws, enacted by Congress, only under certain circumstances, such as when a series of crimes are perpetrated in several states by the same offender or group of offenders, or when the crime occurs on federal property or involves an activity (such as banking) that is under federal regulation and control. The primary law enforcement agency at the federal level is, of course, the Federal Bureau of Investigation, which is part of the Department of Justice. The Secret Service and the Bureau of Alcohol, Tobacco, and Firearms (both parts of the Treasury Department) also have law enforcement duties assigned to them by Congress. In addition, the Drug Enforcement Agency is responsible for enforcing drug abuse and trafficking laws, and there are dozens of other agencies in the Executive Branch that have specific responsibilities for the enforcement of criminal laws in their areas of concern.

Nevertheless, it is the local police department or sheriff's office that performs at least 90 percent of the police services in almost every community in America, and most of those agencies are very small, with limited budgets and limited access to other resources.

For the thousands of very small agencies (those with fewer than 25 commissioned officers), "community policing" is not just a good idea, it is a necessity for survival. As we will see, there are some aspects of a community-oriented policing model that these very small agencies might wish to adopt. However, for the most part their officers and managers are already intimately familiar with the community they serve.

At the other extreme, there are only a dozen or so police departments in the United States that have more than five thousand commissioned officers. Several of these very large agencies, including the largest of them all (New York City), have made significant efforts to implement some variation of community policing. If the results have not always been entirely successful, that is hardly surprising: Implementing any sort of fundamental change in such enormous organizations is a daunting task. Very large organizations, whether in law enforcement or any other field of endeavor, tend to have a momentum of their own that resists change in any direction, even when there is wide agreement as to the kind of changes that are desired.

Between the very small and the very large, there are several thousand county and municipal police agencies that are prime candidates for the transformation from traditional police practices—the so-called professional model—to community policing. These agencies have sufficient resources to make the transition, and they have ample reasons to do so, as we discuss in subsequent chapters. Indeed, most of the successful implementations of community-oriented policing that have been reported in the literature have taken place in these medium-sized agencies. The successes and reputed failures of the major metropolitan agencies—New York, Detroit, Houston, Los Angeles—have gotten the most publicity in the mass media, but only because of the vast numbers of people affected, and perhaps because those huge agencies have better access to the media. Many other positive developments in community policing have occurred in places like Newark; San Diego; Portland, Oregon; Madison, Wisconsin; Flint, Michigan; and Austin, Texas, as well as in dozens of smaller cities and towns.

Community policing is not a single, monolithic scheme for the organization and operation of law enforcement agencies. As we discuss in the next chapter, it is essentially a philosophy of policing, a set of ideas and concepts that can be implemented in many different ways. In fact, over the past two decades, community policing *has been* implemented in many different ways, not all of them widely known. Our purpose in this text is to show how the essential concept of community policing can be, and ought to be, adapted to every county and municipal law enforcement agency.

FOOTNOTES

1. Edward M. Burns, *Western Civilizations: Their History and Their Culture*, 5th ed. (New York: W. W. Norton, 1958), p. 69.
2. New York City Common Council, *Report of the Select Committee of the New York City Board of Aldermen on the New York City Police Department* (New York: Arno Press, 1971, reprint of 1844 report), p. 687.
3. New York City Common Council, *Report*, pp. 710–716.
4. New York City Common Council, *Report*, p. 688.
5. Herbert A. Johnson, *History of Criminal Justice* (New York: Anderson Publishing, 1988), p. 178.
6. New York City Common Council, *Report*, pp. 720–724.
7. Lawrence M. Friedman, *Crime and Punishment in American History* (New York: Basic Books, 1993), p. 204.
8. *Texas Criminal Laws*, 1995–1996 ed. (Austin, TX: Texas Department of Public Safety, 1996). "Computer crime" is listed at Sec. 33 of the Penal Code, pp. 81–83.
9. James Q. Wilson, *Thinking About Crime*, rev. ed. (New York: Basic Books, 1983, 1st ed. 1975, pp. 242–244.
10. Friedman, *Crime and Punishment*, p. 3.
11. Lydia Voigt, William E. Thornton, Jr., Leo Barrile, and Jerrol M. Seaman, *Criminology and Justice* (New York: McGraw-Hill, 1994), p. 38.
12. Voigt et al., *Criminology*, p. 39.
13. Friedman, *Crime and Punishment*, pp. 32–34.
14. T. B. Bottomore, *Elites and Society* (New York: Penguin Books, 1970, reprint of 1964 edition).

15. Parviz Saney, *Crime and Culture in America* (Westport, Conn.: Greenwood Press, 1986), pp. 11–14, 35–40. See also John L. Cooper, *You Can Hear Them Knocking* (Port Washington, N.Y.: Kennikat Press, 1981, pp. 28–40).

16. Friedman, *Crime and Punishment*, p. 99.

17. Friedman, *Crime and Punishment*, pp. 95–96.

18. Mark Whitman, ed., *Removing a Badge of Slavery* (Princeton, N.J.: Markus Wiener, 1993).

19. Friedman, *Crime and Punishment,* p. 365.

20. Samuel Walker, *A Critical History of Police Reform* (Lexington, Mass.: Lexington Books, 1977), p. 4.

21. Friedman, *Crime and Punishment*, p. 105.

22. Friedman, *Crime and Punishment*, p. 134.

23. Macklin Fleming, *Of Crime and Rights* (New York: W. W. Norton, 1978), pp. 21–24.

24. Johnson, *History of Criminal Justice*, pp. 131–132.

25. An example from North Carolina, in 1706, is given by Friedman, *Crime and Punishment*, page 45. For an amusing essay on trial by ordeal and the origins of the jury system, see Barbara Holland, "Trial by Jury, or Have We Got an Ordeal for You!" in *Smithsonian*, 25, no. 12 (March 1995), pp. 108-117.

26. Johnson, *History of Criminal Justice*, p. 139.

27. Mary Jeanette Hageman, *Police-Community Relations* (Beverly Hills, Calif.: Sage, 1985), pp. 22–24.

28. James F. Richardson, *Urban Police in the United States* (Port Washington, N.Y.: Kennikat Press, 1974), pp. 22–25.

29. Friedman, *Crime and Punishment*, pp. 194–196 and elsewhere.

30. Robert Fogelson, *Big City Police* (Cambridge, Mass.: Harvard University Press, 1977), pp. 15–25. See also Clive Emsley, *Policing and Its Context, 1750–1870* (New York: Schocken Books, 1983).

31. Hageman, *Police-Community Relations*, pp. 66–72.

32. Friedman, *Crime and Punishment*, pp. 34–36.

33. Friedman, *Crime and Punishment*, p. 130.

34. Richardson, *Urban Police*, pp. 26–30; Fogelson, *Big City Police*, pp. 20–23. See also Friedman, *Crime and Punishment*, pp. 153–155.

35. For example, the Lexow Committee, named for its chairman, Clarence Lexow, a member of the New York State Legislature, which issued a scathing report on corruption in the New York City Police Department in 1894. State of New York, *Report of the Special Committee Appointed to Investigate the Police Department of the City of New York* (Albany, N.Y.: State of New York, 1895).

36. Walker, *A Critical History of Police Reform*, p. 48.

37. Alfred R. Stone and Stuart M. DeLuca, *Police Administration: An Introduction,* 2nd ed. (Englewood Cliffs, N.J.: Prentice Hall, 1994), p. 9.

38. Ronald J. Waldron, ed., *The Criminal Justice System* (Boston: Houghton Mifflin, 1976), pp. 72–73.

39. August Vollmer, *Law Enforcement in Los Angeles: Annual Report, 1924* (New York: Arno Press, 1974, reprint, pp. 2–3.

40. Vollmer, *Law Enforcement in Los Angeles*, p. 4.

41. Vollmer, *Law Enforcement in Los Angeles*, p. 6.

42. *World Almanac and Book of Facts* (New York: World Almanac, 1995), p. 219. Data for 1910 are not shown, but as of 1920, less than one percent of American adults held a high school diploma.

43. Vollmer, *Law Enforcement in Los Angeles*, pp. 11–12.

44. James N. Gilbert, *Criminal Investigation* (Columbus, Ohio: Charles E. Merrill, 1980), p. 29.

45. Waldron, ed., *The Criminal Justice System*, pp. 72–73.

46 Friedman, *Crime and Punishment*, p. 340.

47. Richardson, *Urban Police*, pp. 86–91.

48. Friedman, *Crime and Punishment*, pp. 354–356.

49. *World Almanac*, pp. 163, 377.

50. Stone and DeLuca, *Police Administration*, pp. 14–15.

51. Tim Brooks and Earle Marsh, *The Complete Directory to Prime Time Network TV Shows,* 5th ed. (New York: Ballantine Books, 1992), pp. 421–422.

52. Friedman, *Crime and Punishment*, pp. 370–372.

53. For example, David McCullough, *Truman* (New York: Simon & Schuster, 1992), p. 773 and elsewhere.

54. McCullough, *Truman*, pp. 551–552.

55. G. Edward White, *Earl Warren: A Public Life* (New York: Oxford University Press, 1982), pp. 263–278. Friedman, *Crime and Punishment,* also contains an excellent discussion of these decisions and their impact on law enforcement; pp. 300–303.

56. McCullough, *Truman*, p. 651.

57. Jack Greenberg, *Crusaders in the Courts* (New York: Basic Books, 1994), pp. 3–84.

58. Greenberg, *Crusaders*, pp. 85–211; also, White, *Earl Warren*, pp. 161–172.

59. Greenberg, *Crusaders*, pp. 212–362.

60. Greenberg, *Crusaders*, pp. 212–213.

61. Greenberg, *Crusaders*, pp. 487–498.

62. Geoffrey P. Alpert and Roger C. Dunham, *Policing Urban America,* 2nd ed. (Prospect Heights, Ill.: Waveland Press, 1992), p. 136.

63. Wilson, *Thinking About Crime*, pp. 66–68.

64. Peter W. Greenwood, Jan M. Chaiken, and Joan Petersilia, *The Criminal Investigation Process* (Lexington, Mass.: D. C. Heath, 1977).

65. John J. Broderick, *Police in a Time of Change* (Prospect Heights, Ill.: Waveland Press, 1987), pp. 198–200.

66. D. F. Gunderson, "Credibility and the Police Uniform," in *Journal of Police Science and Administration*, 15, no. 3 (September 1987), 192–195, discussed experiments with nontraditional, "blazer-style" uniforms.

67. Ellen J. Albright and Larry G. Seigel, *Team Policing: Recommended Approaches* (Washington, D.C.: U.S. Department of Justice, National Institute of Law Enforcement and Criminal Justice, 1979). See also Frank Schmalleger, *Criminal Justice Today* (Englewood Cliffs, N.J.: Prentice Hall, 1991), pp. 183–186.

68. Dennis J. Kenney, "Strategic Approaches," in Larry T. Hoover, ed., *Police Management: Issues and Perspectives* (Washington, D.C.: Police Executive Research Forum, 1992), pp. 212–214. Also, Wilson, *Thinking About Crime*, pp. 68–73.

69. Richardson, *Urban Police*, pp. 158–187. Also see Cooper, *You Can Hear Them Knocking*; Hageman, *Police-Community Relations*.

70. An expanded version of the article is included in Wilson, *Thinking About Crime*, pp. 75–89.
71. Robert Trojanowicz et al., *An Evaluation of the Neighborhood Foot Patrol Program in Flint, Michigan* (East Lansing, Mich.: Michigan State University, 1982).
72. Wilson, *Thinking About Crime*, pp. 62–65.
73. Herman Goldstein, "Improving Policing: A Problem-Oriented Approach," in *Crime and Delinquency*, vol. 25 (1987), pp. 236–258.
74. For example, Kansas City Police Department, *Directed Patrol* (Kansas City, Mo.: Kansas City Police Department, 1974).
75. John E. Eck and William Spelman, *Problem Solving: Problem-Oriented Policing in Newport News* (Washington, D.C.: Police Executive Research Forum, 1987).
76. Kenney, "Strategic Approaches," in Hoover, ed., *Police Management*, pp. 217–218.
77. Herman Goldstein, *Problem-Oriented Policing* (New York: McGraw-Hill, 1990).
78. Bureau of Justice Assistance, *Understanding Community Policing* (Washington, D.C.: U.S. Department of Justice, 1994), pp. 8–9.
79. Timothy N. Oettmeier, "Matching Structure to Objectives," in Hoover, ed., *Police Management*, p. 41. Also, Bureau of Justice Assistance, *Understanding Community Policing*, pp. 8-11.
80. Mary Ann Wycoff and Timothy Oettmeier, *Planning and Implementation Issues for Community-Oriented Policing: The Houston Experience* (Houston: Houston Police Department, 1995).

CHAPTER 2

DEFINING COMMUNITY AND COMMUNITY POLICING

Before we try to discuss the implementation of community policing, it might be a good idea to make certain that we know just what we are talking about. If community policing means, for example, providing law enforcement services to a community, we ought to know just what a "community" is. Then we ought to be as clear as we can be about what we mean by "community policing" and how it differs from any other kind of policing.

Out of the hundreds of books, journal articles, research reports, and monographs that deal with community policing, you might suppose that there would be at least one clear, comprehensible definition of "community." But that is not the case. The few definitions that are presented in the literature are vague and ambiguous. We are not the first to say so: Stephen D. Mastrofski observed nearly a decade ago, "At the core of the [community policing] reform's problem is the need to define community and establish its existence. . . ."[1]

Let us begin, then, by trying to track down an elusive query: a clear concept of what a community is, what it does, and how it affects or is affected by policing.

COMMUNITY AS A PLACE

Among the handful of definitions we have found, most connect the idea of community to geography. For example:

The "community" for which a patrol officer is given responsibility should be a small, well-defined geographical area. Beats should be configured in a manner that preserves. . . the unique geographical and social characterisics of neighborhoods.[2]

Geography and Community

Indeed, one of the landmark texts on community policing, Trojanowicz and Dixon's *Criminal Justice and the Community*, assumes that a community is first of all a geographical area.[3] It is only recently that criminologists and law enforcement scholars have taken notice of what other social scientists discovered long ago: "Geographical areas do not always lend themselves to neat categorisation . . ."[4]

A very different concept of community is represented by Gary Sykes's definition: A community is "a group committed to shared assumptions or. . .fundamental values."[5] This idea—we might call it the sociological perspective—is recognized by others as well.[6]

For that matter, Trojanowicz and Dixon did not stop with their initial, geographical definition; they quickly added that a community is "a group of people with similar character and goals. . ." who may or may not happen to live in close proximity.[7]

Nevertheless, the two concepts—sociological and geographical—of community are inherently linked, simply because people live where they do for a reason, and ". . .a community facilitates a specific kind of social living that more or less satisfies its inhabitants."[8] That is, the geographical community—where people live—provides for its inhabitants a variety of institutions and services that promote social interaction. Indeed, the extent and quality of social interaction in a community becomes one of the community's most significant characteristics.[9]

Sense of Community

Defining a community in terms of geography should not mean that only residents are to be considered. As Kelling and Stewart point out, "Neighbors are not just the residents. . .but also include shopkeepers and their employees, other workers who frequent areas regularly ,. . . and even the homeless."[10] Nevertheless, for criminologist James Q. Wilson, it is the residents of an area whose sense of community is crucial:

> Around one's home, the places where one shops, and the corridors through which one walks, there is for each of us a public space wherein our sense of security, self-esteem, and propriety is either reassured or jeopardized by the people and events we encounter.[11]

Wilson adds that a sense of community depends in large part on "a desire for the observance of standards of right and seemly conduct in. . .public places."[12] In short, people feel some sense of ownership of the area in which they live at least partly because their ideas of proper behavior are upheld in the area. According to Mastrofski, the lack of a sense of community is to be found most often in those neighborhoods that have a serious problem with disorderly behavior.[13]

Former New York City police commissioner Patrick V. Murphy, one of the first innovators to experiment with community policing, goes so far as to define a community as "a network of people exchanging information, assisting one another, observing, cooperating with the police to identify violators, but also to help minor offenders to go straight."[14]

Clearly, there is much more to the idea of "community" than merely a geographical area within which some number of people live. But how can we make sense out of this welter of ideas?

We will begin by offering the broadest possible definition of community: *A community is any group of people who have something in common.* Exactly what they have in common, and to what degree or extent, are open questions to be investigated and answered.

Types of Communities

Within this very broad definition, we can identify several major types of communities. The first and most obvious is the one that we have been discussing: the *geographical community*, a group of people who, as residents or occasional users, occupy a given geographical area. The most important specific example of a geographical community is the *neighborhood*, a term we will define and discuss in some detail later.

But there are other types of communities as well. We can define a *demographic community* as a group of people who have the same, or very similar, demographic characterisics such as age (for example, senior citizens or teenagers), gender (men and women as separate "communities"), and ethnicity.* Examples of ethnic communities would include Hispanic Americans, Asian Americans, and African Americans, and subdivisions such as Mexican Americans, Cuban Americans, and so forth.

Communities also can be defined in terms of *interests*, which might include ideologies (religious, political, and so on), vocations or professions, or even hobbies and personal interests.[15]

Two important points need to be made regarding this typology of communities. The first is that *everyone is a member of multiple communities.* There are, for example, African-American dentists who live in a given neighborhood and coach Little League teams; there are Methodist grocers who live in a given neighborhood and write poetry in their spare time; there are Polish-American housewives who live in a given neighborhood, support Republican candidates and causes, and do volunteer work for the Red Cross. Each of these hypothetical individuals is a member of several "communities" at once, depending on whether we focus on their geographical place of residence (or place of business), their ethnicity, their gender, their age, their ideology, or their personal interests.

The second point is that *all communities are atomistic*: That is, any community, regardless of its type, is composed of individuals and the "connections" or relationships among them. It is a serious mistake, made too often by people who should know better, to forget that there is no monolithic public, but "in fact, many groupings with diverse interests."[16]

---

*In keeping with the conclusions of anthropologists and biologists, we will not use the term *race* to distinguish groups of people. *Ethnicity* is a cultural term, describing people according to their cultural group, which may be based on their national origin or ancestry. For a thorough discussion of the misconceptions that led to the use of *race*, see the November 1994 issue of *Discover Magazine*, a series of articles beginning on p. 56.

WHAT COMMUNITIES DO

In the pages that follow, we do not pretend to offer even a rudimentary review of sociology or social psychology. We merely wish to highlight some of the concepts of social science that bear directly on the subject of communities.

We are very much aware that many police officers vehemently reject the role of "social worker" and deny that enforcing the law has anything to do with social services. Nevertheless, the fact is that police work inescapably concerns social behavior, the way people act toward one another. Effective police officers always have been intuitive psychologists, armchair sociologists, and, in the succinct phrase of William Ker Muir, Jr., "streetcorner politicians."[17] Any understanding of the origins and dynamics of social behavior can only help to make a police officer more effective.

Humans are inherently social beings and always have been. People exist not as isolated entities, but as members of groups. As the philosopher and anthropologist Ashley Montague put it,

> Every human being necessarily forms a network of social interrelationships from which he cannot possibly extricate himself . . .[18]

Indeed, a person's very identity, his or her concept of who he or she is as a human being, depends in large measure on the groups to which he or she has some sort of relationship.[19]

Groups, Roles, and Behaviors

Subjectively, most people feel that they choose their actions at any moment, in whatever circumstances they find themselves, even though they may feel that their range of choices is constrained by outside forces (such as a lack of resources, or the rules imposed on them by others).

Objectively, it is abundantly clear that people behave in recognizable patterns. Most people behave in patterns that are consistent: When faced with similar circumstances, they behave in similar ways. Furthermore, these patterns of behavior are associated with *social roles*, the "positions that people occupy in the social system, accompanied by expectations as to how they should behave."[20]

Not only are these patterns of behavior, these roles, learned in groups, but groups themselves consist of sets of defined roles. To put it another way, roles partition people into defined groups.[21]

For example, within a school (a type of community), there are such roles as teacher, student, and staff member. Teachers are expected to behave differently from students or staff members; their roles prescribe certain behaviors. When one's role changes, so does one's behavior: When a teacher enrolls in a class as a student, he is expected to act like a student, not like a teacher. Conversely, when a student is placed in the role of teacher, she is expected to act like a teacher. People who occupy various roles at different times—such as a student who has a part-time job as a staff member—sometimes have trouble keeping their roles separate, and may be criticized for, perhaps, acting like a student when they are working as a staff member.

School is, in our society, a type of community that is experienced by almost everyone. Another type of community (using our broad definition) that has even greater influence on its members' social behavior is the family.

Family as a Community   "Family," for our purposes, does not mean only the conventional group consisting of Mom, Dad, and two or three children (what social scientists call the "nuclear family"). For better or for worse, the nuclear family is much less prominent today than it was a couple of generations ago.[22] Divorce and remarriage, single parenthood, multigenerational households (where, for example, grandparents bear the primary responsibility for caring for their own grandchildren), and various other arrangements also must be regarded as families.

We will define a *family* as any group of two or more people who maintain a long-term, intimate relationship. Usually but not necessarily, the members of a family occupy a single household. The relationship may be based on biology or marriage, but that is also not necessarily the case.

Again, this definition clearly is not what most people conventionally understand as a "family," and what social scientists mean by the "nuclear family." We have made our definition much broader so that we can look at how the interactions among "family members" affect their social behaviors. For that special purpose, neither biological nor legal relationships are as important as the way people live together.

What is most important about a family is its influence on the development of children's social behaviors. By the time a child reaches school age, he or she has already learned an amazing amount: how to use language, how to eat (what foods to choose, how to use various eating utensils), how to dress (what clothes to wear for several different purposes, how to put them on and take them off), how to treat and deal with other people in numerous roles (parents, siblings, neighbor adults, neighbor children, visiting relatives, and so forth). Clearly, *child* is a well-defined role in every family, and in most families there are extensive and complex ideas about how a child is supposed to behave.

For most children, school is the second community that has significant influence on the development of social behavior, and it is often the first community a child experiences outside of the family. For some children, a religious community—church, synagogue, or mosque—is experienced before or at about the same time as school. Again, both the school and the church are types of communities in which there are several discrete roles, each associated with sets of expected behaviors that the child must learn. These new roles and associated behaviors are added to those learned in the family.

Adolescent Groups

Adolescence brings a major change in a child's relationships with other family members. Usually for the first time, a child's main concern is his or her relationship with *peers*—other young people of the same or similar age. In particular, *hierarchical* relationships develop rapidly in adolescence: Some children achieve a dominant status while others find themselves in a subordinate status from which they may never extricate themselves. At the same time, the adolescent is obsessed with establishing an *autonomous identity*, an idea of who he or she is *other than* a reflection of his or her parents.

The timing, direction, and intensity of these developments probably have their basis in biology and the physiological and neurological changes that accompany puberty. Be that as it may, the effect is that young people between the ages of about 12 and about 18 undergo a series of radical changes in their relationships with family and other people, in their social roles, and in their social behaviors. This effect is by no means peculiar to our present-day society; even ancient texts mention the frustration and confusion faced by parents whose children seem suddenly to become strangers.

Adolescent "rebellion" can take many forms. The one that interests us is the tendency of young people to form or join groups composed mostly of their peers. The overt purpose and structure of a group is almost incidental. It can be a social group, fraternity, sorority, club, or team, and it can be affiliated with a school or church, organized by adults for young people, or organized by the young people themselves (often without adult leadership). For urban young people it is often a gang. Regardless of its purpose or structure, the adolescent group often serves as a *surrogate family*, one in which the adolescent can experiment with roles, relationships, and behaviors that are independent of his or her parents.

The surrogate-family group is, of course, yet another type of community, and it can have a great deal of influence over adolescents' behavior. Often there is constant and strident competition for dominant status within the group (particularly if there is no adult leadership), and there may also be competition between rival groups. Members are required to meet behavioral expectations that may include conformity to unconventional fashions in appearance, unswerving loyalty to fellow members and the group as a whole, extreme risk-taking, and expressions of contempt for adult (that is to say, parentlike) standards of behavior.

Adolescents often act within the group, or under the group's direct influence, in ways that they would not act alone. The result, as law enforcement authorities have known for generations, is that adolescents are responsible for the majority of incidents of vandalism, criminal mischief, minor (and not-so-minor) theft, and other crimes of disorder. Underage drinking, experimentation with illegal drugs, fighting with members of rival groups, and sexual misconduct are among the criminal behaviors that are often associated with adolescent groups.

In recent years, there has been growing concern over the violence that seems to be associated with adolescent crime. Unfortunately, there are no clearly defined causes. Because of the way criminal statistics are collected and categorized, it is not entirely certain that adolescent criminal behavior has become more violent. If it has, among the possible causes are the easy availability of firearms of every sort, and the escalation of competition among rival groups.

Most adolescents eventually outgrow their group affiliations. As they mature, their identifications shift to different communities: those of the workplace, of the adults with whom they associate, and of the neighborhood in which they settle.

Membership and Reference Groups

The importance of the group or community in defining social roles and expected behaviors does not diminish; it is still as important among adults as it is among adolescents.[23] The nature of those roles and expected behaviors usually does change, however. Rebellion against adult authority and contempt for conventional standards of behavior are replaced with a more mature acceptance of social responsibility.

Membership in a community is not necessarily formalized. People can be influenced by groups in which they have no actual membership.

Geographical communities usually have no formal structure. They are simply composed of the people who live or work in, or frequent, a given area. Demographic communities' "membership" is statistically defined: A person is a "member" of a given community if he or she meets the criteria used to define the community.

Interest communities vary in the extent and type of their structure. Some have no formal structure at all. Any number of people might think of themselves as having a particular political ideology—conservative or liberal or independent or what-have-you—and yet there are no national organizations composed exclusively of people who share their ideology. Other interest communities do have a formal structure: for example, the two major political parties. However, relatively few people are actually dues-paying members of either party. Most people consider themselves either Republicans or Democrats on the basis of their voting tendency or their approval of the party's positions on various public issues.

Social scientists point out that people are influenced not only by groups or communities of which they are formally members, but also by communities with which they identify but in which they have no formal affiliation. Conversely, people sometimes maintain membership in formal organizations even though they have little or no interest in the organization or its purposes. When a person strongly identifies with a group, it becomes a *reference group* for that person: He or she adopts one of the roles available in the group and accepts its standards of behavior.[24] Reference groups become extremely important in establishing and maintaining a person's self-concept. People judge their own behavior, as well as the behavior of others, according to the standards of their reference group, and those judgments contribute to—or detract from—the individual's sense of self-worth.[25]

Summing Up: Communities and Social Behavior

Let us sum up what we have said so far. A community is any group of people who have something in common. Some types of communities include:

- Geographical communities—people who live in, work in, and frequent a particular area
- Demographic communities—people who share some statistical category or characteristic
- Interest communities—people who have a common interest such as a type of work, an ideology, a hobby, and so on

A family might be considered as both a demographic community and an interest community.

Individuals may be members of an interest community whether or not there is any formal, structured organization. People also may consider themselves members of a community even though they have no formal affiliation. In either case, a community may serve as a person's reference group, providing roles for a person to play and standards of behavior that the person attempts to emulate. People judge themselves and others by the standards of their reference groups.

Perhaps the concept of reference groups can be clarified by an example. A few years ago, the parents of a teenage girl agreed to let her hold a Valentine's Day party at home. She invited a number of her friends from school, some of whom brought other guests. By late evening, the party was roaring along; everyone was having a grand time.

An uninvited guest showed up at the front door, trying to "crash" the party. The hostess, who knew that the gatecrasher was a member of a gang, became frightened; she called the police. Two police officers arrived a few minutes later, but by then the gatecrasher had decided not to cause trouble, and had left. The police officers observed a large crowd of young people partying, but everything appeared to be in good order, so they started to leave.

As the officers were getting back into their cars, two young men who had been at the party got into an argument on the front lawn of the house. The argument quickly escalated into a shoving match. One of the police officers ran back to break up the fight. Someone (it has never been clear exactly who) struck the officer on the head with either a bottle or a rock. The officer was fairly seriously injured.

The other officer, who had remained in the patrol car, called the dispatcher and reported, "Officer down, officer needs help!" The dispatcher immediately relayed this call, then asked for additional information; the officer giving the report said that the first officer had an apparent head wound.

Soon there were more than a dozen police cars in front of the house; eventually more than fifty police officers showed up, most with sirens screaming. Naturally, the people at the party came streaming out of the house to see what was going on; so did their neighbors for more than a block in every direction. As many police as there were, there may have been two or three times as many neighborhood citizens.

Meanwhile, television reporters listening over their scanners had heard the "officer down" call and the report of an "officer with a head wound." One of the local television stations interrupted its programming with a bulletin that a police officer had been shot in the head at a riot.

In fact, there never was a riot. About a dozen people were arrested, but the charges (either for resisting arrest or for interfering with an arrest) were dropped on all of them a day later. Not one citizen was injured seriously enough to require medical treatment, and the only police officer who was injured was the one who tried to break up the fight.

How did all of this happen? The Valentine's Day party was being held in a working-class, almost entirely African-American neighborhood, and virtually all of the partygoers were black. The first two officers to arrive on the scene and all but one or two of the officers who came later were white or Hispanic.

What the police officers saw, or thought they saw, was a huge number of rowdy black adolescents who had been partying, perhaps drinking or using drugs, and who were interfering with the officers' lawful performance of their duty.

What the young people at the party saw, or thought they saw, was a mob of white people attacking their friends and neighbors for no reason.

Only the fact that cool heads prevailed on both sides kept a genuine riot from exploding, and possibly expanding throughout the neighborhood. As far as could be determined afterward, not one police officer drew a firearm, much less fired a shot. The adults in the neighborhood also did their best to restrain the young people from overreacting. Nevertheless, the incident might very easily have escalated out of control, because of the completely different perceptions on the part of the community residents and the police about what was happening. On both sides, what people saw or thought they saw depended very largely on which group they considered "us."[26]

Of course, reference groups and other communities are not the only source of social behaviors, and we do not mean to suggest that this is a complete explanation of human actions. People behave the way they do for any number of reasons, including their inherited capabilities and potentials, their unique personal histories and experiences, and, ultimately, their preferences and choices. Furthermore, because every person is a member of many different communities, it is impossible to ascribe an individual's behavior solely to membership in a single group.[27]

Nevertheless, an understanding of how groups affect and influence behavior can be valuable to someone, such as a police officer, whose main tasks are to observe, predict, and to a degree control social behavior. There can be little doubt that the members of some groups or communities are more likely to run afoul of the law than are others.[28]

CRIME AND COMMUNITY

In Chapter 1, we discussed how certain behaviors come to be defined as crimes, and why some people tend to reject those definitions. Now we can see that every community has its own distinctive code of behavior, and that the codes of some groups may be in disagreement with the standards of behavior implied by the criminal law.[29] This does not mean that everyone who is a member of such a community or group is necessarily a criminal. It does mean that becoming aware of such groups, their membership, and their influence among their neighbors may be useful to those who are responsible for maintaining social order.

Geographical Communities: Territories

In ancient times, the rule of law extended to whatever territory was controlled by a village chief or the king of a city-state. Later, the great empires were defined by the area over which the emperor's word was enforced. The very word *jurisdiction* (which means the right to exercise authority) is derived from two Latin words that mean "law" and "word" or "speaking." In other words, a jurisdiction is the speaking of a certain law or body of laws. In most contexts, a jurisdiction is a particular territory over which a lawmaking body has authority both to make and to enforce its laws.

Since all political and legal systems are based on the right to exercise authority over a given territory, it was only natural for early police agencies to be organized along territorial lines. Peel's constables and their American counterparts, the patrol officers, were assigned to enforce the law in specific territories, called precincts or beats. By the middle of the present century, most American law enforcement agencies regarded beat boundaries as inviolable walls: A patrol officer was expected to deal with the crimes on his beat and no other.

Modern police agencies usually treat beat and precinct boundaries more flexibly. Officers are encouraged to back up one another, to assist by responding to calls in adjacent beats when possible. In some agencies the concept of a fixed beat for each patrol officer has been all but abandoned: A number of officers are assigned joint responsibility for a district or sector containing several beats.

Advocates of community policing often begin with an assumption that beat assignments should be *less* flexible than is the standard practice today. The idea seems to be that in order for an officer to become intimately acquainted with the community he or she serves, that community must be rigidly defined. Later we will consider whether this idea is true.

Some Definitions

Before we can try to understand how geographical communities affect and are affected by policing, we need some more definitions. Those that follow are essentially our own and they are admittedly rather arbitrary.

We will use *territory* to mean any geographical area of undetermined size, scope, or nature.

Jurisdiction will mean a territory under the authority of a particular governing body. Thus, for example, a state is the territorial jurisdiction of the state's government; a city is the jurisdiction of the city's government. Conversely, a city government has jurisdiction only over the territory of the city.

A *district* will be a more or less recognizable part of a jurisdiction; for example, a large part of a city, recognizable by the presence of many types of industrial facilities, is an industrial district.

A *precinct* is an area established by law or by administrative rule for some legal purpose, such as the election of governmental officials, or such as the assignment of a group of law enforcement personnel. In some cities, a *ward* is essentially the same thing as a precinct.

A *beat* is a specific area assigned to one or more police officers for specific law enforcement purposes. Usually one patrol officer is assigned to provide preventive patrol and complaint response services to his or her assigned beat.

A *neighborhood* is an area in which there is a recognizable similarity in the types of physical structures and the uses made of them. Usually "neighborhood" is understood to mean an area of residences, but we will extend the term to mean areas that are primarily commercial or industrial, too.

Again, these definitions are arbitrary; their sole purpose is to give us a consistent vocabulary to use in discussing geographical communities.

HISTORIES IN CONCRETE

According to Wilson, "It is primarily at the neighborhood level that meaningful opportunities exist for the exercise of urban citizenship."[30] He also points out that, given a free choice, people choose to live in neighborhoods that consist mainly of people like themselves.[31] Thus there is a tendency toward homogeneity. This tendency is by no means accidental; it is an intentional by-product of the way that cities are built.

Rings of Development

The history of a city often can be seen in its physical structures. In almost all cities, large or small, the core is a commercial district, often called the *central business district* or CBD. Here commercial buildings—stores and office buildings—have replaced the city's original settlement of homes, shops, and small industries. Public facilities, such as government buildings, hospitals, and libraries, usually are found in the CBD as well, presumably because this placement makes them equally accessible to all of the city's residents.

Around the CBD is a fringe or *transition zone* containing dilapidated housing, marginal businesses, and obsolete industrial facilities. In some large cities, the transition zone includes a "skid row" of cheap hotels and apartments, taverns, and disreputable businesses; in a few cities, the main entertainment district of night clubs, theaters, and dance halls also can be found in the transition zone. Eventually, investors will buy up the land in this zone, raze the existing buildings, and add new commercial buildings to the city's core.

Around the transition zone are concentric rings of residential and commercial neighborhoods, ranging from the oldest (generally more than fifty years old) to the newest. Old neighborhoods show the greatest variation in physical and social conditions, since much depends on the extent to which owners have maintained their property. Some cities have *gentrified* neighborhoods in which old but sturdy homes have been renovated, creating stable, attractive neighborhoods. More often, the oldest areas are slowly decaying as the upwardly mobile residents move out to newer areas and are replaced by people with lower incomes and less ability to pay high rents.

The newest neighborhoods almost always are found on the edges of the city. The reason is simple: the farther from the core of the city one goes, the lower the cost of land. But the farther from the edge of the city one goes, the higher the cost of developing the infrastructure of roads and utilities. Therefore, the most economically attractive land for new development is at the very edge of the city, where a compromise can be found between land costs and the cost of the infrastructure.

Residential developers buy a large tract of land and subdivide it into as many smaller parcels as they can. It is axiomatic that developers want to obtain the highest possible return for their investment. Usually this means developing the land as a mix of residential and commercial areas.

Subdivision development is something of an art; when it is done well, the developer can attain high profits while providing an attractive environment that will remain stable for generations. When done poorly, a subdivision can be an "instant slum" whose value declines rapidly as cheap, poorly constructed buildings deteriorate in only a few years. Thus, the physical and social character of newer neighborhoods is a reflection of the entrepreneurial abilities, aesthetic values, and the ethics of real estate developers.

Plans and Zones

City planning practices also influence the character of neighborhoods. In all states, most cities have *zoning authority*, which is the right to decide what kinds of structures—residential, commercial, or industrial—may be built in each area. In most states, larger cities exercise zoning authority not only within their boundaries but in an *extraterritorial jurisdiction* (ETJ), typically five miles beyond the present city limits. The purpose of the ETJ is to ensure that areas that eventually will be annexed into the city are developed according to a reasonable plan. Zoning laws and regulations themselves are exceedingly complex, specifying in excruciating detail exactly what kind of structure may be built in a given area.

The generalizations in the preceding paragraphs apply to most American cities, large and small—but not to all. Some cities (Los Angeles and Miami, for example) developed very rapidly, outstripping the ability of local governments to plan their growth. Los Angeles in particular developed not as a single core city, but as a collection of small towns, once widely separated, that grew explosively and coalesced into a huge metropolitan area divided into dozens of separate jurisdictions.

Houston is another exception to our generalizations; the city has no zoning laws and no city planning agency. As a result, the city is a hodgepodge of residential, commercial, and industrial areas scattered almost randomly across the landscape.

Some cities (notably Gary, Indiana) began as "company towns," built and owned by the town's main industry specifically to provide housing and commercial services for factory workers. Although the idea of the company town has fallen into disrepute, the original concept was once considered a major social advance. Industrial capitalists were supposed to ensure the welfare and satisfaction of their workers by providing not just wages but a comfortable, attractive living and social environment as well. Unfortunately, this ideal was rarely attained in the face of economic reality; most company towns turned out to be a collection of the cheapest possible housing and a limited range of company-owned stores selling shoddy merchandise at inflated prices.

Every city, regardless of its physical and social history, is a collection of neighborhoods—residential, commercial, and industrial—each of which exists for a specific set of reasons, mostly having to do with the profits of investors. The character of a neighborhood reflects those reasons and influences the kinds of people who live, work, shop, play, and interact in it. Wilson may be correct in saying that people choose to live in a neighborhood made up of people like themselves, but we cannot ignore the fact that those choices are constrained by several factors, chief among them the cost of living in a particular place.

As we explore in Chapter 3, it is the social character of a neighborhood that most affects the kinds and quantities of law enforcement services it requires.

Neighborhoods

Our definition of neighborhood (an area of similar structures) says nothing about the size of the area to be considered. In most cases, the entire central business district can be considered a single commercial neighborhood. At the other extreme, a single large factory complex might be considered an industrial neighborhood. Residential neighborhoods may vary from a single city block to an area of several square miles.

Most advocates of community policing assume that neighborhoods are more or less self-defined.[32] The assumption is not entirely invalid. In fact, most neighborhoods adopt the identification given to them by the original developers of the area, although over time these identifications may erode. For example, a developer may call a new subdivision "Knollwood Estates." Later, another developer, capitalizing on the popularity of the Knollwood Estates subdivision, may call an adjacent development

"Knollwood Manor"; a commercial developer may call a nearby shopping center "Knollwood Park Mall." Eventually, the entire area may come to be known simply as "Knollwood."

Defining a particular neighborhood and its boundaries can be a significant political issue. In some cities, neighborhood associations—groups of residents who have formed some sort of organization—are recognized by the city government and given some limited role in community planning. But a problem arises when different groups of residents from the same area compete to represent their neighborhood. Portland, Oregon, has gone so far as to establish a rather elaborate procedure by which neighborhood associations become recognized. There are no fewer than 93 associations, organized into seven district "coalitions" under the city's Office of Neighborhood Associations.[33]

Once a neighborhood has been defined, what then? In Chapter 3, we discuss how the physical and social character of a neighborhood affects its needs for police services in a community policing system. But first, we need to gain a better understanding of what a "community policing system" is—or could be.

"NEW AND IMPROVED"?

Whenever a new product is introduced into the marketplace, prospective consumers want to know three things:

- What is it?
- How is it different from the old stuff?
- Is it really better?

Community policing may not be a "product" in the usual sense, but it is a new entry into the marketplace of ideas about law enforcement, and the same three questions apply. Unfortunately, the producers and "marketers" of this new idea seem to have a difficult time answering those three questions.

Defining a Concept of Policing

Patrick Murphy, one of the first to experiment with patrol techniques that are often regarded as community policing, and one of the first to use the term, admits, "Community policing means different things in different cities. . .[but] the community policing idea is fully implemented when all patrol officers participate."[34] In his view, "the function of the police is to assist every neighborhood community to exercise social control."[35]

Greene and Mastrofski agree:

> It should be emphasized that community policing means many things to many people. It is at once an ideology, an organizational framework for many police activities, and a set of individual programs.[36]

Several years ago, criminologists Jerome Skolnick and David Bayley visited and studied metropolitan police departments around the world. They concluded that there was a "bewildering" variety of law enforcement programs that were called "community policing," but there were also some common elements to all of the programs:

- A growing reliance on "community-based crime prevention," through the use of citizen education, neighborhood watches, and similar techniques, as opposed to relying entirely on police patrols to prevent crime
- The reorientation of patrol from being primarily an emergency-response force ("chasing calls") to a greater emphasis on "proactive" techniques such as foot patrol
- Increased police accountability to the citizens they are supposed to serve
- Decentralization of command and police authority, with more discretion allowed to lower-ranking "generalist" officers, and more initiative expected of them[37]

According to a more recent publication by Bayley, "Community policing represents the most serious and sustained attempt to reformulate the purpose and practices of policing since the development of the 'professional' model in the early twentieth century."[38]

Another of the early advocates of community policing is Lee P. Brown, former chief executive of the police departments of Atlanta, Houston, and New York City. Brown regards community policing as "not a particular program within a department, but. . .the dominant philosophy throughout the department."[39] He adds, "Although it is an operating style, community policing is also a *philosophy* of policing that contains several interrelated components. . . [that] help distinguish it from traditional policing."[40] (Emphasis in original.) He goes on to list those "components":

- A problem-solving, results-oriented approach to law enforcement.
- Articulation of police values that incorporate citizen involvement.
- Accountability of the police to each neighborhood.
- Decentralization of authority.
- Police-community partnership and sharing of power.
- Beat boundaries that correspond to neighborhood boundaries.
- Permanent assignment of patrol officers.
- Empowerment of patrol officers to show initiative.
- Coordination of investigations at both neighborhood and citywide levels.
- New roles for supervisors and managers, as supporters of patrol rather than evaluators of patrol officers.
- Changes in the content of training at all levels.
- New systems of performance evaluation, placing much less emphasis on "production" of quantified activities.
- New approaches to "demand management," the response of the agency to calls for service.[41]

This is a long list and it implies a virtually total restructuring of a police agency, its operating policies, and the roles of its personnel. One would suppose that an agency that has adopted community policing and implemented it to the extent Brown describes would look very different from a traditional police department.

But not everyone thinks that community policing requires such wholesale change. The U.S. Department of Justice, in its monograph on community policing, describes it simply as "in essence a collaboration between the police and the community that identifies and solves community problems."[42] Police and citizens could "collaborate" in any number of ways, to a greater or lesser extent, without seriously changing the organizational structure or operating policies of a traditional police agency. All that might be required is an admonition to patrol officers and investigators to listen to what citizens tell them. A few "community liaison officers" assigned to attend public meetings and solicit citizens' comments also might be helpful.

Indeed, that is about all that some "community policing" efforts have included. In Flint, Michigan, in the early 1980s, foot patrols were reintroduced in some high-density residential neighborhoods. Residents were delighted, and even voted to increase the police department's budget to permit the experimental program to continue.[43] But according to some skeptics, such as Bayley, "police foot patrols make people feel better but they do not prevent crime."[44]

Again and again, community policing theorists insist, as David L. Carter puts it, that "community policing is a philosophy, not a tactic."[45] Kelling and Moore describe it as a "paradigm,"[46] a model of the real world. The various definitions we have reviewed characterize community policing as an *idea*, a *philosophy*, a *concept*, and so forth.

Defining a Philosophy of Policing

A philosophy is a set of ideas about what is true and what is important or valuable. All philosophies are based on some set of assumptions about the nature of reality. Often these assumptions are implicit, and therefore difficult to detect and analyze. Even when the assumptions are stated explicitly, it is often impossible to test them, to prove whether or not they are valid. Assumptions that can be tested are called *hypotheses*, and a philosophy that is based primarily on testable hypotheses deserves to be called scientific.

Traditional police practices, sometimes called the "professional model," are based on a philosophy, too. It is a philosophy that developed in American law enforcement early in this century, and was articulated and expressed by several influential theorists. In Chapter 1, we mentioned the role of August Vollmer, who as an active police executive, as a college professor, and as a leader of professional organizations, probably did more than anyone to establish the intellectual and practical foundations of the professional model. One of his most influential disciples was Orlando W. Wilson, who, like his mentor, taught at Berkeley and at Chicago, served as the chief of police in several cities (including Oakland and Chicago), held office in several major professional organizations (including the IACP), and was a prolific writer and speaker. Wilson's textbook on police administration (co-authored by Roy C. McLaren) served as the core curriculum in police academies and colleges for some three decades, and is still in print.

The "Professional" Model

The philosophy espoused by Vollmer and O. W. Wilson was based on assumptions that were almost entirely implicit and untestable. It is impossible to document those assumptions since they were rarely stated openly; we can only infer what the assumptions were from what the theorists said and did. On this basis, we believe that the underlying assumptions of the "professional model" of policing are as follows:

- The primary purpose of the police is to protect the law-abiding public from criminals (that is, people who violate the criminal laws).

- The most effective means of accomplishing this goal is to identify and apprehend criminals, to collect sufficient evidence to ensure that the criminals are convicted of their crimes, and to punish the criminals through incarceration or other methods.

- Given sufficient resources, the police could, in principle, eradicate all crime. However, this would require enormous resources beyond what the public is willing to devote to the police. Therefore, it is most efficient to devote the limited resources of the police to the eradication of serious crimes, those that cause the greatest disruption, injury, loss of life, and property damage (and that are accorded the most severe penalties in the law).

- Serious crimes are committed mainly by bad people who prey upon their innocent, law-abiding neighbors.

- Bad people, in order to avoid punishment, employ various means to make themselves indistinguishable from law-abiding citizens.

- Identifying and apprehending criminals therefore requires the use of sophisticated techniques, which in turn demand highly trained, skilled, and experienced specialists who employ the best available scientific devices and methods.

- Since the specialists cannot be everywhere at once, their essential function must be supported by a corps of generalist patrol officers. The main purpose of the generalists is twofold: first, to prevent crime by their mere presence, thus discouraging would-be criminals; second, when a crime is reported or discovered, to provide the specialists with a minimal amount of information about the nature of the crime, the identity of the victim(s), and, if known, the identity of the perpetrator.

- These limited functions of the generalists do not require any great expertise or competence. Therefore, it is both efficient and safe to assign generalist duties to people who have minimal training, experience, and competence.

- Because the generalist personnel have limited competence, it is necessary to provide them with extensive guidance in the form of policies and procedures that are designed to minimize the risk of dangerous or embarrassing mistakes. The generalist personnel are expected to know and obey these policies and procedures, unquestioningly and without exception.

- The vast majority of law-abiding citizens want nothing from the police except protection from criminals. Constitutional and ethical imperatives demand that the law-abiding public be left strictly alone except when they become victims or there is evidence that they have committed a crime.

- Conversely, law-abiding citizens who are neither victims nor criminals have no business interfering in the legitimate work of the police, since their ignorance of the intricacies of the law and of the sophisticated techniques used by the police are likely to hinder the police in their essential duties.

We have stated these assumptions rather bluntly, and no doubt apologists for the "professional model" would quarrel with some of them. Nevertheless, we think that the foregoing list is a fair representation of the basis for traditional law enforcement practices. We also think that these assumptions are almost entirely false, and that the failure of the "professional model" can be attributed primarily to the lack of validity of these underlying assumptions.

It would be unfair to put all of the blame on Vollmer and O. W. Wilson. The ideas they articulated and espoused were widely shared, not only within the criminal justice field but among the general public. For some three generations, Americans were satisfied that the police were doing the right thing, were doing it reasonably well (except in rare cases of scandalous corruption), and should be doing more of it.

Failure of the Model

The erosion of public confidence came with devastating swiftness in the 1960s, and for the first time, criminal justice scholars and practitioners were forced to reexamine some of their assumptions.

The Kansas City preventive patrol experiment was supposed to help determine which of several patrol techniques would be most efficient. Instead, the experiment demonstrated that *all* "preventive patrol" is a waste of time. Both the experiment and the analysis of the results have been criticized on procedural and methodological grounds, but the fact is that the hypothesis that random vehicular patrol of some sort reduces the incidence of crime was shown to be false. It is false because it relies on assumptions about the nature of crime and criminal behavior, and about the role of generalist police officers, which are themselves false.

The RAND study of criminal investigation is even more disastrous for the "professional model." According to the Vollmer-Wilson theory, scientific methods of collecting and analyzing physical evidence at a crime scene are the best means of identifying the perpetrator. The RAND study found that crime scene evidence is almost entirely useless for that purpose. It is mostly useful, if at all, to corroborate the identification of the perpetrator and persuade a judge or jury of the defendant's guilt. In fact, highly trained, skilled, and experienced specialists rarely use sophisticated techniques to identify criminals. They rely mostly on information volunteered to them by victims and other law-abiding citizens. Collecting such information usually is well within the competence of even the most inexperienced and minimally trained generalist.

In short, the Vollmer-Wilson assumptions about efficient and effective law enforcement practices were simply wrong.

So were their assumptions about the nature of criminals and criminal behavior. Again, we should be fair: The systematic study of criminal psychology and behavior was in its raw infancy when Vollmer began to develop his theories. Nevertheless, the traditional law enforcement system has blithely ignored almost everything that has been learned about crime as a manifestation of social psychology. The seminal work of such criminologists as Edwin Sutherland and Donald Cressey has had virtually no impact on the "professional model" of law enforcement even though they found that the traditional assumptions were mostly false.[47]

New Models, New Assumptions

Of course, the community policing philosophy also is based on a set of assumptions. But many of the assumptions have been made explicit by one or another advocate. Most of the assumptions are testable; some (but not all) have been tested and found to be valid, at least under specified conditions. In a few instances, the assumptions of community policing rest directly on evidence provided by social scientists outside of the criminal justice field.

The differences between community policing and traditional policing—the "old stuff"—are most obvious when the underlying assumptions are compared. The following list represents what we believe to be the most widely shared assumptions of community policing:

- The primary purpose of the police is to assist the public in establishing and maintaining a safe, orderly social environment.[48]
- This goal is accomplished by providing a variety of services to the community. Identifying and apprehending criminals is one of those services; it is important, but not necessarily more important than other services.[49]
- It is not possible, even in principle, for the police or any other governmental agency to eradicate all crime. Crime is simply a manifestation of social disorder, which is in turn a product of complex social interactions.[50]
- Some serious crimes are committed by "bad people," predatory criminals who prey on the innocent. However, many serious crimes are committed by otherwise ordinary, law-abiding individuals. They are indistinguishable from the general population because they *are* the general population.[51]
- People commit crimes, serious and otherwise, for all sorts of reasons, many of which arise directly out of their social relationships. Some other reasons for criminal behavior include financial desperation, emotional illness, limited mental capacity, alcohol or drug intoxication, and the influence of peers. Treating all criminal law violators indiscriminately as "bad people" is both unjust and ineffective.[52]
- Some law enforcement services require the extensive training and expertise of specialists and technical experts. However, by far the greater part of policing involves services that are performed by generalists, usually the patrol force.[53]
- The services performed by the generalist patrol force require a broad range of competencies, most of which can be developed through training. Fortunately, in recent years the quality of the personnel recruited and hired as patrol officers has increased, and they have been given more and better training. Thus it is reasonable to expect patrol officers to have the skills and talents necessary to perform the demanding services expected of them.[54]
- Increasing the range of services performed by generalist patrol officers, and expecting a higher level of performance, also increases the job satisfaction felt by the officers, and thus their motivation to do superior work.[55]
- In every community, citizens need the police to perform various services to help control misbehavior, not all of which is specifically criminal, and to help maintain

social order. These needs are not always obvious; often they must be discovered through the cooperative efforts of the police and citizens.[56]

- Citizens not only make demands on the police for services, but also must take an active role in promoting social order. Ultimately, there must be a close and collaborative relationship between the police and the communities they serve.[57]

There may be other assumptions that we have failed to identify, and some advocates of community policing might argue about our list. Nevertheless, we contend that these assumptions are critical to the philosophy of community policing, that most of them are testable hypotheses, and that in fact most of them have been tested and found to be valid. On that basis, we would argue that the community policing philosophy deserves to be called scientific.

Now we know what community policing is: It is a philosophy, a set of ideas about what is true, important, and valuable, specifically with regard to the role and mission of a law enforcement agency in American society. We also know how this set of ideas is different from the "old stuff," the philosophy of traditional policing.

But in what way is community policing really better?

In fact, the idea of community policing has been around for more than two decades, and numerous approaches to its implementation have been tried. Not all can be considered unqualified successes, but there has been enough experience by enough different police agencies in enough different places and circumstances to say that the concept is practical, appealing to the public, and at least as effective in fulfilling the fundamental mission of law enforcement as the traditional model. Examples of successful implementations of community policing can be found in dozens of books and hundreds of monographs and journal articles.

As one might expect, there are people in the law enforcement profession who are vehemently opposed to changing the way they have been taught to do things, what they have learned to believe is "the right way." There are also people whose enthusiasm for new ideas may have exceeded their capacity to implement those ideas soundly.

Reasonable questions have been raised about some of the specific efforts to implement community policing. Concerns have been expressed about exactly how the police-community collaboration is to be achieved and what it might imply.[58] We have traced the origins of the community policing idea back to the late 1960s, but most of the early experiments took place less than twenty years ago; in the realm of law enforcement, that is only yesterday.

In any case, if the assumptions that underlie the philosophy are valid, the issue becomes how best to implement that philosophy. Platitudes about developing a warm and fuzzy relationship with the citizenry will accomplish nothing if patrol officers still spend much of their time chasing after 911 calls and the rest of their time cruising randomly around their beats. The philosophy of community policing implies substantial changes in the roles of patrol officers and other members of a police agency, but does not specify what those new roles should be. In order to succeed, community policing must involve changes not only in the organizational structure, but in the way people (particularly, but not only, police officers) think about themselves and their work.

MYTHS AND MISCONCEPTIONS ABOUT COMMUNITY POLICING

New ideas, like newborn babies, can be damaged as badly by their friends as by their enemies. They can die of neglect and indifference or they can be smothered by excessive enthusiasm. They can be pushed too fast and too hard by unrealistic expectations, or they can be destroyed by inappropriate criticism. The philosophy of community policing has been subjected to all of these dangers.

In particular, community policing has been the target of some remarkably intransigent resistance within the law enforcement profession itself. Rank-and-file police officers, experienced supervisors, and high-level police executives all have had their own reasons to reject the new model of policing. Some of those reasons may stem from simple self-interest, but others appear to represent a sincere concern that the best ideals of traditional law enforcement are being eroded.

Before we can fully understand what community policing is, we must consider what it is *not*. So many myths and misconceptions about community policing have appeared in the literature or have been expressed by police officers that we cannot address all of them. Instead, we address four that seem to be particularly widespread and potentially damaging.

Myth #1

The first myth is that community policing is so radically different from traditional law enforcement practices that it requires a complete restructuring of a law enforcement agency.

The fact is that almost all law enforcement agencies, even the most traditional, have practiced some aspects of what we now consider community policing. Furthermore, the work of a police officer, in an agency that has adopted the community policing philosophy, still requires most of the same skills, techniques, and practices that are taught in traditional police academies.

Ultimately, as the community policing philosophy is implemented, some changes in an agency's organizational structure, policies, and procedures will occur. Some of them might have changed anyway, even in a traditional agency, although perhaps not in the same directions. There still will be administrators and supervisors and officers on the street; there still will be technical specialists and support personnel.

Organizational restructuring is not the first step in implementing community policing. It may not always be necessary even as the last step.

Myth #2

The second myth is that community policing involves an enormous increase in officers' workload, especially for patrol officers, who are suddenly required to "interact with the community" in addition to all of their ordinary duties of preventive patrol and responding to calls for service.

The truth is that many officers will spend part of their time in different activities, depending on their assignment and the nature of the community in which they are deployed. Patrol officers and their supervisors will be expected to take the initiative in establishing a partnership with the community. However, their ability to perform these new duties will depend on their being relieved of some of the burden of "chasing 9-1-1 calls," plodding through administrative paperwork, or laboring at tasks that either do not need to be done at all, or can be done just as well by someone else.

Ultimately, if community policing lives up to its promise of making neighborhoods safer, most patrol officers should be able to spend most of their time on productive, "proactive" duties without being in any way overburdened.

Myth #3

The third myth is that community policing distracts police officers from their main responsibility of enforcing the law, and therefore leads to an increase in the incidence of crime. Evidence is sometimes offered to support this myth, in the form of crime rate statistics from some of the cities that have implemented one or another form of community policing.

As we discuss in more detail in Chapter 8, crime rate statistics are always subject to many possible interpretations and probably should be regarded with a healthy dose of skepticism. Whether the crime rates go up or down in a given community during a period of one year, two years, or five years may be due to many different factors and it is impossible to say with certainty that the organizational structure, policies, or philosophy of the police department is more significant than any other factor.

However, the underlying misconception is that officers in a community policing agency are "distracted" from "real police work." The first duty of a police officer is to enforce the law by identifying and arresting offenders and gathering evidence to secure a conviction. That is just as true in a community policing agency as in a traditional agency. The question is not *what* police officers should do, but *why* and *how* they do it.

Myth #4

Perhaps the most pernicious myth of all is that community policing turns patrol officers into "social workers."

This myth is triply damning. First, it implies that there is something demeaning about social work. Social work is a respected, honorable, and worthy profession in itself. Its practitioners often hold postgraduate degrees. Social workers devote their careers to alleviating the pain and misery of poverty, social dislocation, and disability. They mobilize a community's resources to help the most disadvantaged members of society. They are—or ought to be—the natural allies of police officers.

Secondly, the myth reflects a profound misconception about the nature of the criminal justice system and the role of police officers in that system. The accusation that community policing "turns cops into social workers" implies that the proper mission of the police is *limited* to catching criminals. In fact, the police have always had a broader role than that in the criminal justice system and in society as a whole.

The philosophy of community policing is based in part on the assumption that the mission of the police is to promote social order in the community. One aspect of that mission is to identify and apprehend people who violate the law.

However, there are other aspects of the police mission, including helping the victims of crime to recover, helping members of the community to protect themselves from predators, and even helping the families of offenders to deal with the disruption in their lives.

The police cannot fulfill all of these roles by themselves. They do not have the resources to do so, and therefore must depend on other segments of the community (including social workers) to participate. But neither can the police afford to ignore any of these aspects of their mission, or inevitably there will be a constant increase in social disorder no matter how many criminals are caught.

If it came to a choice between "acting like social workers" or spending the rest of one's life chasing 9-1-1 calls, we think that most sensible police officers would choose the former.

But again, the myth reflects a misunderstanding of what community policing requires of police officers. In a community policing agency, patrol officers still wear a uniform and a badge. They still carry a gun, a baton, and the other paraphernalia of their trade. They still make traffic stops and issue citations. They still answer 9-1-1 calls, interview victims and witnesses, collect physical evidence, and write incident reports. In short, the differences between what police officers do in a community policing agency and what they do in a traditional agency is so subtle that an uninformed, casual observer might not see any difference at all.

Community policing does not require cops to become social workers. Rather, community policing requires police officers to understand their mission and their tasks in the context of their society. Community policing also requires police officers at every level, from street cop to administrator, to enter into a working partnership with the community they serve.

One aspect of that partnership is that the police must be responsive to the needs of the community. As we have noted, those needs are not always obvious and not always clearly articulated even when the community is invited to express them. Before we attempt to determine what police officers should be doing, perhaps logic dictates that we discuss how the needs of the community should be identified. We will do that in Chapter 3.

FOOTNOTES

1. Stephen D. Mastrofski, "Community Policing as Reform: A Cautionary Tale," in Jack R. Greene and Stephen D. Mastrofski, eds., *Community Policing: Rhetoric or Reality* (New York: Praeger, 1988), p. 49.

2. Bureau of Justice Assistance, *Understanding Community Policing* (Washington, D.C.: U.S. Department of Justice), 1994, p. 13.

3. Robert C. Trojanowicz and Samuel L. Dixon, *Criminal Justice and the Community* (Englewood Cliffs, N.J.: Prentice Hall, 1974), pp. 5–6.

4. Terry Thomas, *The Police and Social Workers*, 2nd ed. (Brookfield, VT: Ashgate Publishing., 1994), p. 138.

5. Gary W. Sykes, "Stability Amid Change," in Larry T. Hoover, ed., *Police Management: Issues and Perspectives* (Washington, D.C.: Police Executive Research Forum, 1992), p. 164.

6. Bureau of Justice Assistance, *Understanding Community Policing*, p. 14.

7. Trojanowicz and Dixon, *Criminal Justice and the Community*, p. 7.

8. Trojanowicz and Dixon, *Criminal Justice and the Community*, p. 7.

9. Trojanowicz and Dixon, *Criminal Justice and the Community*, pp. 12–16.

10. George L. Kelling and James T. Stewart, "Neighborhoods and Police: The Maintenance of Civil Authority," in *Perspectives on Policing* No. 10, U.S. Department of Justice, (May 1989), p. 1.

11. James Q. Wilson, *Thinking About Crime*, rev. ed. (New York: Basic Books, 1983), p. 28.

12. Wilson, *Thinking About Crime*, p. 28.

13. Mastrofski, "Community Policing as Reform," p. 49.

14. Patrick V. Murphy, "Organizing for Community Policing," in John W. Bizzack, ed., *Issues in Policing: New Perspectives* (Lexington, Kentucky: Autumn House, 1991), p. 114.

15. Morris Rosenberg, *Conceiving the Self* (New York: Basic Books, 1979), p. 10.

16. Anthony V. Bouza and Lawrence W. Sherman, "Controlling Police Wrongdoing," in Bizzack, ed., *Issues in Policing*, p. 132.

17. William Ker Muir, Jr., *Police: Streetcorner Politicians* (Chicago: University of Chicago Press, 1977).

18. Ashley Montague, *The Humanization of Man* (Cleveland: World Publishing Co., 1962), p. 63.

19. Rosenberg, *Conceiving the Self*, p. 10.

20. Elisha Y. Babad, Max Birnbaum, and Kenneth D. Benne, *The Social Self*. Sage Library of Social Research, Vol. 144. (Beverly Hills, Calif.: Sage, 1983) p. 211.

21. Babad, Birnbaum, and Benne, *The Social Self*, pp. 224–226.

22. Tamar Lewin, "Global Study Finds Nuclear Family Fading into Past," in *Austin American-Statesman* (from New York Times News Service), May 31, 1995, p. 1.

23. Elliot Aronson, *The Social Animal,* 5th ed. (New York: W. H. Freeman, 1988), pp. 13–55.

24. Babad, Birnbaum, and Benne, *The Social Self*, p. 22.

25. Rosenberg, *Conceiving the Self,* p. 12–13.

26. The incident described here occurred in Austin, Texas, on February 14, 1995, and was extensively reported for the next several days in the *Austin American-Statesman;* it has become known locally as the "Cedar Street incident."

27. Babad, Birnbaum, and Benne, *The Social Self,* p. 31.

28. Parviz Saney, *Crime and Culture in America* (Westport, Conn.: Greenwood Press, 1986), p. 11, p. 36.

29. Wilson, *Thinking About Crime*, p. 33.

30. Wilson, *Thinking About Crime,* p. 29.

31. Wilson, *Thinking About Crime*, p. 33.

32. Bureau of Justice Assistance, *Understanding Community Policing*, p. 34.

33. Diana Dworin, "A Crazy Quilt of Austin Politics," in *Austin American-Statesman*, May 6, 1995, p. 1.

34. Murphy, "Organizing for Community Policing," in Bizzack, ed., *Issues in Policing*, pp. 118–119.

35. Murphy, "Organizing for Community Policing," in Bizzack, ed., *Issues in Policing*, p. 121.

36. Greene and Mastrofski, *Community Policing: Rhetoric or Reality*, p. xiii.

37. Jerome H. Skolnick and David H. Bayley, "Community Policing: Issues and Practices Around the World," in *Issues and Practices in Criminal Justice*, May 1988 (Washington: National Institute of Justice, U.S. Dept. of Justice, 1988)

38. David H. Bayley, *Police for the Future* (New York: Oxford University Press, 1994), p. 104.

39. Lee P. Brown, "Community Policing: A Practical Guide for Police Officials," in *Perspectives on Policing*, no. 12 (September 1989), p. 1.

40. Brown, "Community Policing: Practical Guide," p. 5.

41. Brown, "Community Policing: Practical Guide," pp. 5–6.

42. Bureau of Justice Assistance, *Understanding Community Policing*, p. vii.

43. Robert C. Trojanowicz, *An Evaluation of the Neighborhood Foot Patrol Program in Flint, Michigan* (East Lansing, Mich.: Michigan State University, 1982). Also reported in Trojanowicz, "An Evaluation of a Neighborhood Foot Patrol Program," in *Journal of Police Science and Administration*, November, 1983, pp. 410–419.

44. Bayley, *Police for the Future*, p. 6.

45. David L. Carter, "Community Alliance," in Hoover, ed., *Police Management* p. 78.

46. George L. Kelling and Mark H. Moore, "The Evolving Strategy of Policing," in *Perspectives on Policing*, no. 4 (November 1988).

47. Edwin H. Sutherland and Donald R. Cressey, *Criminology*, 10th ed. (Philadelphia: J. B. Lippincott, 1978).

48. Skolnick and Bayley, "Community Policing: Issues and Practices Around the World," p. 3: police and the public are "co-producers" of public safety and order. Bureau of Justice Assistance, *Understanding Community Policing*, p. vii: "Community policing is, in essence, a collaboration between the police and the community that identifies and solves community problems." Murphy, "Organizing for Community Policing," in Bizzack, ed., *Issues in Policing,* p. 121: "The function of the police is to assist every neighborhood community to exercise social control."

49. Frank J. Remington, "The Limits and Possibilities of the Criminal Law," in University of Notre Dame Law School, *The Challenge of Crime in a Free Society* (New York: DaCapo Press, 1971), p. 56: "When we talk about. . . the philosophy of the criminal law, it is sort of like talking about the philosophy of the wastebasket. It is the place where all things go that are not wanted. . . it is filled with all kinds of stuff that has been rejected by other less drastic methods of social control whether governmental, family, or religious." Wilson, *Thinking About Crime*, p. 56: Most police activity involves minor crimes and noncriminal events.

50. George L. Kelling and Elizabeth M. Watson, "Creativity with Accountability," in Hoover, ed., *Police Management*, pp. 141–142: "Street crime. . . is not only the predatory behavior of persons who are so predisposed, but includes criminal activities by people who are familiar with each other. . . . The problems enshrouded by the phrase 'street crime' are fraught with complexity and ambiguity. . . . Many of the critical issues society and police are now confronting. . . place police in the middle of family, sexual, and neighborhood relationships."

51. Saney, *Crime and Culture in America*, p. 11, p. 36. Stuart A. Scheingold, *The Politics of Street Crime* (Philadelphia: Temple University Press, 1991), pp. 1–28. Alfred Blumstein, Jacqueline Cohen, Jeffrey A. Roth, and Christy A. Visher, eds., *Criminal Careers and "Career Criminals"* (Washington, D.C.: National Academy Press, 1986) is a monumental summary of current research in criminology.

52. Henry S. Ruth, Jr., "To Dust Shall Ye Return?" in Notre Dame Law School, *The Challenge of Crime,* p. 18: "To speak of controlling crime only in terms of the work of the police, the courts, and the correctional apparatus is to refuse to face the fact that widespread crime implies a widespread failure of society as a whole." Bayley, *Police for the Future,* p. 10: "Most—perhaps as much as 90 percent—of the differences in crime rates can be explained by differences in such factors" as employment status, income, educational levels, gender, age, ethnic mix, and family composition.

53. Kelling and Moore, "Evolving Strategy," p. 11.

54. Wilson, *Thinking About Crime*, pp. 111–112; also, p. 113: "Properly trained and organized, the police may help evoke a sense of community and a capacity for self-regulation where none is now found."

55. Bureau of Justice Assistance, *Understanding Community Policing*, p. 48: "Patrol officers will experience greater job satisfaction as they accept higher levels of responsibility and accountability. Officers are often able to resolve issues quickly, allowing them to see the immediate results of their efforts. With high morale and greater job satisfaction, patrol officers will more effectively mobilize the community . . . . The job satisfaction they experience will help make the community policing strategy a success."

56. Murphy, "Organizing for Community Policing," in Bizzack, ed., *Issues in Policing* p. 113: "It is a cardinal principle of democratic societies that ultimate responsibility for peace, good order, and law observance rests with the community of citizens of that society, not with an organized police force." Kelling and Watson, "Creativity with Accountability," pp. 143–144: "Disorder, as well as serious crime, creates citizen fear. . . . Fear, stimulated by disorder, not just street crime, drives citizens from alleys, streets, parks, public transportation, and cities." Wilson, *Thinking About Crime*, p. 29: "It is the breakdown of neighborhood controls. . .that accounts for the principal concerns of many urban citizens." Lisa M. Riechers and Roy R. Roberg, "Community Policing: A Critical Review," in *Journal of Police Science and Administration* 17, no. 2 (June 1990), 107–108.

57. Sykes, "Stability Amid Change," p. 165: "At the heart of this community policing collection of ideas is the yearning that police and citizens can have an intimate, cooperative, and nonauthoritarian relationship." George L. Kelling, "Police and Communities: The Quiet Revolution," in *Perspectives on Policing*, no. 1. (Washington, D.C.: National Institute of Justice, U.S. Dept. of Justice, June 1988), p. 7: "Officers must create for themselves the best responses to problems; and police must become intimately involved with citizens." Herman Goldstein, *Problem-Oriented Policing* (New York: McGraw-Hill, 1990), pp. 32–49.

58. Bayley, *Police for the Future*, p. 117. George L. Kelling, Robert Wasserman, and Hubert Williams, "Police Accountability and Community Policing," in *Perspectives on Policing*, no. 7, (November 1988), pp. 2–3. Larry T. Hoover, "The Police Mission," in Hoover, ed., *Police Management*.

CHAPTER 3

UNDERSTANDING COMMUNITY NEEDS

If there is any one point on which virtually all of the advocates of community policing agree, it is this: The police should tailor the services they provide to fit the specific needs of each community they serve.[1]

The difference between community policing and the traditional law enforcement philosophy could hardly be clearer. From Peel to Vollmer to the present day defenders of the *status quo*, the assumption always has been that the most significant "service" provided by the police consists of two elements: responding to complaints and arresting offenders.

This assumption, in turn, rests on several implicit assumptions about the nature of criminal behavior and the role of law enforcement. One such implicit assumption is that crimes are committed mostly by "bad people" who, once they have been identified, can be removed from society through arrest, conviction, and incarceration. Presumably, if the police can just catch enough of these "bad people," they will all be in prison and crime will disappear from society.

A second assumption is that identifying criminals (unless they are caught in the act) depends mainly on the technical expertise of highly trained, experienced specialists. In Vollmer's organizational scheme, which has served as the basis for virtually all American police agencies since the beginning of this century, the role of the generalists (that is, the patrol force) is limited to gathering essential information about crimes and forwarding that information to the specialist detectives; the latter then are supposed to solve every crime that can be solved. Of course, generalist patrol officers also are supposed to arrest criminals who are caught in the act, and when officers are not otherwise engaged, they are supposed to deter criminals by the "technique" of random patrolling.

Even before the Kansas City study of patrol's effectiveness and the RAND study of police investigators' effectiveness, there were serious questions raised about all of these assumptions. But the assumptions themselves have been so deeply entrenched in the American police culture that few people could imagine any alternatives. As long as the primary duty of the police was to respond to complaints and arrest offenders, the best that could be done was to make incremental improvements in the speed with which the police responded and the efficiency with which they identified and arrested criminals.

Everything else that the police do, according to this philosophy, is at best supplemental (such as traffic enforcement) and at worst a distraction from "real policing." Furthermore, the traditional philosophy assumes that all communities have essentially the same "need," to be free of criminal activity, though perhaps to different degrees and with varying emphasis on specific types of crimes.[2]

But what exactly do the community policing people mean by "services"? And why should communities differ in their "needs" for those services? If they do, how can you tell which services a community needs?

POLICE SERVICES

A *police service,* as we will use the term, means *any action performed by the police for the benefit of the public.* This definition omits the activities that necessarily take place within a police agency for its own benefit or in support of the services provided to the public, but otherwise includes almost everything that a law enforcement agency does.

Law Enforcement Services

Of course, the most essential and universal types of law enforcement services are those that involve enforcing the criminal laws. In broad terms, this includes:

- *Complaint response and initial investigation.* Answering a complaint (usually made by telephone) that a crime has been committed, determining whether the complaint has substance, and obtaining as much information as possible from the victim, witnesses, and crime scene[3]
- *Continuing investigation.* When the perpetrator is not identified during the initial investigation, follow-up efforts aimed at identifying and locating a suspect, gathering evidence, making an arrest, and presenting the suspect and evidence for prosecution[4]
- *Surreptitious investigation.* For criminal enterprises, when it is unlikely that a complaint will be made, the use of "undercover" and other surveillance techniques to determine what crimes are being committed and by whom
- *Directed patrol.* The use of intensive patrol and related techniques to prevent specific crimes, usually as a result of the analysis of a series of similar incidents

There are few intrinsic differences between these services as offered or performed by officers in a traditional police agency and those in a community policing agency.

Regulatory Enforcement Services

American municipal police agencies also perform services that have little to do with "crime" as it is popularly understood. Nearly all American police agencies are responsible for enforcing traffic laws, and many agencies are also responsible for the enforcement of dozens or hundreds of regulatory statutes and ordinances.

Legislators define the violation of these laws as "crimes" and set criminal penalties (usually fines and short jail sentences). However, to the general public, such violations as speeding, overstaying a parking meter, or buying a bottle of beer at the wrong time of day are not "crimes" in the same sense as committing a burglary or armed robbery; they are merely infractions of regulations that are essentially arbitrary in nature. For that reason, we will call these "regulatory enforcement services." In a traditional police agency, most of these services (other than traffic enforcement) are considered a nuisance and a burden.[5]

Nonenforcement Services

Even in the most traditional agencies, the police also perform a variety of nonenforcement services. One of the most common is noncriminal emergency response: answering calls about every conceivable sort of personal or community crisis, including some that are more or less imaginary. One of the co-authors was riding with a patrol officer one afternoon when the officer was dispatched to see a woman who had found a "stick of dynamite" in her flowerbed. The "stick of dynamite," to the officer's intense relief—and that of the complainant—proved to be a not-so-dangerous highway flare.

We will categorize "crime prevention" as another type of nonenforcement service, in the sense that it is not a service performed in response to a specific crime. Again, traditional agencies regard random patrolling as the standard form of crime prevention, despite the evidence of the Kansas City experiments that cast considerable doubt on the usefulness of this practice.[6] Public education about self-protection and related subjects also is a type of crime prevention service offered by many agencies. According to traditional law enforcement theorists, juvenile services such as counseling and diversion are also crime prevention services.

Aside from crime prevention, many police agencies are involved to some extent in providing safety education services to their communities. Some police agencies conduct traffic safety classes, including driver training and defensive driving programs. Many agencies conduct traffic safety educational and promotional campaigns. A few police agencies are responsible for the actual engineering design of roadways in their communities.

Finally, there are all sorts of nonenforcement services that have little or nothing to do with crime: escorting funeral processions, inspecting boilers, registering taxicab drivers, licensing bicycles, and on and on. Some police agencies operate their community's emergency medical service or search-and-rescue service. In each case, assigning the responsibility for these services to the police department usually is justified by the *possibility* that criminal activity will be either detected or averted (for example, a serial ax murderer might try to get a job as a taxicab driver). Realistically, the best reason for giving these jobs to the police is simply that they are there, twenty-four hours a day, seven days a week.

An agency that adopts the community policing philosophy does not necessarily provide a different "menu" of services. Most agencies provide all of the same types of services we have listed. The significant differences lie in *how* the services are provided, *by whom*, and *when*.[7]

Random automotive patrol is one service that, if not entirely abandoned, is at least given a much lower priority in a community policing agency. However, foot patrol and other nonautomotive patrolling techniques (such as bicycle patrol and, in some areas, horse patrol) are often used to a far greater extent than in a traditional agency, although the effectiveness of these techniques in preventing crime remains highly arguable.[8]

ORDER MAINTENANCE

If there is some debate over the use of foot patrol, another aspect of community policing arouses frenzied controversy: the role of the police in noncriminal *order maintenance*.

Traditional Views

According to the traditional philosophy of policing, police officers have no right or authority to interfere with any citizen's lawful behavior, even if that behavior is to some degree annoying to others in the vicinity. Unless and until a specific law is violated, a citizen has an absolute right to be left alone.[9] When a violation is observed by or reported to a police officer (who acts as an agent of the state, and thus as a representative of the whole society), the only proper response is to arrest the violator and turn him or her over to the criminal justice system.

The very concept of community policing began with the explicit recognition that effective policing goes beyond the impersonal, almost cybernetic enforcement of the law.[10] In fact, police officers have always provided some degree of social order maintenance that does not immediately involve courts and prisons. In some instances, it is the threat of enforcement that an officer may use to dissuade a citizen from annoying the neighbors: "If you don't stop, I'm going to have to run you in." But at least as often, no explicit threat is necessary; the officer's uniform and equipment, including the badge, the gun, and the baton, symbolize an authority that most people do not care to challenge. A police officer obtains a very high degree of compliance merely by *looking* at someone who otherwise might have slipped through a red light.

What the Community Wants

Advocates of community policing and problem-oriented policing not only recognize this aspect of law enforcement, but legitimize and encourage it.[11] According to this view, the role of the police is to assist the community in maintaining order *as defined by the community*. Some "definitions of order" are expressed in laws, but there are also informal "definitions" that are nowhere explicitly stated, yet are widely shared among members of a community. Likewise, the community grants to its police officers not only the authority to enforce laws, but also the authority to enforce these informal standards of social behavior. The community *expects* a police officer to stop people from acting in annoying or potentially dangerous ways, even if the behavior is not precisely illegal.[12]

This aspect of the community policing philosophy is summarized in a publication of the U.S. Department of Justice:

> Community partnership means adopting a police perspective that exceeds the standard law-enforcement emphasis. This broadened outlook recognizes the value of activities that contribute to the orderliness and well-being of a neighborhood.[13]

For those who are steeped in the traditional law enforcement philosophy, the alarm bells set off by such a pronouncement are deafening. Criminology professor Larry T. Hoover worries that the police are taking, or being given, too much responsibility for "neighborhood management."[14] Others recall the days a century ago when the neighborhood cop had almost unlimited authority and discretion. One result was an era of corruption that no one wants to see repeated.[15]

The traditional view requires a police officer, when confronted with behavior that is socially unacceptable, to either *arrest* or *ignore*. Of course, in order for an arrest to be made, there must be a law that specifies the behavior as criminal; if there is not, the officer has no choice but to ignore the behavior, no matter how offensive it may be to the community. That is why the law books are filled with statutes and ordinances specifying in excruciating detail what kinds of social behavior are permissible and what kinds are not.*

Seeking an Alternative

There must be some middle ground, some third choice an officer can make, neither to arrest nor to ignore but to *advise* the disorderly citizen that his or her behavior is unacceptable and must stop, but without necessarily implying a threat of arrest. Again, there is ample evidence that even in the most traditional police agencies, officers on the street employ this "third choice" routinely and generally to good effect. All that is needed to meet the requirements of community policing is an explicit recognition of the officer's right to make this choice, and appropriate training and supervision to guide officers in using it appropriately.

Some of the debate surrounding the issue of social order maintenance, and the closely related topic of an officer's discretion, can be attributed to a misunderstanding that goes back to Wilson and Kelling's seminal article in *Atlantic* magazine, "Broken Windows."[16] The point of the article was that social conditions in a neighborhood have visible manifestations. In the traditional view, the police have no responsibility for the physical conditions of people's private property; if broken windows and other signs of deterioration are allowed to proliferate, that is no concern of the police.

---

*The courts also have contributed to what we might call the Blizzard of Trivial Offenses, by applying with great zeal the principle of prior notice: that is, a person cannot be convicted of an offense unless the law clearly defined the offense in advance. The principle is an important safeguard against the arbitrary application of vague, ambiguous laws, but it also means that legislators must sometimes belabor the obvious to define impermissible conduct in a way that satisfies the courts.

Wilson and Kelling argued that the police ought to take notice of such matters, and should regard them as symptoms of growing social disorder that invariably accompanies growing incidence of crime. At the very least, the police ought to take the time to bring the physical deterioration of the neighborhood to the attention of local authorities, such as the building inspectors, whose job it is to maintain a healthy and safe physical environment. By ignoring the broken windows, the police implicitly—and unintentionally—give a signal that they are just as likely to ignore social disorder, and that signal is too easily read by those who would prey upon their neighbors.

The misunderstanding arises in the minds of those who understood Wilson and Kelling to mean that the police should assume responsibility for getting broken windows fixed. Indeed, there are some community policing and problem-oriented policing advocates who might see this as a logical extension of community-oriented policing, and it is this concept of "neighborhood management" that Hoover criticizes as an unwarranted, and impractical, expansion of the police mission.[17]

Here, too, it may be possible to explore some middle ground. Many neighborhoods do not need to be "managed" by the police or anyone else; they are doing just fine on their own. Indeed, too much police involvement in some neighborhoods would be construed by the residents as invasive and objectionable. At the other extreme, there are neighborhoods that may be too far gone to be redeemed by the efforts of the police or any other single agency. Massive action by local government, probably with at least financial support from state and federal agencies, is needed to rebuild some of the country's worst slums; broken windows are indeed too trivial to notice.[18]

Where the police can be pivotal is the *transitional* neighborhood, where changes in demographic composition, patterns of property ownership, and other factors are causing a deterioration in both the physical and social structure.[19] In such cases, the police may very well have a crucial role to play, either in support of existing community managers,[20] or, where there are none, as neighborhood managers themselves.[21] At the very least, we would agree with Wilson and Kelling that the physical condition of neighborhoods should not be ignored by the police; it is a critical indicator of the social conditions that affect the way people live.

Thus we conclude that the police do have reason to consider the character, physical and social condition, and needs of the neighborhoods and communities they serve, and that not all communities have the same needs.

COMMUNITY AND NEIGHBORHOOD CHARACTERISTICS

In Chapter 2, we discussed the differences between geographical communities, such as neighborhoods, and nongeographical communities such as interest groups. Much of what we say in this section applies equally to both kinds of communities, and it is important to remember that a community is *any* group of people who have something in common. Thus, a neighborhood is invariably composed of many different nongeographical communities, and residents of a given neighborhood are also members of nongeographical communities that extend across neighborhood boundaries.

Precincts and Neighborhoods

However, it is also true that for both historical and practical reasons, police agencies necessarily are organized along geographical lines. In large cities, the police department usually is divided into precincts or districts, which are further divided into sectors or areas, which are further divided into beats; all of these divisions can be represented on a map. Even in small towns and rural areas, it is standard practice to assign each patrol officer to a specific geographical area.

That these neighborhoods differ in character is hardly a major revelation. People always have chosen to live, when they have had a choice, among people like themselves,[22] and always have tended to avoid neighborhoods where the people are perceived as significantly different.[23] One reason many people prefer to live in a small town rather than a large city is that they expect to have more influence over the character of their neighborhood and the social behavior of their neighbors.[24]

Sociology and Demography

The systematic study of differences among social groups such as neighborhoods is the business of two branches of science: sociology and demography. Sociology, which has numerous subbranches, is particularly concerned with the organization and structure of social groups, how they change over time, and the forces that help to preserve order and stability. Demography, a branch of statistics, consists of the careful measurement of quantifiable aspects of a population. These two sciences have much to say to each other; the findings of one often influence the methods and the conclusions of the other. Nevertheless, they look at a social group such as a neighborhood from different perspectives, both of which may prove valuable to police officers.

For our purposes, one key insight of sociology is that stable social groups tend to be comprised of people who are similar in *socioeconomic status*, or *class*.[25] In other words, people who are alike in income (not only how much they earn, but how they earn it) and wealth (not how much they earn, but how much they keep or have kept from previous generations) also tend to be alike in their educational attainment, their influence (or perceived influence) over the rest of society, and even in such matters as values, beliefs, interests, and personal tastes. All of these factors and characteristics interact with one another to an extent that is almost incomprehensibly complex, which is one reason that sociologists rarely are able to make hard-and-fast predictions about individual or group behavior based on only one or two such factors.

Demographers generally avoid drawing sociological conclusions from their studies; they are content to compile the statistics and let the numbers speak for themselves. Among the factors that demographers study are birth and death rates, marriage and divorce rates, the age composition of a group, patterns of migration, income and educational levels, and so forth. The census taken every ten years throughout the United States is the master fount of these statistics, but demographers also conduct a vast array of statistical studies of parts of the population, or specific aspects of the national population.[26]

Crime and Poverty

More than a century and a half ago, early sociologists paid attention to crime as the most common form of social disorder, and began to elaborate theories about the sources and nature of criminal behavior. The earliest theorizing consisted more of conjecture than disciplined investigation, but eventually the use of field research brought a few facts into the discussion (thanks in part to the information contributed by demographers). By the end of the nineteenth century, most sociologists concluded that *crime is strongly associated with poverty.*[27]

This conclusion, supported by statistical studies of prison inmate populations and some limited studies of arrestees, appealed greatly to commonsense notions about social behavior. After all, it seemed obvious that poor people, desperate to survive, would be more prone to disregard normal morality and would succumb to the temptation to take what they wanted and needed from their wealthier neighbors. Furthermore, there always has been a deep-seated suspicion that people are poor because of defects of character, which also are assumed to promote criminality.

The association of poverty with crime led to the idea that much if not all criminal behavior could be eradicated by eliminating poverty. One result was that some police departments, around the end of the nineteenth century, began to operate soup kitchens, employment agencies, and shelters for the poor. Most of these efforts were discontinued or turned over to other private or public agencies by the end of World War I, but they illustrate the lengths to which the police would go in a futile attempt at crime prevention: If poverty causes crime, then it must be the responsibility of the police to eliminate poverty.

But that is not at all what the sociologists were saying, or, at any rate, it is not what their evidence proved. It is one thing to say that criminal behavior is *associated* with poverty, and it is quite another to say that poor people tend to be criminals. More careful studies have shown repeatedly that the vast majority of poor people are as honest and law-abiding as the people of any other class.

Furthermore, criminal behavior is not primarily a matter of poor people preying on wealthier citizens. Most crimes *for which an arrest is made*—both property crimes and crimes against persons—involve perpetrators and victims who know each other, often live in the same neighborhood, and have the same socioeconomic status.[28] Obviously, no real conclusions can be drawn about the vast number of crimes that are never "solved," although here, too, the majority of victims are not the wealthy.

In short, no single sociological factor "causes" crime.[29] Criminal behavior is the product of many different causative factors, some of them social and some psychological. Employment status, income, educational levels, gender, age, ethnicity, and family composition are among the factors that influence the difference in crime rates among different neighborhoods, but there is no known equation that can be applied to these factors to predict the number or types of crimes that will occur.[30]

A more sophisticated view is that crime is not the product of any one sociological or psychological factor, but rather is simply one of several manifestations of a more general social disorder. *Social disorder* is a broad and rather ambiguous term, and it is relativistic: There is no absolute index of disorder.

Any given social group, such as a neighborhood, exhibits some degree of social order, the opposite of which is disorder. In a perfectly orderly social group, not only is there no crime, but no long-standing disagreements among members, no significant changes in the composition of the group, and no conflicts with other groups. Of course, such perfect social order is exceedingly rare. Virtually all social groups exhibit some degree of social disorder from time to time.

Stability

One of the most important indicators of social order is *stability*, the extent to which a social group remains much the same over time.

It is a biological fact that babies are born, grow up, grow old, and eventually die, and this fact obviously affects the character of a social group. In a neighborhood that contains many young children, it is usually the case that the children's parents are themselves young adults, striving to advance their families' incomes and their personal careers. Young parents typically are very concerned about their children's safety and education; schools and playgrounds are important to them. They are also typically concerned about their own economic success, which may depend on convenient access to the kinds of jobs that they are capable of holding (or that they prefer), or on access to markets for the goods or services that they produce. Thus traffic and transportation issues are important to them, as well as more general economic matters.

In a neighborhood that contains a large number of older children and adolescents, different concerns become prominent. There is ample documentation to show that adolescent males are involved in and responsible for a disproportionate amount of what is sometimes called "street crime": burglaries, thefts, armed robberies, auto thefts, and assaults.[31] Furthermore, adolescent males appear to be responsible for a very high proportion of noncriminal or barely criminal incidents of disorderly behavior, and it is just this sort of behavior that arouses the greatest public indignation and fear.[32] The parents of adolescents usually are themselves reaching middle age, in the midst of their careers.

Mobility

In the past, as children became adults they rarely moved very far from their places of origin. However, that changed dramatically in America in the mid-nineteenth century as millions of young families and single adults sought their fortunes in the expanding West. Especially after the Civil War, emigration from the East to the frontier reached unprecedented proportions. By the end of the century, the western expansion had come to an end, but not the restlessness of the American people. Nearly a century later, American young people are much more likely to relocate as they reach adulthood, in search of opportunity or just to get away from what they perceive as a limited or oppressive home environment. The tendency is encouraged by businesses that treat their employees as chess pieces, to be moved around as the company's needs dictate. Each year, between 35 million and 40 million people change their place of residence, out of a total population of about 250 million; that is an average rate of migration of about 15 percent. To put it another way, the average person moves about once every six or seven years.[33]

Consequently, the young adult population of any given community is likely to consist mostly of newcomers, many of whom are likely to move again not just once, but two or three times before they reach middle age.

Furthermore, people in the lower socioeconomic classes—both the very poor and the "working poor"—seem to be more mobile than people in the middle and upper classes. People who cannot afford to own a home and may have difficulty even in keeping up rent payments have little choice but to move frequently, and of course they may move in search of better economic conditions and opportunities.

In general, sociologists assume that a stable community is likely to maintain a higher degree of social order than an unstable community. In a stable community, residents know one another and, presumably, care about one another; they also care about the opinion that others have of themselves. In many well-established neighborhoods, a few individuals take on the role of "neighborhood caretaker," protecting the interests of their neighbors, offering assistance to those who suffer some misfortune, and generally promoting social order.[34]

Limited Choices

However, stability is not always the product of the free choice of a group's members. For example, the oldest residential districts of many large cities have become "ghettos" (a term we will discuss in a moment) for hundreds of thousands of people who have nowhere else to go and no prospect of improving their place in society. Merely surviving from day to day becomes a desperate struggle. Under these circumstances, people have little interest in the welfare of others and little concern for the good opinion of their neighbors. Despite the fact that these masses of people share a common and extremely bleak fate, they "have no interest, or face special disabilities, in creating and maintaining a sense of community," as Wilson puts it.[35]

In short, stability alone does not ensure domestic tranquility. On the other hand, there is little chance for a sense of community and social order to develop in a community that is undergoing rapid and substantial change.

Around the core of many large cities there is a wide transitional zone. Homes, businesses, and public facilities have not yet reached the point that they are hopeless slums, but there is steady deterioration of the physical environment. As residents move away in search of new opportunities or a more pleasant atmosphere, they are replaced by people with lower incomes and less positive prospects for the future. Landlords, faced with increasing demands and costs for maintenance at the same time that the market is less capable of paying high rents, cut their losses wherever possible. Banks and mortgage companies become reluctant to lend money to people who want to buy homes or businesses in areas that are unlikely to be attractive and productive in the future.

Increasing social disorder in such a transitional neighborhood is all but unavoidable.

Transitions are not always from good to bad. At the outer fringe of most large cities, a different kind of transition is taking place: from rural to suburban patterns. At the same time, somewhere between the central core and the suburban fringe, neighborhoods that were once considered suburbs, or even rural villages, are slowly being transformed into urbanized districts. Each of these transitions involves and is accompanied by changes in the composition of the population.

Degrees of Difference

Another characteristic of communities, and especially of neighborhoods, that sociologists believe to be related to social disorder is the degree of *homogeneity* (made up of similar elements) or *heterogeneity* (composed of many different elements).

In the mid-sixteenth century, Jewish people in Europe were experiencing yet another periodic wave of persecution. Pope Paul IV decreed that a wall should be built around the main Jewish neighborhood in Rome and that all Jews must live within that district. His decree was framed as a law that also required the gates in the wall to be locked at night, and all residents of the Jewish sector to wear an identifying insignia whenever they left the district. The Jewish district came to be called a *ghetto*, from an Italian word that originally meant simply a camp or settlement outside of a city's walls.

Within a few years, most of the larger cities in Europe had adopted similar laws establishing ghettos. Pope Paul's original decree may have been intended in part to give the Roman Jews some protection from their persecutors, but in most cases the ghettos, usually located in the poorest and most undesirable areas, became instruments of oppression. Legal ghettos were abolished in France during the Revolution of 1792-1793, but the last legal ghetto in Europe, the one in Rome, was not officially abandoned until 1870. (In Germany, Poland, and other parts of eastern Europe, before and during World War II, Jews and other ethnic groups were confined, by law, to specific areas that were effectively ghettos, but the term was not used.)

De facto ghettos, maintained in fact but not according to any law, have persisted in many cities to the present day.

De Facto Ghettos

The United States has never had legal ghettos, but each new wave of immigrants has faced a similar experience. In part, the existence of de facto ghettos can be attributed to the tendency Wilson mentioned: Given a free choice, people tend to live among people like themselves. However, it is abundantly clear that people do not always have a free choice.

Until the passage of civil rights laws in 1964 and 1965, prohibiting discrimination in housing, American landlords were given almost unlimited freedom to select their tenants not just on the basis of their ability to pay rent, but on whatever ethnic, religious, or other criteria the landlord chose to apply. Thus newly arrived immigrants usually found that the only places they could live were in neighborhoods made up of people of the same, or very similar, ethnic background or national origin.

The great cities of the Northeast and Midwest each had its enclaves of Irish, German, Jewish, Italian, Chinese, and Hispanic people. When large numbers of African-Americans migrated from the South to the North after the Civil War, especially after World War I, they, too, found that the only housing available to them was in all-black neighborhoods.[36] Most recently, immigrants from Vietnam, Cambodia, Taiwan, and Korea have had the same experience.[37]

Again, it is important to understand that none of these ethnic, religious, or national origin neighborhoods was a legal ghetto. Nevertheless, the effects were much the same. There were no walls around these ghettos, but anyone who ventured out of them—except under certain conditions—could expect to face a hostile public.[38]

Over time, immigrants tend to become assimilated into their new society. They acquire the language, dress, fashions, occupations, and habits of the general population, and lose their original cultural identity. That is, they become assimilated *provided* they are not visibly different from the members of the larger society.[39]

For African Americans, Hispanic Americans, and Asian-Americans, assimilation has proven to be extremely difficult, for the obvious reason that they are visibly different from the white Europeans who have dominated American society from its beginnings. It would be very difficult to find large, homogeneous Irish or German or Polish neighborhoods even in the largest cities, but not at all difficult to find black, Hispanic, and Asian ghettos.

Ghettos and Heterogeneity

Ghettos are peculiar in one respect that greatly affects their social stability and order: They tend to be extremely homogeneous, but only for one characteristic.

In the European legal ghettos, only Jews were permitted, and all Jews were required to live in the prescribed district. Thus the Jewish ghetto was almost perfectly homogeneous for ethnicity and religious background. But since *all* Jews were required to live in the ghetto, the population was highly heterogeneous for such characteristics as socioeconomic status and educational level.

Aside from the existence of the ghetto itself, widespread discrimination against Jews meant that the Jewish people were disproportionately poor: They were not permitted to hold the best jobs and were denied access to the best markets for their goods or services. Nevertheless, some Jews were wealthy, and some were able to earn a better-than-average income, usually by providing goods and services to their ghetto neighbors—goods and services that non-Jews refused to offer.

De facto ghettos show exactly the same pattern: They are highly homogeneous for the single characteristic that defines the ghetto, but highly heterogeneous for almost all other characteristics. In effect, the ghetto becomes a miniature analogue of the larger society, with its own stratification into socioeconomic classes. In particular, the de facto African-American, Hispanic, and Asian-American ghettos in the United States historically have shown nearly as much variation in elements of culture (beliefs, values, interests, fashions, and so on) as the entire society. One important result is that the ghetto society develops its own leadership structure, comprised of a "ghetto elite" (generally the wealthier, better educated, and more socially adept individuals) that sets and enforces community standards of social behavior, and helps to moderate conflicts among ghetto residents.[40]

People Left Behind

When the earlier de facto ghettos of white European immigrants dissolved, as the immigrants and their descendants became assimilated into the larger culture, very few people were "left behind" to fend for themselves. But the de facto ghettos of today have not dissolved due to assimilation. The civil rights laws that prohibit discrimination in housing, employment, and other areas of social life have allowed the "ghetto elite" to move out into the larger society, but they have left behind large numbers of people who do not have the resources and skills to succeed in that larger society.[41]

This is a profound problem that directly affects law enforcement and for which our society has yet to find a practical solution.[42] By adopting a social policy of prohibiting housing discrimination, we have inadvertently increased the level of socioeconomic homogeneity in the remaining ghetto population. There can be no question that prohibiting discrimination is morally and politically necessary; we are not suggesting that the civil rights laws ought to be abandoned. However, the unintended consequences also must be recognized and addressed. The alternative is to tolerate increasing levels of social disorder among the "left-behind" ghetto population, as that population becomes increasingly composed of the poorest, least educated, and least socially competent individuals.[43]

At the same time, we must realize that merely passing laws to prohibit discrimination does not magically produce assimilation. Blacks, Hispanics, and Asian Americans who have moved out of the ghetto often have encountered new problems. Their presence in formerly all-white neighborhoods may be resented, even if not to the extent of violent rejection. They often find themselves isolated, separated from family and longtime friends, and unable to break through the social barriers to establish friendships among their new neighbors.[44] In a few instances, violent rejection has indeed occurred, which requires police intervention to protect the rights and the lives of the newcomers. The police may be able to put down the violence, but only a continued police presence ensures the safety of the newcomers, and even that does nothing to promote acceptance of the newcomers by hostile neighbors.

Furthermore, the changing composition of the newly arriving immigrant population has had unintended consequences for minority Americans. In particular, new Asian immigrants, especially those from rural areas of Southeast Asia, have faced monumental difficulties in adapting to the English-language American culture.[45] Meanwhile, African Americans mired in poverty have seen waves of Hispanic immigrants, both legal and illegal, as competitors for low-skill jobs and for government assistance.[46]

The conclusion we can draw is that a high level of homogeneity does not ensure, and a high level of heterogeneity does not prevent, an orderly community. A neighborhood may be highly homogeneous in one characteristic and highly heterogeneous in all others, yet maintain an acceptable degree of social order through the influence of the neighborhood's own elite. On the other hand, a neighborhood may be composed of people who are homogeneous in socioeconomic status, education, values, and many other characteristics, but the lack of homogeneity in one characteristic—such as ethnicity—may result in a great deal of social disorder. Much depends not only on how sociologists or demographers would classify people, but on how the people perceive themselves and their neighbors.[47]

GIVING THE CUSTOMERS WHAT THEY WANT

Public perceptions about their neighborhoods, about crime, and about the role of the police have all influenced the development of the community policing philosophy.

Up to this point, we have discussed the theory and philosophy of community policing; we have mentioned, briefly, some of the early attempts to implement this philosophy in actual police agencies; and we have presented some of the arguments both for and against community policing. The rest of this book is devoted to explaining how to transform an existing police agency into one that practices community policing.

Most of the information in the chapters that follow is based on the experience and observations of co-author Elizabeth Watson. As deputy chief of the Houston Police Department, she was responsible for implementing community policing (under the title, "Neighborhood-Oriented Policing") in one fourth of that city's police department.

Later, as chief, she began the process of expanding Neighborhood-Oriented Policing throughout the department. For four years she was chief of the Austin, Texas, Police Department and was responsible for the implementation of community policing there.

The adoption of community policing in a traditional police department is not merely a matter of shuffling the boxes on the organization chart, nor is it mostly a matter of issuing new policies and procedures. Ultimately, the organization chart and the policy manuals do change, but only as a result of a more fundamental transformation.

Implementing community policing requires changing the attitudes and values of the agency's personnel, from the street level to the executive office. It involves changing the public's expectations of what the police do and how they do it.

In short, adopting community policing in an existing agency means nothing less than transforming the *culture* of policing, both within and outside of the department.

Community policing developed in reaction to the social upheavals of the 1960s and early 1970s, during a time when both police officials and street cops believed that the public regarded them with hostility and suspicion. In fact, the public probably never had as poor an opinion of the police as the police thought. On the other hand, the police, especially in major urban areas, seem to have had an extraordinarily low opinion of the citizens whose lives and property they were sworn to protect.[48]

In Seattle, a city with a national reputation as virtually a model of civic tranquility, citizens began to clamor for the police to "do something" about what they perceived to be rampant crime. In 1985, several citizens' groups formed the South Seattle Crime Prevention Council (SSCPC) and began lobbying the police department to address several specific crime problems in the southern part of the city. When the police responded that they did not have the resources necessary to the task, the SSCPC lobbied the city council for more money for the police.

The initial results of the South Seattle police project were sufficiently impressive that, in 1989, the people of Seattle passed a referendum to increase their taxes, so that money would be available to hire additional police officers and to expand the South Seattle program to the rest of the city.[49]

The Seattle experience is not unique, although few cities' voters have endorsed a particular police system by raising their taxes. The point is that the police responded to the community's demands for specific services. Under the traditional philosophy of law enforcement, such a response might be regarded as an unconscionable abandonment of professional judgment. After all, "civilians" are not supposed to know anything about policing strategies, and a police executive who gives in to community demands is little better than the politicians who hired him.

But according to the community-policing philosophy, citizens are the police department's "clientele," and their concerns should be respected by the police. It is not that "the customer is always right," but rather that the customer always has a right to be heard. After all, if a police department's "customers" are sufficiently dissatisfied, they have the right and the power, as citizens, to see that changes are made.

For all of the reasons we have cited, then, it is not only desirable but essential for the police to find out what the public wants and needs. Of course professional judgment is still required; the police have access to information, and the background of training and experience to evaluate that information, which the public does not have. In part, the police must interpret the public's needs and wishes in terms of the kinds of police services that are feasible, known to be effective, and legally acceptable. But first, the police must find out what the public wants and needs. The person who is best able to direct that inquiry is the police executive, the chief of police or sheriff.

Before any substantial change can be made in an existing institution such as a police agency, a plan to accomplish the change must be devised. Such a plan should be based on an assessment of the agency's present condition and about the kinds of changes that are desired. The process of making that assessment involves interviewing three segments of the community:

- *The parent authority.* The elected officials and the appointed managers who have authority over the police agency
- *The internal community.* The personnel of the agency itself
- *The external community.* The citizens who are served by the agency

Both one-on-one, face-to-face interviews and group meetings may be used, depending on the number of people whose knowledge, perceptions, and insights are to be tapped.

Asking the Boss

All of the elected officials and appointed managers who have authority over the police agency should be interviewed individually. In fact, everyone who has any substantial degree of power or influence over the police department should have an opportunity to contribute to the assessment of community needs.

Usually one appointed official—the city manager or county supervisor—has direct authority over the police agency. Where this is not the case (generally only in the largest cities), everyone in the chain of authority over the police should be interviewed individually.

The police executive also may find it desirable to interview a few city or county department heads who are not in the direct chain of authority over the police, but whose agency has similar concerns or related areas of responsibility. Before concluding each interview, the person being interviewed should be asked, "Is there anyone else we should talk to about these matters?"

Questions for the Troops

The procedure for soliciting information within the police agency must take into account the tendency of subordinates to feel uncomfortable about offering opinions or suggestions that could be construed as criticism of their superiors. For this reason, in agencies that are too large for individual interviews at all levels, group meetings should be stratified by rank. The chief executive may meet with all executive-level personnel (such as deputy chiefs or assistant chiefs) at one time, but separate meetings should be held for upper-level managers (captains and majors), first-line supervisors (lieutenants and sergeants, plus operating personnel of equivalent rank, such as detectives), and lower-level personnel (patrol officers, plus most noncommissioned personnel).

Assessing the Community

Both individual interviews and group meetings should be used to determine the community's perceptions of their police service. Group meetings should be open to the public, and every effort should be made to publicize the meetings extensively and to encourage the broadest possible public participation.

The site for each group meeting must be selected with care: It must be readily accessible, with ample parking for the number of people expected; it must be large enough to accommodate more people than are likely to attend; and it must be reasonably comfortable for those who do attend. A school auditorium or cafeteria may be a good choice, since almost everyone will know the location and usually there is plenty of parking. Some other possibilities include a community recreational center, the community meeting rooms provided by some banks and libraries, or a meeting room in a police precinct station or neighborhood substation.

Except in a small community, the group meetings should be held in all parts of the city. If the agency itself is divided into large geographic areas, a meeting should be held in each precinct or sector.

The police executive himself or herself should conduct each of these meetings; precinct or sector commanders, and as many lower-ranking personnel as wish to attend, also may participate. However, the presence of the police chief or sheriff reinforces the importance of these meetings and assures the public that they are not merely "show-and-tell" sessions. Media coverage should be encouraged, especially for the first few meetings. If the community has a public access cable channel, its staff may be willing to cablecast the meetings "live" and videotape them for later use.

The public meetings are only part of the assessment of community perceptions; the other half consists of individual interviews with community leaders.

Choosing whom to interview should not be difficult in small- to medium-sized communities. Usually there is a relatively small number of individuals who are well known in the community for their leadership. They may be businesspeople, retired politicians, civic activists, or leaders of service clubs. School administrators and members of the clergy also may be widely respected and regarded as influential.

In larger cities, identifying community leaders may be more difficult, since there are often a few individuals whose names appear in the newspaper often but who actually have little influence in the community, and there may be other individuals whose opinions are widely respected but who maintain a low profile.

Fortunately, there is a simple technique for identifying community leaders who otherwise might be overlooked. At the end of each individual interview, the interviewer should ask the interviewee, "Is there anyone else I should talk to about these issues?" In fact, this question should be asked not only in interviews with community leaders, but in *every* individual interview (including those with elected and appointed officials, and with members of the police agency itself), and even in some group meetings. These referrals can be extremely valuable, not only in pointing the executive to individuals with significant insights, but also in developing a sense of the relationships that exist among the community. When several people mention the same name, that is a good indication that the person named is widely respected in the community. When someone who seems to have a high public profile is rarely mentioned, that is a good indication that the person's influence is much less than might be supposed.

All of the interviews—both individual and group, and including those with the parent authority, those within the agency, and those with the public—should be scheduled in advance, with allowance to add names to the list. In a small community, the process might be completed in two or three months. In a large city, especially when the executive conducting the assessment has day-to-day management responsibilities as well, the process may take as much as a year. At some point, however, the assessment must be brought to a close, or there is the danger that it will go on indefinitely to no real purpose. (However, as we discuss in later chapters, there is also a need for a continuing dialogue between the police agency and all segments of the community. The initial assessment may serve as the launching pad for this dialogue, but the implementation of it usually takes a somewhat different form.)

What to Ask

The purpose of the assessment is to address three sets of questions:

- *What is the present condition of the agency?* How well is the agency presently performing? What does it do well? What does it do poorly or not at all? What activities or services meet the community's expectations, and in what areas is the agency failing to satisfy the community?
- *What should the agency do to improve its service?* Which of the agency's present activities and services should be expanded? Which should be reduced or eliminated?
- *What would be an ideal police service?* If there were no constraints, such as limited resources, how would the police service be different from the present service? What would it look like? How would police officers at every level interact with the community?

Each of these areas should be addressed with a series of follow-up questions, based on or drawn from the specific situation of the particular community and the agency itself. For example, if the agency has recently conducted a major operation to suppress drug trafficking, that may be high in the public's awareness. Interviewees might be asked if they approved of the way in which the operation was performed, and whether they would like to see more or less police effort devoted to similar activities.

In individual interviews, and to some extent in public meetings, people should be asked to discuss their specific, personal experiences with the police. How were they treated by a police officer or deputy? Did they feel that they were treated with courtesy and professionalism? If they were the victim of a crime, did they feel confident that the agency would do as much as possible to resolve the crime? If they were a witness to a police action, such as an arrest, what was their impression of the officers' behavior? If they were stopped for a traffic violation, how were they treated? Did they feel that the stop was justified?

Especially in public meetings, people should be encouraged to suggest activities that the police should undertake. Some of the specific suggestions may be unfeasible or simply inappropriate for a law enforcement agency, but the responses to this question can be indicative of the public's attitudes toward and expectations of the police agency.

Both in the group meetings within the agency and in the public meetings, *who* shows up may be as significant as what they say. If the group meetings of personnel are poorly attended (on a voluntary basis), that should ring loud alarms: Communication within the agency has broken down, probably because of a lack of trust and confidence in one's superiors. If the only people who show up are those who have a degree of official status as representatives of the rank-and-file (for example, officers of the police union or association), there may be barriers between the agency's management and its personnel.

In public meetings, both the size of the attendance and its composition may be significant. Unfortunately, the number of people who turn out for a public meeting with the police chief may depend on a great many factors, including the extent to which the meeting is publicized, the attractiveness of the meeting site, the competition from other events (including popular TV shows!), and the weather. In some communities, *low* attendance could be taken as a positive sign: The citizens are so well satisfied with their present police service that they feel no particular interest in discussing it. More often, low attendance indicates a lack of confidence and trust, resulting in skepticism toward the police chief's intentions and the likelihood of significant reform.

Some public meetings, intended to gauge the public's perceptions of the police service, quickly degenerate into "gripe sessions," often monopolized by a few individuals who come to the meeting prepared with their own agenda. The level of hostility that can be produced may undermine the executive's effort to gather credible information. Unfortunately, once an invitation is issued for the public to comment, there is nothing much that can be done to stop the comments from flowing, even if they are hostile and unhelpful. Of course, flagrantly disruptive behavior should not be tolerated; in most states, deliberately disrupting a public meeting is in itself a criminal offense. But if the speakers refrain from being overtly disruptive, the only recourse is to listen patiently until they have said whatever they want to say.

However, the role of the executive in a public meeting should not be confined entirely to passive listening. Sometimes citizens, who may have little experience in participating actively in a community meeting and who may be nervous about "public speaking," can be encouraged to participate by posing questions to individuals rather than to the group as a whole. The executive should respond in some way to every comment from citizens; at the very least, to thank them for their contributions, to answer their questions (or promise to get an answer and call them within a day or two), and so forth. The executive probably should not respond defensively to critical comments. If there is a valid explanation for some police action that a citizen has criticized, the explanation should be given as briefly and objectively as possible; if a citizen criticizes something that (if true) was in fact wrong, the executive should say so, and if necessary should promise to investigate further. It should go without saying that a promise to answer a question or to investigate a complaint must be fulfilled!

During individual interviews, the interviewer (that is, usually the police chief or sheriff) should keep notes. If the interviewee does not object, a small tape recorder might be used; this is preferable to having a secretary or other third person in the interview. However, in all group meetings, someone—usually a secretary—should be assigned to keep detailed notes of what was said, and an audiotape recording might be made as well.

Several months might be spent in making this initial assessment of the community's perceptions and wishes. It is fair to ask whether the expenditure of so much time and effort is truly justified, especially if the police executive has served in that office for several years or has "come up through the ranks" in the agency and is already familiar with the community.

Our response is an unqualified "Yes!" Transforming the culture of a police agency from the traditional orientation, usually called "professional law enforcement," to the very different set of values and attitudes that characterize community policing, is a substantial undertaking. It is a journey that requires the best possible road map. Even for an experienced police chief or sheriff who feels that he or she knows the community "like the back of his (or her) hand," the assessment provides a rational process by which critical issues can be identified and priorities established. For someone newly appointed to lead the police agency, the assessment is simply indispensable.

When the last interview has been completed and the last group meeting has been held, the executive should have a considerable fund of information. How to analyze and apply that information is the subject of our next chapter.

FOOTNOTES

1. For example, Herman Goldstein, *Problem-Oriented Policing* (New York: McGraw-Hill 1990), pp. 32–49.

2. Bureau of Justice Assistance, *Understanding Community Policing* (Washington, D.C.: U.S. Dept. of Justice, 1994), p. 6.

3. David H. Bayley, *Police for the Future* (New York: Oxford University Press, 1994), p. 17.

4. Bayley, *Police for the Future*, p. 20.

5. James Q. Wilson, *Thinking About Crime,* rev. ed. (New York: Basic Books, 1983), p. 61.

6. Dennis J. Kenney, "Strategic Approaches," in Larry T. Hoover, ed., *Police Management Issues and Perspectives* (Washington, D.C.: Police Executive Research Forum, 1992), pp. 205- 206.

7. National Institute of Justice, *Community Policing in Seattle* (Washington, D.C.: U.S. Department of Justice, 1992), p. 9.

8. George L. Kelling and Mark H. Moore, "The Evolving Strategy of Policing," in *Perspectives on Policing,* no. 4 (November 1988), 12. Also see Wilson, *Thinking About Crime*, pp. 63–65, 76; and Lisa M. Reichers and Roy R. Roberg, "Community Policing: A Critical Review," in *Journal of Police Science and Administration*, 17, no. 2 (June 1990), 110.

9. Sam S. Souryal, *Police Administration and Management* (St. Paul, Minn.: West Publishing, 1977), pp. 35–38.

10. Bayley, *Police for the Future*, pp. 18–19.

11. Goldstein, *Problem-Oriented Policing*, pp. 10–11.

12. Wilson, *Thinking About Crime*, pp. 77, 83.

13. Bureau of Justice Assistance, *Understanding Community Policing*, p. 15.

14. Larry T. Hoover, "Police Mission: An Era of Debate," in Hoover, ed., *Police Management*, pp. 10, 25.

15. Reichers and Roberg, "Community Policing: A Critical Review," pp. 108, 111.

16. James Q. Wilson and George L. Kelling, "Broken Windows," in *Atlantic*, March 1982; also, in revised version, in Wilson, *Thinking About Crime*.

17. Hoover, "Police Mission: An Era of Debate," pp. 8–11.

18. Elisha Y. Babad, Max Birnbaum, and Kenneth D. Benne, *The Social Self* (Sage Library of Social Research, Vol. 144) (Beverly Hills, Calif.: Sage, 1983), p. 31.

19. Patrick V. Murphy, "Organizing for Community Policing," in John W. Bizzack, ed., *Issues in Policing: New Perspectives* (Lexington, Ky.: Autumn House Publishing, 1991), p. 115.

20. George L. Kelling and James K. Stewart, "Neighborhoods and Police: The Maintenance of Civil Authority," in *Perspectives on Policing,* no. 10, May 1989 (Washington, D.C.: U.S. Dept. of Justice, 1989), p. 5.

21. Kelling and Moore, "Evolving Strategy," p. 12.

22. Wilson, *Thinking About Crime*, p. 33.

23. Babad, Birnbaum, and Benne, *The Social Self*, p. 25.

24. Wilson, *Thinking About Crime*, p. 29.

25. Mary Jeanette Hageman, *Police-Community Relations* (Beverly Hills, Calif.: Sage, 1985), pp. 54-70.

26. Sam Roberts, *Who We Are* (New York: Times Books/Random House), 1994, p. 3.

27. Roberts, *Who We Are*, pp. 190–192.

28. George L. Kelling and Elizabeth M. Watson, "Creativity with Accountability," in Hoover, ed., *Police Management*, pp. 141–143.

29. Parviz Saney, *Crime and Culture in America* (Westport, Conn.: Greenwood Press, 1986), p. 11.

30. Bayley, *Police for the Future*, p. 10.

31. Macklin Fleming, *Of Crime and Rights* (New York: W. W. Norton), 1978, p. 44.

32. Kelling and Watson, "Creativity with Accountability," in Hoover, ed., *Police Management,* p. 153.

33. Roberts, *Who We Are*, pp. 8–9.

34. Kelling and Stewart, "Neighborhoods and Police," p. 5.

35. Wilson, *Thinking About Crime*, p. 33; also pp. 38–39.

36. William Julius Wilson, *The Declining Significance of Race* (Chicago: University of Chicago Press, 1978), pp. 65–70.

37. Bartholomew Lahiff, "A Plea for Selfishness," in Robert Emmet Long, ed., *Immigration to the United States* (The Reference Shelf, vol. 64, no. 4) (New York: H. W. Wilson, 1992), pp. 102–104.

38. W. J. Wilson, *Declining Significance of Race*, pp. 78–82.

39. James Fallows, "Immigration: How It's Affecting Us," in Steven Anzovin, ed., *The Problem of Immigration* The Reference Shelf, vol. 57, no. 1 (New York: H. W. Wilson, 1985), p. 13.

40. W. J. Wilson, *Declining Significance of Race*, p. 20.

41. Wilson, *Thinking About Crime*, p. 39.

42. Allen D. Sapp, "Alternative Futures," in Hoover, ed., *Police Management*, p. 178. Also, W. J. Wilson, *Declining Significance of Race*, pp. 99–109.

43. Babad, Birnbaum, and Benne, *The Social Self*, pp. 30–32.

44. Wilson, *Thinking About Crime*, p. 35.

45. Robert Lindsey, "The New Asian Immigrants," in Anzovin, ed., *The Problem of Immigration*, pp. 13–27.

46. Alex Prud'homme, "Browns vs. Blacks," in Long, ed., *Immigration to the United States*, pp. 29–33.

47. Babad, Birnbaum, and Benne, *The Social Self*, p. 25: "People experience great difficulty in understanding others who are significantly 'different' from themselves. The basis for understanding others is our understanding of ourselves."

48. Wilson, *Thinking About Crime*, pp. 90–97.

49. National Institute of Justice, *Community Policing in Seattle* (Washington, D.C.: U.S. Department of Justice, 1992).

CHAPTER 4

DEVELOPING A PLAN

If it ain't broke, don't fix it!

This bit of homespun wisdom has become the mantra of traditionalists, the defenders of the status quo. Of course, there is an element of truth to it: If something is working well, "fixing it" may make it worse instead of better. Change involves risks that are often unforeseeable and it should not be undertaken lightly.

But defending the status quo simply is no longer an option for most police executives. Change is already taking place, on a massive scale, throughout American society. For most police agencies, it is already too late to lead the charge. The choice lies between "going with the flow" or racing to catch up.

Furthermore, there is a substantial consensus that the changes already occurring in society are not an isolated or temporary phenomenon. Executives and managers of every sort of enterprise, in both the private and public sectors, are urged to make *change itself* a fundamental characteristic of their organizations. The call is for *continuous* change. In other words: *If it ain't perfect, make it better.*

DEALING WITH CHANGE

Management theorist Leon Martel discusses two basic types of change: cyclical change, which involves temporary fluctuations around a "normal" state of affairs, and structural change, which is permanent and irreversible.[1] Short-term economic changes, such as periods of recession or inflation, are clearly examples of cyclical change, and most alert managers know how to deal with them effectively.

Structural change, however, can be slow, gradual, and difficult to recognize. It is easy to ignore evidence of structural change until it has become overwhelming.

As Martel points out, assuming that current conditions will continue is almost always wrong—sooner or later.[2] Instead, one must recognize that changes are taking place, identify which of them are significant to one's own enterprise, and find ways to *use* the fact of change to one's own benefit.

That major structural changes have occurred in the United States during the past quarter-century is undeniable. There have been massive changes in technology (especially, but not only, in communications and electronic computers); the demographic composition of society (in general, a population that is growing older but living longer); the economy (competition on a global scale for many industries, and the increasing dominance of service industries over manufacturing industries); and culture (the virtually universal practice of two-income families, the growing number of single parents, and changing attitudes about an enormous range of social behaviors). The underlying reasons for all these changes are beyond the scope of this text. What concerns us now is their impact on the business of policing.

New technologies unquestionably have had a profound impact on policing. Computer-assisted dispatching, digital two-way radios, and computerized report generation are now almost commonplace. Interconnected computer databases give officers on the street almost instantaneous access to enormous quantities of information. In-vehicle video camcorders provide documentation of police actions for use in court.

But new technologies also affect crime, creating new opportunities for criminality (ATM muggings, computer chip theft), creating entirely new types of crimes (cellular phone number interception and fraudulent use), and facilitating criminal activities (digital pagers used to arrange drug deals).

Decades of demographic and sociological research have shown that public crimes (that is, crimes committed by people who generally do not know the victim) and violent crimes are both committed preponderantly by young men, ages 18 to 25. If the demographic trend continues, young men will make up a smaller proportion of the population, and therefore one might expect crime rates to fall, as they have been for the past few years. However, elderly citizens, with some justification, tend to be more concerned about their personal safety, and therefore make more demands on the police, than do younger citizens.

The globalization of the economy may not seem to have much to do with municipal law enforcement. However, globalization has meant unprecedented competitive pressure on American businesses, and that has produced a response that often includes "downsizing"—the *permanent* elimination of thousands, tens of thousands, even hundreds of thousands of jobs. In the past, industries sometimes resorted to large "layoffs" of superfluous workers during cyclical downturns, but it was always understood that the laid-off workers would be rehired as soon as business conditions improved. "Downsizing" involves not just factory workers, but, often, middle- and upper-management personnel and their support staffs of clerks, secretaries, accountants, lawyers, and technicians. And they will not be hired back.[3]

A community that depends heavily on a few major employers may face the horrific prospect of having a substantial part of the population suddenly unemployed, with little prospect of regaining their high-salaried, privileged positions. The resulting economic dislocations may be reflected in the incidence of crime.

Furthermore, when foreign companies establish factories and offices in a community, they often bring a core of critical-function employees. Some companies go to great lengths to ensure that their relocated employees are prepared to adapt to a new culture, but other companies make no such effort. The result can be an influx of hundreds or even thousands of people who have lived their entire lives in a culture that is substantially different. Misunderstandings, conflicts, and potential disorder may be the result.

The technological, demographic, and economic changes that began in the 1960s and continue at present have had a profound influence on the values, attitudes, and beliefs of many Americans. One consequence has been a general pessimism that is very different from the attitudes of Americans a generation ago. Another result has been a widespread impatience with promises of a better future. Americans as citizens and as consumers demand products and services that live up to the manufacturers' or sellers' claims—and disappointed consumers are quick to take their complaints to court. Increasingly, people regard themselves as "consumers" of government services as well as of commercial products, and here, too, there is little patience for unfulfilled expectations.[4]

For the police executive, a skeptical and demanding public is both boon and curse. On one hand, people insist on the highest quality of law enforcement service, and thus local political leaders are pressed to support improvements. On the other hand, the public will not be satisfied with glib promises that fail to materialize.

Given the breadth and depth of the changes in these four areas that the United States has experienced over the past two or three decades, few police administrators can expect to get by with bland reassurances that "everything is fine," that "the system ain't broke and doesn't need fixing." Whether "the system is broke" is not the point. The public is saying, "If it ain't perfect, make it better"—and they want it "better" *right now*.

Change and Crisis

Some management theorists have suggested that change is most easily accomplished when there is the perception of a crisis, when the present system or practice or policy clearly has failed and must be replaced or the entire enterprise may be lost.[5] Most management experts today have rejected the "crisis" theory.

Fortunately, it is not necessary to prove that the traditional system has completely failed in order to justify change. Nor is it necessary to prove that the alternative, community policing, is perfect. It is only necessary to demonstrate to the public, and all of the various constituencies within the agency itself, that *improvement* is both possible and desirable, and that the executive—as an agent for change—has adopted a vision of a better way to serve the real needs of the community.[6]

The vision of an ideal future, by its very nature, represents something other than, and indeed better than, the conditions that presently exist. If there is no such vision, and if no one can imagine a better state of affairs, there is little hope of improving. By the very act of articulating a vision of a better world, one creates a certain dissatisfaction with the present world, a desire to see the vision fulfilled. It is that dissatisfaction, fueled by the distance between what is desired and what already exists, that makes change both necessary and desirable.[7]

Measuring that distance, between what is desired and what already exists, is the primary purpose of the initial assessment process we discussed in Chapter 3.

ANALYZING AND INTERPRETING THE ASSESSMENT

The initial assessment consists of individual interviews and group meetings with officials of the parent authority, members of the agency itself, and representatives of the community (both influential citizens and the general public).

Identifying Common Themes

Specific comments, suggestions, criticisms, and complaints, culled from the notes and records of each interview and meeting, should be listed and categorized. The particular scheme of categorization is not very important. The purpose is to identify common themes in terms of what the community wants and expects of its police agency. Usually these common themes can be reduced to a single statement of a few key words, such as, "More police visibility in neighborhoods," or, "Officers more sensitive to cultural differences."

When these common themes have been identified and sorted into categories, the number of times each theme was mentioned should be tallied. When one of the common themes was mentioned in a group meeting, there should be a notation as to whether the rest of the group appeared to agree or disagree. The tally also might indicate whether a theme was mentioned by an official of the parent authority, by a member of the agency's staff, by an influential citizen, or by a member of the general public.

Criticisms and complaints should be treated primarily as statements, in negative form, of the community's expectations and desires. For example, if a citizen complains, "I asked a police officer for directions, and he answered me in a rude and abrupt manner," the citizen in effect is saying, "I expect police officers, even when they are merely giving someone information, to treat people in a courteous and helpful manner." Similarly, if a citizen says, "There's just never a police officer around when you want one," in effect the citizen is saying, "The police need to be more visible in the community."

At the same time, specific complaints, especially if they clearly violate the agency's policies and regulations, may require appropriate investigation. Criticisms and complaints should never be dismissed out of hand, but neither should citizens, especially in group meetings, be encouraged to turn the meeting into nothing but a "gripe session."

The first product of this analysis should be a list of statements, each of which represents something that the community expects or wants from its police agency, organized into general categories, and listed in the order of frequency (that is, how often an item was mentioned).

Identifying Constraints

The list of statements provides an index of what the community wants, but it may tell more than that.

Some of the items on the list may be unfeasible. For example, there might be a widespread belief in the community that the police should be responsible for stopping the incursion of weapons into the public schools. However, in many states the public schools are managed by an independent governmental agency. The city or county police may not have the authority to intrude onto school campuses unless invited by the school administrators, and the latter may not be willing to acknowledge that the problem is as serious as the public thinks it is.

Another problem may arise if different segments of the community have widely different, and opposing, perceptions of what the police should be doing. For example, if elected officials of the parent government have put great emphasis on reducing budgets and "living within our means," while community leaders and the general public have emphasized the need to expand the police presence by putting more officers on the street, the discrepancy portends a serious political problem for the police executive.

Both unfeasible or impractical expectations and disparities among segments of the community should be viewed as constraints on the direction that change can take. Nothing is more likely to lead to disaster than raising expectations that cannot be fulfilled. No matter how much the community may want something, if it is legally impermissible, financially impractical, or functionally impossible, that expectation cannot serve as the basis for planned change. Instead, the police executive must first find some way either to make the desired practice or condition attainable, or must educate the community to realize that it is not possible.

Similarly, if there is a serious disparity among different segments of the community as to what is expected and wanted, the police executive must not succumb to the temptation to do what the majority (or the most powerful) want and ignore the rest. Instead, the police executive must find some way to bring the community together, to mediate among the different segments until they find some common ground.

Meanwhile, the police executive can concentrate on the themes, identified and categorized from the initial assessment, that are most common throughout the community, that represent change in the desired direction, and that are most feasible and likely to be successful.

Identifying Potential Resistance

Another product of the initial assessment should be the identification of probable areas of resistance.

Discrepancies in expectations or desires among different segments of the community are almost certain to produce resistance, if the desires of one segment are honored while those of another segment are ignored or discounted. If business owners want the police to be less visible and intrusive, while the city council wants more intensive patrols in commercial districts, attempting to satisfy one constituency is sure to bring resistance from the other.

Similarly, if one segment of the community has nothing good to say about any aspect of the police, but merely recites a list of criticisms, complaints, and grievances at every meeting, even positive changes are likely to be greeted with skepticism, mistrust, and resistance.

Sometimes resistance can be indicated by what people do not say, more than what they do say. This is especially true with regard to members of the agency's staff. When they are given an opportunity to suggest areas of improvement, or asked to describe their ideals, failing to respond—or responding with nothing but a laundry list of trivial, superficial items—may indicate that the personnel are opposed to any significant change, and are likely to resist change vigorously.

Some resistance to change probably is inevitable; it is a reflection of basic human nature. People who have devoted a large part of their lives to learning to perform their roles in a particular social structure, and who have been rewarded for their success, are not eager to abandon those roles, to give up everything they thought they knew in favor of something that seems to them untested and uncertain. Particularly in an institution, such as a traditional police agency, that is structured on the framework of "command-and-control," supervisors and managers may be legitimately afraid of a system that seems to require them to abdicate control altogether.[8]

Resistance may have, or at least appear to have, a reasonable basis in fear of the unknown. But as management expert James O'Toole points out, there is another factor that may be operating as well: the simple fact that people do not like to be told what to do. If change, regardless of its nature, is imposed on people without their consent, resistance is certain.[9]

The possibility, even the probability, of resistance to change cannot prevent change from being contemplated and need not prevent change from being successful. It is not necessary, after all, to have complete unanimity among the agency's personnel (or any other constituency) before any change can be implemented. Once a change has taken place, some of the dissenters will discover that it is not as bad as they feared; they may change their minds. Others eventually will realize that, whatever their views, the change has taken place and will not be reversed, and that their continued resistance will only be to their personal detriment. As long as the number of dissenters is relatively small and the level of resistance is relatively low, grumbling and foot-dragging can be tolerated.

Thus it is not the task of the executive to eliminate resistance altogether, but merely to reduce it to the point that it does not seriously interfere with the desired changes. This can be done mostly by involving as many people as possible in deciding what changes are desirable and how they are to be implemented. People who have contributed to these decisions almost always will support them, and will encourage their peers to support them as well. By including as many people as possible in the decision-making process, the executive empowers both the rank-and-file officers and the members of the community, giving them both a responsibility for and an investment in their own future.[10]

Identifying Allies and Resources

Finally, the initial assessment should produce some prospective allies and may help in identifying resources.

Allies are, naturally, those who already favor the kinds of change that the police executive contemplates. Allies in the parent government, in the agency's own staff, and in the general public all may play a significant role in implementing the changes that they have called for.

By "resources," we mean individuals and groups who can make a specific contribution to the change process. In the course of interviewing influential citizens, the police executive may find someone who has expertise in some area that could help implement the change. For example, if the executive has identified communications as one of the areas in which change is needed, and happens to meet a person who has broad knowledge of communications systems, that person might be willing to volunteer his or her time and expertise in designing an improved communications system. Another example: If members of a particular ethnic group complain that the police officers in their neighborhood are insensitive to the group's culture, the group could be invited to help develop and implement a training curriculum for those police officers.

MAKING A STATEMENT

The purpose of the assessment process is to determine what kinds of changes in a police agency are desired by the community. When that has been completed, the next stage is to describe the intended outcome: what the police agency will look like as a result of the planned change.

In fact, three different but related statements should be developed:

- A *vision statement*, representing a description of an ideal future to which the agency aspires
- A *mission statement*, defining the agency's role and function in society
- A *values statement*, expressing the core values that will form the basis of the agency's policies and serve as the standard against which its performance, and that of its personnel, will be measured

Each of these statements serves as a pledge to the community, a public declaration of the kind of police service that the citizens should expect to receive. The statements are not merely public relations slogans. Considerable forethought and care should go into developing each of the statements.

Articulating a Vision

The vision statement usually is formulated by one person: the agency's chief executive. Indeed, many authorities on management have identified the ability to articulate a vision of a desirable future as a critical skill of leaders.[11] Especially during a period of transition, subordinates and even the general public, who also have a vested interest in the agency, want to be reassured that the leadership has a clear goal in mind.

The vision statement should be succinct and unambiguous. It should describe, in one sentence, what the executive believes would be an ideal state. It should go beyond the immediate desires of the community, but should reflect the community's ultimate aspirations.[12]

Although the vision statement should be formulated by the chief executive, and should be identified with him or her as a personal expression of the agency's ultimate goals, it also must represent the shared purposes of subordinates. It should express not only "what the Chief wants," but, for members of the agency, "what we want for ourselves and our community." Therefore, we would urge the executive to consult with the agency's managers and with representatives of all elements of the agency before finally adopting the vision statement. Changing a word or a phrase may clarify the statement's meaning, or may evoke an image that subordinates find particularly appealing.

Stating the Mission

The mission statement defines the agency's present role or function. It answers the question, "How will this vision be achieved?" Like the vision statement, it should be clear and concise.

The mission statement also should represent a consensus among the agency's leadership. Usually it should be developed by a committee composed of all of the agency's top-level administrators and representatives of upper- and mid-level management. Except in very large agencies where such broad participation would be unwieldy, the committee also might include representatives of first-line supervisors and operating personnel.

We recommend the use of a facilitator to lead the development process: someone from outside of the agency who has experience in this process. In some respects, it is the process of developing the mission statement, more than the product, that is significant.

The process begins by considering the value and importance of a mission statement in defining the agency's essential purpose. Mission statements from other police agencies and from organizations outside of law enforcement should be examined and compared. If the agency previously has developed some sort of mission statement, it, too, should be examined.

The committee's task initially seems simple: to define the agency's essential purpose. However, in order to carry out that assignment, the committee must plunge deeply into the consideration of several critical questions:

- What does this agency do that no other agency does or can do?
- What function of this agency is indispensable to the community? What do we do that, if we failed to do it, would cause the community to suffer?
- How are we striving toward the achievement of our ideal vision?

Finally, the mission statement should take the form, "The mission of the _____ Police Department is . . ." The remainder of the statement should be no more than a single sentence.

Expressing Values

The values statement usually is the longest and most complex of the three statements, and may be the most difficult to develop. It is an expression of the values that the agency regards as central to its mission and essential to the achievement of its ultimate goals.

A *value* is simply an idea about what is important or worthy. There can be many different ideas about how people should act; the values statement identifies those behaviors that the agency regards as appropriate and desirable. It also defines how the agency's mission, as given in the mission statement, is to be carried out and how the agency intends to achieve its ultimate purpose, as expressed in the vision statement.

Again, broad participation in developing the values statement is important, to be certain that it represents the views of all elements of the agency, and to promote acceptance of and commitment to the stated values. This is not a statement that any one person should formulate.[13] In a large agency, participation usually must be limited to representatives of the various levels and units, but it is still important to make the process as inclusive as possible.

Again, as with developing the mission statement, the process of developing the values statement may be more important than the product. Especially in a traditional agency, managed according to the command-and-control philosophy, the mere fact that subordinates are asked to express their opinions may be revolutionary. Possibly for the first time, agency personnel at every level are being told, implicitly, that their interests, their needs, and their beliefs are important and will be respected.

At the same time, opening the process to maximum participation is important in gaining commitment to the resulting values statement. People naturally feel a stronger obligation to live up to standards that they have helped to formulate, rather than standards that have been handed down from on high.[14]

The values statement should not be merely a laundry list of noble sentiments. Limiting the statement to a single sentence may be impractical, but it needs to be short enough to be memorable. Otherwise, the statement will suffer the same fate as so many other such declarations: It will languish in file drawers, or as the frontispiece to policy manuals, ignored and forgotten.

The values statement represents the agency's commitment to a standard of performance. Officers, when they are contemplating a certain action, should instinctively ask themselves, "Is this action consistent with the values I have promised to uphold?" Supervisors and managers, as they instruct and guide their subordinates, should refer frequently to the values statement and explain how specific policies and procedures reflect and implement the values of the agency. Administrators, when called upon to explain or justify the agency's activities, should be able to relate those activities to the standards expressed in the values statement.

Examples of the Three Statements

We reproduce here the vision, mission, and values statements adopted by the Austin Police Department, not because they are necessarily the best possible models, but because they are products of the process we have described in the past few pages.

We do not recommend that any other agency simply copy them; as we have stressed, the process by which these statements are developed is at least as important as the product.

The Vision
Working with neighborhoods to create a safe city.

The Mission
To protect and to serve through community partnerships.

The Values
To treat all persons with fairness, respect, and dignity through:

Professionalism
Open, honest commmunication
Loyalty
Integrity
Courage
Ethical behavior

In this case, adopting a values statement that includes the acronym, POLICE, may seem gimmicky. However, the acronym has the great advantage of making the statement as a whole easy to remember. The fact that some elements of the statement, such as "professionalism" and "loyalty," require further definition is not a drawback. On the contrary: All six terms in the acronym raise questions that demand to be discussed in training sessions and in everyday interactions between supervisors and subordinates.

No matter what list of values an agency adopts, the process of setting standards of performance is not finished: It is just begun. The vision, mission, and values statements are only words on paper until they are put into action through the activities of the agency's personnel.

Even just as words on paper, these statements are important because they represent the agency's commitment, and that of its personnel, to an explicit set of standards. Those standards must reflect not just congenial ideals, but the very highest aspirations of the people who, through their everyday actions, will make these statements a living reality—or will deny and repudiate them.

ESTABLISHING PRIORITIES

The three statements—the vision, mission, and values statements—serve as the foundation for the transformation of the police agency from a traditional philosophy to that of community policing. In a sense, these statements are similar to the platforms adopted by political parties: They identify the issues that the agency must address in becoming community-oriented.

Transforming the agency then becomes a matter of *aligning* the agency's structure, policies, and practices with the ideas embodied in the three statements and with the expectations and desires of the community, as expressed during the initial assessment.

This concept of alignment is the key to deciding what changes are needed and in what order they should occur.

The lists of community expectations and desires serve as a guide to the kinds of changes that are desired. The vision, mission, and values statements provide a specification of the direction in which change is needed.

Establishing priorities for change is ultimately the responsibility of the executive. Given the list of community desires, the executive must determine:

- What does everyone want? What specific expectations are most widely held in the community? What specific changes in the police agency are most often mentioned by the officials of the parent government, by the public, and by the agency's own personnel?
- What changes are possible? Given the present structure and resources of the agency, which of the most widely desired changes can be accomplished most readily? Which of them, if any, would be difficult or impossible to accomplish?
- What comes first? Is there a natural order to the changes that are widely desired and possible? Which changes can be made only after other changes have been accomplished?

The first decision should be based directly on the analysis of the initial assessment, the lists of community expectations and desires we discussed previously. Out of all the one-on-one interviews and group meetings, the executive should be able to identify the one or two or three items that were most frequently mentioned and that appeared to meet with universal approval.

Deciding what is possible may be more difficult. Earlier we discussed the constraints that may be imposed if there are conflicting expectations or incompatible desires: If one segment of the community has a very different view from another segment about what the police should be doing.

There are also other factors that may limit the executive's ability to bring about positive change. One such factor, almost always, is the availability of sufficient funds.

Some changes might require an expenditure that is unreasonably disproportionate to the benefit that could be derived. For example, suppose that citizens express a desire for the police to adopt two-person patrols (that is, two officers assigned to each patrol beat). That idea might be received very favorably by the agency's personnel. However, the cost of two-person patrol, except on a limited basis in specific areas, is impossible to justify in terms of effective policing.

Other possible changes might be perfectly justifiable but simply beyond the means available to the agency in the foreseeable future. Of course, much depends on the community's general economic condition and on the ability and willingness of the political authority to raise funds. There is not much point in planning a change if the money to carry it out does not exist.

Financial constraints are not the only factors to be considered. For example, there may be a broad consensus in the community that the agency is understaffed and should be enlarged. There may even be a willingness, as there was in Seattle, to increase taxes enough to pay for more officers. However, it takes time to recruit, select, train, and deploy police officers. They are not, after all, interchangeable parts that can be bought off the shelf.

There may be purely physical constraints, such as buildings and other facilities that are overcrowded, deteriorating, or unsuitable for the uses that might be contemplated. The public may be unaware of these conditions and may not realize that some of the agency's policies and practices are limited by the lack of appropriate facilities. In this case, correcting the facility problems may have to take a higher priority than some of the other changes that the community has identified.

In some cases, there may be constitutional, legal, and contractual constraints. It is a fundamental tenet of American government that the police power of the state is limited: The police cannot do whatever they wish to do. In addition, many large police agencies are subject to collective bargaining agreements (usually between the city government and the police officers' organization) or civil service rules (usually embodied in state laws) that are based, naturally enough, on the traditional system of police organizational structure. Before changes can be made in the agency's structure and policies, either the agreements must be renegotiated—a process that is likely to be time-consuming and fractious—or the laws must be changed.

These constraints should not be used as excuses to avoid the transformation to community policing. Granted, the transition will be more difficult, but once the constraints have been recognized, action can be taken to remove or alleviate them. The very fact that the community has expressed its desire to see certain changes can provide motivation for political authorities to correct long-standing deficiencies in the police agency.

Still, until the constraints have been removed, they must dictate the kinds of changes that the executive chooses to initiate, or at least the order in which changes are to take place.

All else being equal, the first changes to be made should be the easiest and quickest to accomplish, with the greatest visibility and likelihood of public approval. Success in the earliest stages of transforming the agency gives powerful leverage for later, more difficult changes to be accomplished.

At this point, the executive should be able to compile a list of specific changes that are to be implemented, in a particular order. Each change on the list should satisfy these criteria:

- It is something that is widely desired by the parent government, the public, and the agency's personnel.
- It is something that can be accomplished in a reasonable period of time, preferably with minimal disruption of the agency's ongoing operations.
- It is something that is not constrained by financial, practical, or legal factors that would have to be addressed first.
- It is something that will produce visible or tangible results.
- It is something that will help to bring the agency's policies or practices into alignment with the agency's vision, mission, and values statements.

This initial list, which may include no more than two or three items, should not be mistaken for a complete description of the transformation from a traditional police agency to a community policing agency. The changes on the list represent only a first step in the desired direction, a kind of "down payment" on the much more comprehensive changes that will be needed.

In a medium-sized or larger agency, these initial changes do not have to be implemented throughout the agency all at once.

As a general rule, we do not advocate the technique of identifying one area as a "test bed" or "experimental district" in which various changes will be implemented before they are disseminated throughout the agency (assuming that they prove to be successful). We believe that this practice incurs too many risks and disadvantages: The public may perceive that the administrators are unsure whether the "experiments" are likely to be successful; personnel in the rest of the agency may resent the special attention (and perceived benefits) that the "experimental district" is given; and, perhaps most importantly, the operations and policies of the agency are likely to become confused and inconsistent.

However, it is not necessary for every change to be implemented throughout the agency all at once, especially when the changes are substantial and involve rearranging physical facilities, extensive training of personnel, and so forth. Major changes can be implemented on a scheduled "roll-out," established in advance but subject to modification as they are implemented in the first areas. In other words, a specific change or set of related changes can be implemented in a single district or in a small number of districts. After a reasonable period for the change to be implemented and any rough spots smoothed out, the changes can be introduced into another district or group of districts. The schedule for the "roll-out" should be established in advance and made generally known. Modifications of the schedule should be avoided, since delaying implementation at any point will encourage resistance in the next area that is due to be affected.

Furthermore, some types of change may not be needed or desired in some areas. The basic concept of community policing, after all, is predicated on the idea that communities may have different needs for police services. Insofar as possible, each neighborhood should have the opportunity to decide what specific changes it wants, and what priorities it wants to observe in bringing about a series of changes. For a large agency, these decisions might be made in each sector, through consultations between the agency's administrators, sector commanders, and representatives of the neighborhoods. Some neighborhoods, for example, might feel that they would be better served by having more officers on the street, assigned to smaller beats. Another neighborhood might feel that the present level of patrol is sufficient, but that the agency should provide more preventive services, such as workshops on self-protection, organization of crime watches, and so on.

Eventually, as the community policing philosophy is fully implemented, decisions about police services and practices should be made directly at the neighborhood level, by sector or area commanders in consultation with residents. During the initial stages of the transformation, a good deal of "hand-holding" will be needed. Residents may have no clear idea of what kinds of changes in police service they want, and neighborhood-level police commanders are likely to be uncertain about how much authority they have to change traditional policing practices. Many decisions that could be made at the neighborhood or sector level are likely to be "passed up" the chain of command.

For many mid- and upper-level managers, the easiest response is to make the decisions that are passed up to them. The police executive must encourage the managers, first, to approve the requests for change as far as possible; second, to begin refer-ring the decisions back down to the neighborhood level as quickly as possible. Neigh-borhood-level commanders must be reassured that they do indeed have the authority to make most of the decisions on their own, provided only that they do not violate the agency's basic policies nor create conflicts with essential agency-wide operations.

Some of the issues raised by neighborhood residents may not involve law enforcement at all, or only peripherally. In areas that have relatively little serious crime, residents often cite "quality-of-life" concerns such as graffiti, noise, poorly maintained vacant lots, and so forth. These concerns may or may not involve viola-tions of local ordinances. Even when there are specific laws against, for example, teenagers cruising the streets in cars with overly loud stereo systems, more vigorous law enforcement is unlikely to solve the problem. The real solution lies with the res-idents themselves, working together to define the behaviors that they consider accept-able and unacceptable.

SETTING GOALS AND OBJECTIVES

A prioritized list of changes to be implemented, identifying which of them are to be agency-wide and which may be limited to particular neighborhoods or sectors, and indicating the sequence in which they are to be initiated, serves as the basis for the plan to transform a police agency from the traditional philosophy to community policing.

As with the three statements, the prioritized list should be a group product. Upper- and mid-level managers and representatives of the supervisory and opera-tional levels should have ample opportunities to contribute their ideas and concerns. For some administrators, making the process inclusive may seem burdensome and inefficient: It is a lot faster and easier just to make all the decisions oneself. But it is a false economy.

Including as many elements of the agency as possible in these initial decision-making processes will pay off handsomely in the next phase: defining goals and objectives for the full implementation of planned change.

When there is already a broad understanding of what is to be accomplished, based on a consensus as to the agency's mission and values, and a commitment at every level to make the changes successful, setting goals becomes a relatively simple exercise in translating broad ideals into specific prescriptions. The goals are then translated into even more specific, measurable operating objectives.

Earlier we presented the vision, mission, and values statements adopted by the Austin Police Department, not as a model to be copied but simply as an example of what such statements look like. These three statements, we said, form the foundation for planned, positive changes.*

---

*In point of fact, the three statements we reproduced on pages 88–91 were adopted by the Austin Police Department in 1996. Shortly before Chief Watson came to Austin in 1992, the department had just completed the process of developing a set of vision, mission, and values statements. These statements were relatively verbose and ambiguous, but it seemed inappropriate to expect the department to go through the same process all over again. The three statements were re-examined in 1995 and the version we present here was adopted. The general intent of both sets of statements is essentially the same.

The initial assessment conducted by co-author Elizabeth Watson when she became chief of the department produced a long list of community expectations and desires. The list was reduced to those few items that were virtually universal:

- A desire for a more visible police presence on the streets
- A desire for the police to address a wide range of neighborhood-specific problems (many of which were "quality- of-life" issues more than crime problems)
- An expectation that police officers would continue to operate, as they have for many years, with a high level of professionalism and respect for the rights and dignity of citizens, and with an attitude of cooperation with neighborhood residents
- A desire for the police service to operate as efficiently as possible, so as to minimize the burden on the taxpayers

A committee of the department's administrators and managers then condensed this list into three global goals:

- *Goal One: Determine the difference between what citizens want and what police can provide.* This goal is based on the finding that the agency's resources probably would not be sufficient to fulfill all of the citizens' expectations and desires. However, there was a feeling that some of the agency's resources could be used more efficiently, thereby freeing some capacity to satisfy the citizens' wants. Identifying underutilized resources and determining the best way to use the agency's personnel would be determined through a continuing self-assessment process.
- *Goal Two: Enrich the work experience for personnel.* This goal addresses two issues, one of which was frequently mentioned by citizens (the importance of maintaining professionalism and respect for individuals). The other issue was not mentioned as often but was raised by several individuals: the need to expand training and career opportunities for police officers.
- *Goal Three: Optimize resources through the investment in technology and long-range planning for unresolved budget issues.* This goal directly concerns the issue, raised by many citizens and officials of the parent government, of maximizing the use of resources to minimize the burden on taxpayers. The planning committee anticipated that better use of new technologies might resolve some of these problems.

These three goals represent the three major areas in which planned changes were to be made over a five-year period. The goals are stated in broad, general terms. The planning committee next tackled the difficult task of restating the goals in terms of relatively specific, measurable, operational objectives. The list they produced is given here only as an example of the kinds of objectives that should be included in a transformational plan.

- *Goal One*
  - Initiate a Department-wide Self-Assessment
    - Determine resources needed at the district level
    - Reevaluate job functions and responsibilities

- Develop Neighborhood-based Policing Strategies
- Analyze Organizational Structure
- Establish Communication Mechanisms to Receive Regular Input [from citizens, and within the department]
- Revise, Condense, and Eliminate Policies and Procedures that Are Not Compatible with Community and Police Department Values

- *Goal Two*
  - Modify Recruiting Efforts to Attract Applicants Temperamentally Suited to the Tenets of Community Policing that Reflect the Diversity of Austin
  - Invest in Training
  - Reexamine Systems Relating to Rewards, Promotion, and Career Development

- *Goal Three*
  - Information Management
    - Revamp 9-1-1
    - Consolidate police information systems
  - Identify, Prioritize, and Develop a Plan to Integrate Technological Improvements in the Area of Forensic Science
  - Coordinate and Integrate the Use and Acquisition of Personal Computers with the Departmental Information System
  - [Improve] Facilities and Equipment
  - [Determine Long-range] Staffing and Support
  - [Identify] Alternative Funding Sources

(*Note:* In reproducing this list of objectives, we have made minor editorial changes in the interest of clarity and consistency.)

Some of the items in the list of objectives may not be self-explanatory. However, even a cursory review of the list demonstrates the point we wish to make: that the planning process begins with the initial assessment of the public's expectations and desires, and ends—for the moment—with the kind of list we have shown here.

Of course, this is not the end of the planning process, much less of the process of transforming the agency. However, it is a good place to pause and to share the results with the public.

GOING PUBLIC

Probably the most neglected aspect of the planning process is sharing the results, the plans themselves, with the public before implementation begins.

Planners, whether individuals or committees, seem reluctant to disclose the details of their product. Perhaps the reason is that subconsciously the planners fear that their work will be rejected after all, or that someone will find some inherent flaw that ruins the plan and requires that they start over.

Whatever the psychology may be, we are certain that "going public" is an essential part of the transformational process.

Circulating a Draft

Before the plan is considered complete and final, a draft version should be prepared and distributed to everyone who has participated in its development. After they have reviewed the full plan and concurred on its details, the draft should be circulated to three groups of people: key officials of the parent government, influential citizens and community leaders, and representatives of the various elements within the agency (such as the officers' association). The recipients of the draft should be specifically asked to comment, and a deadline for their responses should be specified.

Despite the planners' fears, severely critical responses are unlikely (unless the planners have truly botched the job). Some useful criticisms and suggestions may be received, and may be incorporated into the plan. However, the most common, and in some ways the most important, response is likely to be an expression of approval or agreement to the draft plan.

With whatever revisions seem appropriate, a final plan can be compiled and printed. It is now ready for broader publication.

Copies of the entire, detailed plan for the transformation of the agency should be made available to all members of the agency's staff and to all interested officials in the parent government. These are, after all, the people whose interests will be most directly affected by the changes that are to be implemented, and they have a right to know what to expect.

If the complete plan is too lengthy and intricate for broad publication, a "condensed version" omitting extraneous details may be prepared. This version should then be sent to all of the people who were individually interviewed in the early stages of the planning process, and to selected community leaders. A cover letter or memo should invite comments, and should indicate that the police executive will appreciate having an opportunity to discuss the plan in person. A week or so after the copies are sent out, follow-up telephone calls should be made, first to ensure that the plan was received, and then to ask for an appointment to answer any questions that the recipient may have.

Many of the recipients are likely to decline an appointment. They may not have read the plan at all, or may have read it and found nothing in it that they feel an urge to discuss. If an appointment is made, the executive should take full advantage of the opportunity to clarify, explain, and essentially to "sell" the plan. Those who have received a copy and have responded positively should be asked for their continued support as the plan is implemented.

Finally, the plan should be made available to the general public. Copies might be distributed through the local library system. A news conference should introduce the plan to the general public, and there should be follow-up meetings in each part of town to present the plan and receive citizens' reactions.

Again, it is certainly possible that some reactions will be negative, and potential sources of resistance will be given an opportunity to frame their attack. Some of the criticisms may prove to be valid, and could lead to beneficial modifications. If nothing else, the executive will have an opportunity to draw out some of the factions that are hostile to the plan, and may gain a preview of their objections and tactics.

Nevertheless, the very willingness of the police department to make its plans public will encourage the community to have confidence that the agency's managers know what they are doing. We do not mean to overemphasize the risks in taking one's plans to the public; in our view, the risks are minimal and vastly outweighed by the benefits. Nothing is more important to the success of the transformation process than the enduring support of the community. The best way to gain that support is to make certain that the public is fully informed; this too is part of the process of making the community full partners with the police.

FOOTNOTES

1. Leon Martel, *Mastering Change: The Key to Business Success* (New York: Simon & Schuster, 1986), pp. 32–44.

2. Martel, *Mastering Change*, pp. 251–252.

3. James Champy, *Reengineering Management* (New York: Harper Business, 1995), p. 23. Champy believes that at least some of the "downsizing" will prove to be only temporary, that corporations will rebuild as their profitability rises. Some economists have begun to use the term *corporate anorexia* to describe companies that have downsized too far (*NBC Nightly News*, Monday, February 5, 1996).

4. Champy, *Reengineering Management*, pp. 16–17.

5. Ernest Dale, *Management: Theory and Practice* (New York: McGraw-Hill, 1965), p. 325. Dale also points out that, even in a crisis, planned, gradual changes are more likely to be successful than sudden, sweeping changes.

6. James O'Toole, *Leading Change* (San Francisco: Jossey-Bass Publishers, 1995), p. 195.

7. Sue Barton, *Austin's Concept for Community Policing: Achieving Self-Reliant Neighborhoods through Community Policing* (Austin, TX: Austin Police Deptartment, 1993), pp. 26–27.

8. Champy, *Reengineering Management*, p. 26.

9. O'Toole, *Leading Change*, p. 15; also pp. 161–164.

10. Champy, *Reengineering Management*, pp. 115–119, 133.

11. O'Toole, *Leading Change*, p. xiii.

12. O'Toole, *Leading Change*, p. 10.

13. Robert W. Rogers and William C. Byham, "Diagnosing Organizational Cultures for Realignment," in Ann Howard, ed., *Diagnosis for Organizational Change* (New York: Guilford Press, 1994), pp. 187–189.

14. O'Toole, *Leading Change*, p. 14.

C H A P T E R 5

MANAGING CHANGE: STRUCTURES AND SYSTEMS

Whenever changes are contemplated in a bureaucratic organization, there is a natural tendency to assume that the changes will be reflected first of all in the organizational structure. Moving boxes around on the organization chart seems to be the first inclination of administrators, the easiest and most obvious way to "shake up" the organization and impose a new system of command and control.

The transformation from a traditional law enforcement agency to one that expresses the philosophy of community policing may very well require some structural changes. However, it is not the structure of an agency—where the boxes are placed on the chart—that matters so much as what the people in the boxes do.

Nevertheless, some changes in organizational structure may be necessary, or at least desirable, in order to bring the agency's structure into alignment with its goals. To see what may need to be done, we will first examine the typical organizational structure of traditional American police agencies.

ALIGNING THE ORGANIZATION AND ITS GOALS

The organizational structures of local police agencies usually are subject to the dictates of the parent government and its budgetary process, which determine what kinds of tasks the agency is expected to perform and what resources it has available, particularly the number of people at each rank or salary level.

The organizational structures of actual agencies evolve over time as different tasks are assigned, as budget levels rise and fall, and as different administrators apply their own ideas about the best way to manage the organization. Furthermore, every agency is more or less free to adopt its own system of naming the various organizational elements. In a broad sense, there is no such thing as a "typical" American law enforcement agency. Each agency has its own history, its own local conditions to deal with, and its own peculiarities. However, there are some features that are common to many traditional police agencies.[1]

Most local police agencies are organized into three or four main elements: Patrol, Investigations, and Support Services. The last of these is sometimes divided into Technical Services and Administrative Services. In some medium-sized and smaller agencies, Patrol and Investigations make up one Operations unit, with everything else lumped into Support Services.

Support Services, whether one element or three, usually is divided into functional units according to their technical specialty or type of service: forensics, communications, fleet, public information, accounting, personnel, training, and so forth.

The Investigations element in almost all traditional police agencies is divided into crime-specific units, the number of which depends mostly on the overall size of the agency and its jurisdiction: the larger the agency, the more numerous and specific the units. Within the Investigations Division of a large agency, there may be three or four major units (Crimes Against Persons, Crimes Against Property, Organized Crimes/Vice, and, sometimes, Criminal Intelligence), each of which is further divided into as many crime-specific subunits as the agency can afford to manage.

The greatest variation in organizational structures is found in patrol. Some agencies' Patrol element is divided chronologically, into *watches*, with each watch divided geographically, into precincts or districts and beats. Other agencies, especially most large municipal police departments, divide Patrol geographically, into sectors, precincts or districts, and beats, with work schedules throughout the unit organized into shifts. The distinction between the time-based structure and the geography-based structure is that it may be easier to vary the number of geographical units (beats) from watch to watch, according to variations in the workload, in a time-based structure. However, the practical effect of the two systems is about the same.[2]

Figure 5.1 presents an organization chart for a hypothetical municipal police department, similar to what would be found in most medium-sized or larger American police agencies.

Commanding and Controlling

The organizational structure shown in Figure 5.1 represents the answer to a problem that bedevilled American police reformers at the end of the nineteenth century: How can one person, the police executive, who is answerable to the parent government and thus to the public, control the behavior of dozens or hundreds of employees who are scattered about the city and who necessarily perform their most important duties independently, with little or no direct supervision? This question assumed great

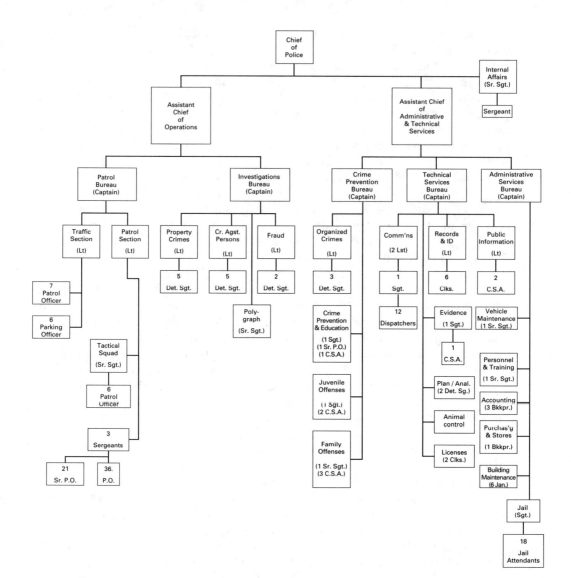

Figure 5-1

urgency in light of the considerable evidence, at the time, of corruption and ineffectuality in American policing.

The answer was to adopt the military model of command, whose origins can be traced back at least to the Roman Empire. This model of bureaucracy already had been adapted to the similar needs of industrial capitalism, beginning around the middle of the nineteenth century, and was further described and elaborated by the German sociologist Max Weber.[3]

The success of the military-corporate bureaucratic model depends on two features: the chain of command and the rules that define performance.

In theory, the people in each box on the chart exercise authority over all of the people in the boxes below them, and are responsible to all of the people in the boxes above them. Thus, for example, the lieutenants in the Patrol Division have the authority to issue orders and give directions to the sergeants and patrol officers under their command, and the lieutenants are answerable to their captain for the performance of those sergeants and patrol officers. These relationships of authority and responsibility provide a unified, unbroken chain of command from the person in the topmost box to the people in the bottommost boxes.

Secondly, the people in all of the boxes perform their duties according to a predefined set of systematic, rational rules, policies, and procedures, which may be expressed in the form of job descriptions, regulations, orders, and on and on. Again, there is no standardized terminology used consistently by all law enforcement agencies. However, in general, *rules* are statements of absolute requirements or prohibitions, often based on statutory law and constitutional principles, that cannot be violated. *Procedures* are regulations that define routine tasks, such as making out a duty schedule or filling out a form; following the proper procedure simply enables necessary work to be done consistently and (one hopes) efficiently.

Policies are statements that are grounded in a department's core values, and that set behavioral parameters within which officers are expected to operate. The policies are intended to guide the exercise of discretion and to aid decision making in complex or unforeseen situations. In other words, policies represent the manner in which the policing philosophy of the department is expressed.

This system of command and control became the foundation of the reformers' concept of police professionalism. The system is so much a part of traditional law enforcement practices that it is taken for granted, as if it were part of the natural order.

Unfortunately, the command and control system has two fundamental flaws: It promotes an inefficient use of resources, and it is prone to break down just when it is needed most.

The inefficient use of resources results from the fact that almost all of the actual work of the organization—the work of providing law enforcement services to the public—is performed by the people in the bottommost boxes on the chart. At the topmost level in the agency, administrators make new policies and regulations, and review the reports of the agency's operations to make sure that the existing policies and regulations are being followed. The people in the middle levels of the organization chart often wind up with hardly anything to do, and even that little is uncreative, tedious, and mostly pointless.

The second, and perhaps more serious, flaw is that no set of rules and regulations can anticipate every situation encountered by police officers in the course of their work. The system breaks down under any of several predictable conditions, such as a novel, unanticipated situation. In principle, all policies should form a coherent, rational system, based on the organization's core values. In practice, most policies are made *after the fact*, when something has gone wrong: when employees have acted inappropriately in some unforeseen situation, or when employees acted correctly but the results were different from what the policy anticipated.

Over time, policies become increasingly numerous, and if there ever was any coherent, rational system to them, it is lost in a welter of after-the-fact decisions about what employees should have done in some specific situation. The distinction between policies and procedures becomes blurred as new policies, designed to prohibit particular behaviors, are increasingly and unnecessarily specific. Predictably, employees become confused about what policies apply to which situations—if they can even remember all of the policies. As a result, employees become frustrated by a "system" that, from their point of view, is incomprehensible, irrational, and designed mainly to give their superiors an opportunity to catch them in a violation.

Evidence that the command and control system actually was breaking down, and in some cases had broken down disastrously, became impossible to ignore during the turbulent 1960s. The military-corporate organizational structure has come under scrutiny and there has been a considerable effort to find alternatives, better answers to the problems that plagued American law enforcement a century ago. Some of those answers are collected under the general heading of community policing.

ORGANIZATION AND COMMUNITY

The concept of community policing, which we describe in considerable detail in Chapter 2, can be summarized in a simple statement: *The police should engage the community in a partnership, a joint effort to maintain social order.* This simple statement, however, has several implications, some of which may affect the organizational structure of a police agency:

- Engaging the community in a partnership with the police usually does not happen spontaneously. Citizens have many concerns and demands on their time. Even though crime and disorder may be a major concern, citizens are not always prepared to devote the time and effort necessary to play an active role in policing. To make matters worse, the traditional concept of police professionalism has discouraged citizen involvement.

- The people in a police department who are naturally in the best position to engage the community are those who already have the most direct contact with citizens: that is, the generalist patrol officers. However, patrol officers usually have not been trained nor directed to perform the tasks that are required to engage the community.

- The distribution of resources, particularly personnel, under the command and control system of the traditional police agency limits the resources that are available at the lower levels. Thus most police agencies have been impelled to maintain the smallest possible patrol force, applying technology and rule-based management to extract the most work possible out of the fewest personnel. One way to satisfy this need is to limit the tasks that the operating personnel are expected to perform. In practice, most police agencies expect their patrol officers to perform only two primary tasks: responding to calls for assistance (including, but not limited to, complaints of crimes), and preparing reports (including, but not limited to, reports about crimes to be investigated by crime-specific specialists). Time for other tasks, such as problem solving, is allotted only after these two primary duties have been completed—or, more accurately, when there happen to be no calls requiring a response, and all reports have been filed.

- All new employees are hired at the patrol level. In many states, law enforcement agencies are prohibited by law or civil service rules from hiring experienced officers at higher ranks (except for the position of chief). Since patrol officers must serve in that rank for a specified minimum period, usually three or five years, a rapidly-growing department may have problems in filling supervisory positions with qualified personnel. Furthermore, because so much emphasis is placed on expanding the patrol force, little attention is paid to providing adequate infrastructure (such as the radio communications system) and support services.

- Most people in any organization naturally seek to improve their position in life by gaining promotions that bring higher salary and other personal benefits. In the traditional police agency, all personnel enter the agency as patrol officers; the first supervisory rank is sergeant. In some agencies, including the Austin Police Department, a patrol officer must first be promoted to detective and be assigned to Investigations before he or she is eligible for promotion to sergeant. Thus the *only* path for advancement is through Investigations.

- The role of the police detective has accrued an aura of glamor and a tradition of autonomy that makes the position even more attractive. Detectives wear suits instead of uniforms, they usually work only during the normal workday, and they have considerable discretion in deciding which cases they will spend their time and effort investigating.

Thus in many American police departments, the most appealing route of advancement for the most competent and ambitious patrol officers is through Investigations. In fact, it is unusual to find an upper-level manager in a police agency (except in some specialized technical support fields) who has not spent part of his or her career in Investigations. One result is that the patrol force is staffed predominantly with two groups of officers: those who have just entered the police force, and those who either do not want or cannot achieve promotion out of the patrol force. Another result is that investigators, having attained a position of autonomy within the law enforcement system, have little inclination to collaborate with the patrol force.

Reinforcing the Backbone

There is a considerable irony here. Law enforcement theorists, scholars, and administrators have always maintained, in the common cliché, that "patrol is the backbone of the police force." No less an authority than August Vollmer made that observation in 1924.[4] Yet the practical effect of the traditional command and control system, with its reliance on crime-specific specialists and technical experts, has been to diminish the role of the patrol force.

Because of the promotional policies we have just discussed, and in some cases the state laws and civil service regulations that govern police personnel assignment and promotions, the patrol force becomes in effect a resource pool for the rest of the department. The best and brightest officers are drawn from Patrol to fill vacancies in Investigations and other specialized units. In some agencies, Patrol even becomes a dumping ground for personnel who have been unsuccessful in other assignments, or who are being punished for some infraction of departmental policy.

Achieving the goals of community policing requires a reversal of this situation. To a very substantial degree, community policing demands that the pious sentiment of 1924 be made a practical reality: The patrol force must be not only the backbone but also the heart and arteries of the police agency.

We discuss at length, in Chapter 6, the new role of the patrol force in community policing. For now, we will focus on those aspects of the patrol force's role that affect the organizational structure.

First and foremost, patrol officers must have sufficient time to carry out an expanded range of duties. Chief among those duties will be eliciting the cooperation of the community, which can be accomplished only through a variety of formal and informal contacts with citizens.

There are three ways to increase the time available to patrol officers for new duties. The number of patrol officers can be increased by hiring new personnel, thereby reducing the service workload (that is, responding to calls and preparing reports) each officer must bear. Second, the workload itself (particularly the administrative workload) can be reduced through better management and the application of new technologies. Third, there may be substantial opportunities for the reallocation of personnel. In many agencies, commissioned officers are assigned to a variety of support services that could be performed as well, or better, by noncommissioned clerical and professional employees. "Civilianization," replacing sworn personnel with properly trained noncommissioned employees where possible, may allow more police officers to be assigned to patrol and other operational units.

Secondly, patrol officers need more than just time. Interacting with the community to maintain social order is a far broader role than merely collecting information and arresting offenders. Officers must have greater flexibility and discretion to decide for themselves how to perform the work assigned to them.

In general, decision-making authority in a community policing agency should be "pushed down" the chain of command. To the maximum extent possible, every decision should be made at the lowest level at which the personnel have sufficient information. Increasing the size of the patrol force, expanding the role of patrol officers, and increasing the discretionary authority of patrol officers all have significant implications for the agency's organizational structure.

First of all, there may not be quite as much of it.

Recapturing Resources

If patrol officers and their immediate superiors are given the authority to direct much of their own activity without waiting for instructions or permission, then the workload of their supervisors is reduced, and the work itself is accomplished more quickly and efficiently. It may be possible to prune the organizational tree, eliminating positions that are no longer needed. It may even be possible to lop off entire branches, eliminating one or more layers of management.

We do not minimize the difficulty in achieving this step. Eliminating high-level positions in a police agency can be a painful experience, a kind of organizational root canal. Nevertheless, the changes often are necessary, and eventually the personnel should see that the results are worth the cost. Eliminating upper-level positions can mean the freeing up of substantial resources. For example, eliminating a single captain's position may "recapture" a salary equivalent to at least two patrol officers.

Notice that eliminating a *position* does not necessarily mean eliminating, or even demoting, the people who currently hold the position. In Houston, an entire level of middle management was eliminated by promoting all of the deputy chiefs to newly created assistant chief positions. In this case, there was no immediate financial payoff; rather, the purpose was to flatten the organizational structure and reduce the bottleneck effect of an unnecessary layer of management.

Another way to free resources is to consolidate programs. For example, in Figure 5.1 (page 102), the Crime Prevention Bureau consists of four sections: Organized Crimes, Crime Prevention and Education, Juvenile Offenses, and Family Offenses. At the very least, the latter two sections could be combined and the personnel cross-trained. It is possible that four or five people could do the same volume of work that is currently divided among seven people.

Police agencies, like other bureaucratic organizations, accumulate specialized programs over the years. Each program may have been necessary and worthwhile when it was begun. However, there is a tendency to continue every program indefinitely, without seriously examining whether it is still needed, whether the benefits it produces are justified, or whether changes in the program's structure or methods might be desired. The close evaluation of all specialized programs in an agency may reveal many opportunities to recapture and redirect resources.

For example, referring again to Figure 5.1, the entire Crime Prevention and Education section might be eliminated if its duties—organizing neighborhood crime watches and personal safety workshops—are taken over by the patrol force.

Finally, one of the most effective ways to recapture resources is to determine what jobs, or even parts of jobs, can be performed by noncommissioned personnel rather than by police officers. In general, noncommissioned employees are paid lower salaries than even entry-level patrol officers, yet they often bring special competencies and experience that most police officers do not have. More importantly, this "civilianization" frees police officers to do the work for which they are specially trained.

Redesigning Beats and Shifts

Reallocating resources to increase the number of patrol officers has another implication for the agency's organizational structure. As more personnel are added to the patrol force, the area to which each officer is assigned will be reduced. In the process of redesigning patrol beats, two more changes can be made.

First, each patrol beat should be designed to take into account the geography of neighborhoods. In a traditional police agency, patrol beats usually are designed only to equalize the service workload. The neighborhood boundaries recognized by citizens usually are ignored. In a community policing agency, those neighborhood boundaries must be recognized and respected. As far as possible, each patrol officer should be responsible for a broad range of policing services to a single, unified community.

Second, patrol officers should be assigned more or less permanently to their beats. The common practice of moving officers from beat to beat every few months, or more often, should be abandoned simply because it prevents officers from establishing a partnership with citizens and impairs the officers' ability to develop a thorough understanding of the community to which they are assigned.

For much the same reason, we believe that the traditional practice of "rotating" from shift to shift every few months also should be abandoned. We realize that there are many difficulties in adopting fixed shifts, not the least of which is that officers do not want to be assigned for months or years to the less desirable shifts. We also recognize that there may be some benefit in rotating shifts; if nothing else, officers have an opportunity to observe their assigned neighborhoods at all hours of the day. Nevertheless, we consider the disadvantages to far outweigh the advantages.

In some neighborhoods, especially those that characteristically have a higher-than-average crime rate, the service workload may vary dramatically from one part of the day to another. Typically, the volume of calls for service rises from late afternoon until shortly after midnight, then falls off rapidly. Where this is the case, it is obviously impractical to expect one officer to handle two or three times the workload of another, when both are assigned to the same area. One solution is to establish a team of patrol officers who have no permanent beat assignment, but "float" from area to area, answering calls and assisting the beat officers. Another solution, where the service workload varies in reasonably predictable cycles, is to assign two or more officers to the selected beats during the high-incidence hours.

Beyond Patrol

Organizational changes to align the agency's structure with the goals of community policing involve more than just the patrol force, and more than just pruning the organizational tree.

If the patrol force is to be truly the backbone of the agency, in fact as well as in theory, then the roles and functions of the other elements of the agency must change. *Every* element of the agency must redefine its role in terms of supporting the patrol force.

Again, this step will not be taken without a certain amount of pain. The criminal investigations element may have the most difficulty in accepting what will be, for them, a virtual reversal of the traditional relationship.

In a traditional police agency, one of the primary duties of the generalist patrol force is to collect information at the crime scene (mostly consisting of the report of the alleged victim) and forward it to the specialist investigators. The investigators then are responsible for applying their scientific technology, crime-specific expertise, and investigative techniques to identify the perpetrator, thereby solving the crime. It is this concept of investigation that has been glorified in popular literature and the mass media, from Edgar Allen Poe and Arthur Conan Doyle to television's *Murder One* and *Homicide: Life on the Street*.

The mere fact that, according to the RAND study in the 1970s, police detectives rarely do any of those things has not diminished the popularity of the idea, not only among the general public but among the police themselves.

We are not suggesting that crime investigators will no longer be needed, or that their expertise is valueless. On the contrary, the experience and technical skill of investigators should be put to better use than merely reviewing an endless stream of reports of crimes that are mostly unsolvable.

Police authorities for several decades have recognized that the best opportunity to solve a crime and identify the perpetrator exists when the crime is first reported. The first officer on the scene—almost always the beat patrol officer—has that opportunity and should take full advantage of it. If there are witnesses present or likely to be found nearby, the patrol officer should interview them. If there is likely to be physical evidence at the crime scene, the patrol officer should collect it. If special techniques are needed to locate and develop evidence, the patrol officer should decide immediately whether the expenditure of time and effort is justified by the nature and scope of the crime, and, if so, should call in the specialists.

If a crime is clearly unsolvable for lack of information, the officer should do what most do now: prepare a report of whatever information is available and submit it to the investigators. The report also should be available to crime analysts for pattern analysis. In many cases, the report will be filed away and nothing will come of it, but occasionally there will be just enough information in a series of reports of unsolvable crimes to solve them all at once.

The role of the investigator becomes that of a technical consultant to the patrol officer. Instead of passively receiving information from patrol, the investigator's job is to give information to patrol as it is needed.

There still will be crimes that are solvable, but require lengthy or complex investigation beyond what can be reasonably expected of patrol officers. There also will be patterns of crime that go beyond a single beat, that may affect the entire community, and therefore require the attention of specialist investigators. And there will be criminal enterprises such as drug trafficking and organized theft rings that can only be attacked by the special techniques, such as undercover surveillance, of specialists. We would hope that freeing the specialist investigators of the constant stream of routine cases would enable them to concentrate more attention, more productively, on the kinds of criminal activity that they are best able to address.

But if investigators are to serve as a resource for patrol officers, some organizational changes may be necessary.

First, depending on the agency's past practices, some investigators may need to be relocated from the central headquarters to precinct or neighborhood stations, where they will be more accessible to the patrol officers. In a few large metropolitan agencies, detectives are already assigned to precinct stations, but they remain under the command of the central headquarters. In such cases, the structural change may not even require moving furniture; placing the detectives under the command of the precinct captain will be sufficient.

Secondly, since the patrol force operates around the clock, so should the investigative force. There should be at least a small support staff of investigators available at all hours to advise and assist patrol officers.

Again, these changes are much easier to describe than to accomplish. Some resistance, especially among the more experienced investigators, may be expected. One of the best ways to overcome resistance is to involve the personnel themselves in planning the changes. If they see for themselves the need for change, and the benefits that they may receive from the change, their resistance may evaporate. For specialist investigators, the most important benefits from the structural changes we have discussed are twofold: they will be more effective in solving crimes by concentrating more of their attention on difficult but solvable cases, and their expertise and skill will be highly valued by the patrol officers whose work they support.

CASE IN POINT: AUSTIN

Since every police agency is unique and has its own history and local conditions, it is impossible to prescribe a general scheme of organizational and structural changes that might be needed in transforming a traditional agency into one that practices community policing. However, we can describe some of the structural changes that have taken place in the Austin Police Department, and two that are planned for the near future.

In 1993, the department formed an Organizational Design Team (ODT) consisting of some twenty officers, representing all ranks and every element of the agency. The team spent two days in an initial "retreat," at a conference center away from the police headquarters. A consultant, acting as a facilitator, presented information about organizational structure and led the ODT in an intensive evaluation of the department's existing structure.

The task of the ODT was to design a police department for the city of Austin as if one did not already exist. Information about the community—its geographical size, population, and so forth—was provided, and the members of the ODT divided the task into specific assignments. Over a period of several weeks, the ODT members interviewed more than two hundred of their colleagues, collecting individual experiences and opinions about the best way to organize a police department.

The ODT also had before them an important set of guidelines: the mission statement and values statement that members of the department had already adopted. Thus, their task involved not just designing a police department "from scratch" to serve a particular community, but also to express the policing philosophy embodied in the mission and values statements—essentially a philosophy of community policing.

In many respects, the organizational design produced by the ODT was not very different from the organizational structure that already existed. The team concluded that the department still needed a patrol force, an investigations unit, and various technical and support services units. However, the team also decided that some significant changes in organizational structure were desirable.

Two such changes were the gradual elimination of the deputy chief rank and one-third of the Captain positions. The reasons for these changes involved, in part, recapturing resources that could then be applied to the need for more street-level officers. However, there were other reasons as well.

Previously, the upper-level management of the department consisted of the chief, two assistant chiefs, five deputy chiefs, and fifteen captains.

One of the conclusions reached by the ODT was that the deputy chief position was redundant. Most of the work done by the deputy chiefs consisted of approving decisions made by the captains (or their subordinates), and transmitting orders and policy changes from the chief and assistant chiefs to the lower ranks. The decision was made to phase out the position entirely.

In the past year, one deputy chief has been promoted to a newly-created third assistant chief position, and two deputy chiefs have retired. A third deputy chief continues to supervise the elements under his command, and the remaining deputy chief is involved primarily in planning. Most of the managerial responsibilities of the deputy chiefs have been assumed by captains. The assistant chiefs' duties also have expanded somewhat to fill the gap.

The decision to eliminate several captain positions was made for several reasons, including the opportunity to redirect funds (that is, the salaries and benefits that would have been paid to captains) to other ranks, especially lieutenants. Because many of the kinds of operational decisions that formerly had been made by captains were to be made by lieutenants and sergeants, the ODT concluded that some captain positions would be redundant.

Possibly the most significant structural change in the department involved Patrol. The city was divided into six sectors commanded by two captains. For each sector there was a lieutenant commanding each of three shifts (plus a fourth relief shift). Under each lieutenant were three to five sergeants and varying numbers of patrol officers.

Under this command-and-control-oriented system, the chain of command from captains down through sergeants was concerned primarily with the supervision of the patrol officers: constantly checking to be sure that they were performing their assigned duties according to the department's rules. No one in the system was specifically responsible for determining and responding to the needs of the community.

The ODT very quickly recognized a need for more street-level officers to handle calls for service more expeditiously and to make time available for the expanded role of the patrol force in community policing. The decision was made to divide one large sector into two. The addition of more patrol officers also permitted patrol beats to be rearranged to respect existing neighborhood boundaries.

Each of the city's six patrol sectors was placed under the direct command of a single lieutenant. The sector lieutenant was made responsible for all patrol activities, twenty-four hours a day, in his or her sector. Instead of two captains, there would be three—one for every two sectors.

Each sector lieutenant was responsible for all of the patrol sergeants and officers, on all shifts, in his or her sector. Naturally, this did not mean that sector lieutenants were expected to be on duty twenty-four hours a day. Rather, they were left free to determine their own working hours, provided only that their work was completed and that they were available a minimum of forty hours per week. When a sector lieutenant was not on duty, the sergeants assumed full responsibility for supervising their patrol officers. (There is also a watch commander—either a captain or a lieutenant—on duty at all times and responsible for incident command.) In practice, the sector lieutenants often spent a few hours each week on the "off-shifts" to stay abreast of any problems that might develop and to become thoroughly familiar with the needs of their communities.

Each sector lieutenant became a *single point of contact* for every sort of information about his or her assigned community. They were expected to learn as much about each neighborhood as possible, through reports from their officers and sergeants and through direct contact with citizens. They organized and conducted community meetings to engage the citizens in the community-policing partnership.

One responsibility of the sector lieutenants was to assist their sergeants and officers in identifying crime problems that required resources beyond those of Patrol. Like most agencies with a long history of commitment to serving the public, the Austin Police Department had accumulated a variety of specialized programs in crime prevention and tactical operations. But when a Sector Lieutenant identified a need to involve one or more of these specialized programs, or when help from the Investigations Division was needed, it was necessary to go through two or more chains of command for approval.

This potential bottleneck was eliminated by making two more structural changes. A support lieutenant was added to each sector pair and assigned responsibility for providing any kind of additional resource or assistance that might be needed by the sector lieutenants and their subordinates. At the same time, some of the specialized programs (specifically traffic, crime prevention, and CrimeNET*) were reorganized, placing personnel directly in each sector pair under the command of the support lieutenant.

Creating the sector lieutenant position and reorganizing the entire Patrol division brought about other structural changes. Decision-making authority was moved down from the third-highest level in the department (the deputy chief position) to the third-lowest (lieutenant), with much authority transferred even lower, to sergeants and patrol officers.

One other significant structural change is being implemented as this is written. In addition to moving some investigators from the central headquarters to the sectors, where they will serve as a resource to the neighborhood patrol officers, the department will create a new position, *street detective*. Street detectives will be promoted from the patrol force and will remain in the patrol force. Each patrol sergeant will have a uniformed street detective assigned to his or her platoon. The detective will respond along with the patrol officer to reports of serious crimes, assist in the investigation, and provide liaison to the specialist investigators at the sector level and those in the centralized investigative units.

The purpose in creating this new position is twofold: first, to create a bridge between the decentralized investigative personnel and the patrol officers; second, to create a career path for patrol officers who want, and can handle, expanded crime investigation responsibilities but who do not want to leave the patrol force.[5]

MAKING THE SYSTEM WORK

Structural changes in the police agency's organization, of the kind we have discussed so far in this chapter, affect virtually every aspect of the agency's operations. They

---

*CrimeNET is a crime-targeting project, funded by a federal grant, in which a team of officers identify a specific crime problem, develop and implement a solution, and evaluate the results, all within a ninety-day time limit.

must be planned and implemented with considerable care, to avoid unnecessary disruption and to ensure that the changes are successful in aligning the agency with its community policing goals.

At the same time, a variety of changes in operating procedures and policies may be required. Ultimately there are likely to be more of these systematic changes than changes in structure.

Historically, American law enforcement agencies have not been reluctant to make procedural and operational changes. In most cases the changes have been designed to improve efficiency through better management of the service workload. New technologies in communications, weaponry, personal defense and safety, and information management have been adopted as rapidly as possible, given the limited funding available from parent governments. Many of the systems changes that may be implemented in the transformation toward community policing might have been adopted anyway. The difference is that the changes must be consistent with, and supportive of, the community policing philosophy and the reorientation of the agency.

Managing the Workload

One of the most important communications technologies in American policing has been the introduction, now almost universal, of the 9-1-1 telephone system. For many larger police agencies, the system has been entirely too successful.

The 9-1-1 system was developed to improve communications between the public and the public safety agencies by providing a single, easily remembered telephone number that citizens could use in any sort of emergency.**

Today, almost everyone knows that help is available in an emergency by dialing 9-1-1. What most people do not know is that the 9-1-1 system is supposed to be used *only* in an emergency, which is defined as an event or condition that threatens life, safety, or property. In fact, the vast bulk of calls to 9-1-1 centers do not involve an emergency at all, and often do not require an immediate response by any public safety agency.

The volume of nonemergency calls to 9-1-1 centers would be merely an expensive annoyance but for one serious consequence. Every 9-1-1 system has a fixed, limited number of telephone lines on which calls can be received, and a limited number of operators available at any given time to receive calls. When the volume of calls exceeds the system's capacity, additional calls are greeted by a recording and then placed on "hold" until an operator is available. When the holding "queue" is filled, any additional calls simply go unanswered. There is no way for the telephone equipment to distinguish between a genuine emergency that requires an urgent response and a routine, nonemergency call.

**Few people realize that an important, but usually unstated, purpose of the 9-1-1 system was to relieve the telephone companies of the expense of having their operators receive and relay emergency calls. Before the 9-1-1 system, people generally dialed "O" in an emergency, and the telephone operator was responsible for determining the type of emergency and the appropriate public safety agency. As the volume of emergency calls rose, this became a substantial training problem for telephone companies and a burden on their operators.

Adding more telephone lines and operators may be necessary but it does not solve the underlying problem, which is the misuse of the system.

Several methods of dealing with this problem can be identified. The first, and possibly the simplest, is to educate the public about the kinds of calls that are appropriate for 9-1-1, and how nonemergency calls (such as requests for street directions or information about how to obtain a driver's license) should be made. The appropriate number for nonemergency calls should be as widely publicized as 9-1-1.

A second, related solution is to establish a single telephone number for non-emergency calls when the caller does not know what agency is needed or where the desired information can be obtained. There have been several proposals to establish a universal number, similar to but distinct from 9-1-1 (such as 3-1-1) for this purpose. However, at the time of this writing, there has not yet been any general agreement on what number should be used, how it should be used, or how this non-emergency system should be established.

Still, there is nothing to prevent a local police department, or perhaps several public safety agencies working together, from establishing and publicizing its own nonemergency referral number. Every call that can be diverted from the 9-1-1 system would be potentially lifesaving.

A third solution, also related to the first two, is to establish a specific unit to receive and handle nonemergency police information. In many cases, information about a crime or traffic accident can be taken over the telephone; there is no real need for a police officer to go to the scene.

Establishing such a telephone service unit (sometimes called "teleserve") can reduce the burden on the 9-1-1 operators considerably by enabling them to dispose of nonemergency calls in a matter of seconds. The staff of the teleserve unit must be thoroughly trained, whether the personnel are sworn officers or noncommissioned, to determine quickly the nature of the incident being reported, whether the presence of an officer is needed, and, if not, what information must be obtained from the caller. The use of standardized report forms, either printed or computerized, is essential. At the end of each call, the teleserve operator should give the caller a report number that can be used for follow-up calls, if the caller discovers new information or merely wants to know the status of the case.

If a teleserve unit has been established, the 9-1-1 operators must be trained in the proper way to redirect calls. When a call is received, the 9-1-1 operator should determine as quickly as possible whether it involves an emergency; if so, the call should be handled according to the standard emergency procedure. If there is not an emergency, the operator must determine whether it is a police matter (that is, a complaint of a crime or traffic accident), or merely a request for information or whatever. If it is a police matter but not an emergency, the operator must determine whether the presence of a police officer is necessary; this decision should be based on a well-developed set of standard procedures and policies.

For example, when a store manager discovers the theft of some merchandise, even if there is a substantial probability of identifying the thief, usually there is no need for a police officer to visit the scene. All of the relevant information can be taken over the telephone, and quickly disseminated to other officers in the area.

When the presence of a police officer is not required, the 9-1-1 operator should advise the caller, "It will take [an estimate of the amount of time] for a police officer to respond, and from what you have said, a police response probably is not necessary. If you wish, we can take the information over the telephone and make an official report the same as an officer on the scene would make." The majority of callers not only will accept this offer but also will appreciate the opportunity to have the problem resolved quickly and efficiently. (However, the callers' response will be very different if the 9-1-1 operator says something like, "That's not an emergency. I'm going to switch you to the teleserve unit.")

Calls that do not involve a police matter as such, but merely requests for information, also should be diverted from the emergency response system. Noncommissioned personnel, officers on temporary light duty due to an injury or some other reason, or even volunteers could staff a desk that handles requests for street directions, information about court procedures, and the myriad of other matters that misguided citizens call 9-1-1 about.

Almost all 9-1-1 centers already have some sort of priority system, to distinguish between genuine emergencies that require an immediate response, and lesser problems that require some police attention but not on an urgent basis. If any changes are needed, usually they will involve making the system more effective and ensuring that genuine emergencies receive the immediate attention they require. However, citizens who have asked for police assistance should not be left waiting for an unreasonable amount of time. If it will take more than ten or fifteen minutes for a patrol officer to respond to a nonemergency request for assistance, some effort should be made to contact the citizen and determine whether help can be provided in some other way—or even whether help is still needed at all.

In a busy communications center, at least one person, preferably a commissioned officer, should be responsible for *call intervention*. He or she should have access to a computer terminal displaying all of the currently pending calls (that is, calls to which an officer has not yet responded). When it is apparent that an officer will not be available for an unreasonable length of time, the call intervention officer should re-contact the complainant to determine whether there is still a need for an officer, or whether the problem can be resolved over the telephone (or has already resolved itself). In some cases, it is possible that a problem (such as loud noises in the neighborhood) will have escalated to the point that it is genuinely an emergency. In many other cases, however, the citizen will decide that police assistance is not needed after all. Usually citizens are appreciative of the department's attention and concern even when no other service has been performed.

Some of the changes we have discussed (educating the public, establishing a nonemergency number, and diverting nonpolice calls out of the emergency system) reduce the burden on the 9-1-1 operators but have little direct effect on the rest of the police department, since many of the calls would not require a police response in any case.

The other changes (establishing a teleserve unit, call intervention, and prioritizing calls) may have a substantial effect on police operations, especially in patrol, by reducing to a minimum the volume of calls to which officers must be dispatched, and by giving officers considerable discretion in the way they respond to nonemergency calls.

Managing the patrol officers' service workload is a major concern in a community policing agency for the simple reason that neighborhood patrol officers must have sufficient time to carry out their expanded duties. Those duties include developing contacts within the community, both on a formal and informal basis, and working with citizens to identify crime and disorder problems, to develop solutions, to assemble the resources needed to carry out the solutions, and to implement the solutions.

Increasing the number of patrol officers and correspondingly decreasing the area each officer serves will help, of course, to reduce each officer's service workload. Unfortunately, in some agencies the result may simply be that officers are expected to respond more quickly to every call, including those that formerly would have been regarded as having a low priority.

No one questions the necessity of responding to emergency calls as quickly as possible, and that must be the highest priority of the patrol force. When an emergency call is received at the 9-1-1 center or police dispatch center, the nearest available patrol unit must be notified and the officer given as much information as is available. Depending on agency policy and the availability of personnel on the street, additional back-up officers may be dispatched to any emergency that is likely to require more than one officer.

We suggest one policy change here. If the "nearest *available* unit" is not the patrol officer on whose beat an emergency incident is reported because that officer is busy on another, lower-priority call or temporarily off-duty, the beat officer still should be notified of the call. It may be possible for the beat officer to interrupt his or her current business and respond to the emergency immediately. Even if that is not possible, if beat officers are expected to be responsible for everything that happens in their assigned neighborhood, as is true in community policing, then it follows that they must be fully informed of emergency incidents and anything else that affects their neighborhood. The public expects their neighborhood officers to know what is going on; a community police officer's credibility is impaired if he or she is unaware of all of the police activities on the beat.

Better Use of Technology

Advances in technology have been made at an ever-increasing rate for several decades, especially in the areas of communications and information management. Indeed, the advances have come so rapidly that many departments have found it difficult to take full advantage of one advance before the next advance makes the last one obsolete!

There are any number of new and improved technologies that have significant applications in community policing. In broad terms, these technologies serve two purposes: first, to expand the opportunities for direct communications and contact between citizens and patrol officers or other police personnel; second, to improve the management of the service workload.

Some examples, again from the Austin Police Department, will illustrate how both purposes can be served.

The Austin 9-1-1 system was considerably improved by adding more incoming lines and increasing the staff substantially. At the same time, the call priority system was revised, and operators were retrained in the proper use of the call diversion (teleserve) system. The teleserve unit also was expanded and policies were revised to make it more effective in handling calls that do not require a patrol officer's response. Both call diversion (for nonpolice matters) and call intervention (for re-contacting citizens when a police response is delayed and may be unnecessary) procedures also were established.

More than three hundred portable "laptop" computers were purchased and distributed, mostly to the patrol force. The computers are preloaded with software containing the various standardized reporting forms. Thus officers in the field can prepare a report, mostly by "filling in the blanks," on their computer. When there is an opportunity, such as at the end of their shift, they can transfer the information from the laptop, on a diskette, to the department's crime reporting system. The time required to prepare and file routine reports has been reduced dramatically. The next step will be to enable the laptop computers to transmit information directly to the agency's main computer system through wireless modems.

The success of the laptop computers has been built largely on the foundation of an integrated crime reporting system and database. The system, which resides on a mainframe computer, enables officers at any of several hundred desktop and mobile terminals to access current and recent crime reports, plus databases of repeat offenders' criminal histories, pawn tickets, photographs, and other information. Previously, the department had not one but half a dozen separate database systems, none of which were connected to the others because they were mutually incompatible. Creating a single system was a massive undertaking, but one that had immediate and endless benefits.

Many members of the department, including noncommissioned employees, now have "voicemail" numbers (essentially a computer-based answering system within the telephone system) so that they can receive messages from citizens directly. All patrol officers and other personnel who work away from an office also have alphanumeric pagers, enabling them to receive messages almost instantaneously. Sergeants are provided with cellular telephones so that they can communicate directly with citizens.

Other technological improvements have been made in support service units, particularly in forensics and traffic law enforcement.

Again, some of these improvements probably would be adopted in a traditional police agency. However, the sheer number of changes in structure, systems, and technology is a result of the concerted effort, throughout the agency, to become more fully community-oriented.

Furthermore, many of the changes have been suggested or requested by the personnel at the street level and lower levels of management. As far as possible, personnel have been encouraged to initiate changes within the broad framework of the department's announced goals and objectives. The result has been virtually a competition among personnel to come up with better ways of operating and managing their work. The role of upper-level management likewise has been transformed, from commanding and controlling to encouraging and promoting positive change.

Not every change has been completely successful. Some of the structural changes we have described have produced periods of confusion and outright resistance as some personnel perceived their interests to be threatened. There are still many issues that have not been completely resolved, and there are still goals and objectives to be pursued in coming years. We make no claim that the changes we have described should be taken as a model; they are merely illustrations of the principles we have presented in the earlier chapters of this text.

In short, no police agency, including the Austin Police Department, is perfect. But it is becoming better.

FOOTNOTES

1. Alfred R. Stone and Stuart M. DeLuca, *Police Administration: An Introduction* 2nd ed. (Englewood Cliffs, N.J.: Prentice Hall, 1994), pp. 61-87.

2. Several examples of police organizational structures, in agencies large and small and from all parts of the country, are included in Stone and DeLuca, *Police Administration*, pp. 75–86.

3. Max Weber, *Theory of Social and Economic Organization*, trans. A. M. Henderson and Talcott Parsons (New York: Oxford University Press, 1947). Also see James Q. Wilson, *Bureaucracy* (New York: Basic Books, 1989), for a modern approach to the subject.

4. August Vollmer, *Law Enforcement in Los Angeles: Annual Report*, 1924, Reprinted. (New York: Arco Press, 1974), pp. 2–3.

5. For a thorough discussion of the structural changes in the Austin Police Department, see Sue Barton, *Self-Reliant Neighborhoods: A Bridge to the Future* (Austin, Tex.: Austin Police Department, 1996).

CHAPTER 6

MANAGING CHANGE: HUMAN RESOURCES

The most important and far-reaching differences between a conventional law enforcement agency and a community-policing agency involve the roles of the agency's personnel. Changes in organizational structure and operating systems reflect these changes in role, which in turn affect the tasks that officers are expected to perform, the manner in which they are expected to act, and ultimately the skills and personal qualities they are expected to bring to their work.[1]

It is extremely important to understand this concept. Merely changing the job description of patrol officers, instructing them to "learn about the neighborhood" or "interact with the community," will accomplish very little unless those instructions are accompanied by a change in the fundamental role and function of the patrol force. Such a change involves, and requires, changes in the roles of the personnel in every other element of the agency. Only when those changes have been implemented will the patrol force be able to carry out effectively the tasks that accompany their new role.

Unfortunately, these also may be the most difficult changes to make, and the most subject to restrictions and constraints.

OBSTACLES, ROADBLOCKS, AND BRICK WALLS

A century ago, the first generation of police reformers adopted as one of their major goals the insulation of the police from political interference. They attempted to achieve this goal in two ways.

119

First, the reformers changed the way new police officers were recruited and selected. Previously, new officers were hired by precinct captains, usually on the recommendation of the political bosses. Whenever one party lost a municipal election to another party, the entire police force was required to resign and be replaced with the new bosses' favorites.[2] The reformers, by enacting state laws and local ordinances, established a *merit system* governed by an independent, nonpartisan civil service commission. The commission developed written tests and other means to determine whether applicants for police employment were qualified. In principle, all applicants were to be treated equally, fairly, and objectively, and only those who were the best qualified would be hired.

Secondly, the same mechanism was used to control the promotion of police officers from rank to rank and, in some cases, their assignment to specialized fields. Written civil service tests, usually consisting mainly of multiple-choice questions (because they can be graded easily), were used to determine which candidates were best qualified for promotion or special assignments.

Over time, the civil service system became increasingly cumbersome. In some states, almost every decision regarding a police officer's employment—hiring, training, promotion, reassignment, disciplinary action, termination, and retirement—is subject to civil service laws and regulations. What is not covered by state laws and regulations may be covered by local ordinances. Union contracts, or their equivalent, also may impose constraints.

Early in the present century, police officers began to form organizations to protect their own interests (sometimes in opposition to the reformers and their "merit" system). Technically, these organizations were not trade unions; in most states, public employees were prohibited from forming or joining unions or engaging in such union-like activities as strikes. Nevertheless, the purpose of the police organizations usually was to negotiate with local governments for improvements in working conditions and other employment benefits. In some states, the organizations still are not considered unions, yet they exercise most of the same powers and responsibilities as unions; in a few states, police unions are legal and commonplace.[3]

Whatever they may be called, the police organizations' primary purpose is to negotiate a contract (which may be called something else) with the employing government. The contract specifies a salary scale, benefits such as insurance and pensions, and, in some cases, "working conditions." The latter term can embrace anything from the number of officers assigned to each patrol beat, to promotion policies, training curricula, the design of uniforms, and anything else the organization considers important to its members' interests.

Just as the civil service laws and regulations were intended to protect the police from improper political interference, the union contract (whatever it may be called) is intended to protect individual officers from favoritism, arbitrary and unfair actions by managers, and unsafe and debilitating working conditions.

Of course, from the point of view of the police administrator, both the civil service system and the union contract impose severe restrictions on the administrator's ability to make decisions about the most crucial issues in a police department: who is hired and how they are expected to discharge their duties.

These laws, regulations, and contracts all have been enacted or negotiated in the context of the traditional system of law enforcement, since that is the system that the police reformers and their successors worked so hard to establish. To a considerable degree, the civil service laws and regulations *are* the "professional" law enforcement system, or at least provide its foundation. The union contracts have been negotiated by parties representing the police officers and the governmental managers who may disagree about almost everything, but agree that the "professional" model—the traditional policing system—is the basis of policing.

But community policing is an entirely different model, and it raises very different expectations about the kinds of people who ought to be hired as police officers, how they ought to be trained, how they should be assigned to their duties and supervised, what qualities and behaviors should be rewarded by promotions, and how they should be disciplined.

It would be difficult enough to implement community policing if one could begin with a "blank slate," a newly formed police department with no existing system, no preconceptions about how personnel were to be deployed, and nothing to inhibit the development of a unique approach to policing. In fact, even a completely new police department still must comply with state laws and civil service regulations. More to the point: Very few police administrators have the opportunity to start a new agency from scratch. Existing agencies not only are subject to state laws, but often to local ordinances and employer-employee agreements that severely restrict the kinds of changes that can be introduced. And we have not even mentioned the purely natural and individual resistance to change that occurs in every organization.

We do not mean to be overly pessimistic or discouraging. Of course it is possible to introduce change even in the most conservative and restrictive system. One merely needs to recognize the constraints and find ways either to remove them or to work around them. Patience, persistence, and a willingness to accept less-than-ideal solutions may be required.

It is generally easier to change regulations than laws. Legislatures routinely enact broadly-worded statutes, then give to some administrative agency (such as a civil service commission) the authority to implement the law by developing and enforcing detailed regulations. As long as the essential purpose and spirit of the law is not violated, the regulations can be changed with relative ease, once the administrative agency is convinced that the changes are desirable.

Likewise, it is almost always easier to change local ordinances than state laws. City and county governments have varying lawmaking powers. In general, local ordinances must conform to state laws but may be more restrictive in some respects. It is a rare city or county government that does not regard law enforcement as one of its most critical functions. Thus local officials usually are at least willing to consider the proposals of the police executive, and usually are willing to make necessary changes in local ordinances—provided the changes do not conflict with state laws.

Persuading a state legislature to change civil service laws and other statutes that concern law enforcement is not impossible, but it is always a substantial undertaking. Usually it is much less difficult if the proposed changes are presented by a professional organization, or at least by a group of police officials (including representatives of the rank and file), and not just by one police executive.

The fewer changes that are required, the easier they will be to accomplish. Usually it is easier to delete restrictive provisions in the law than it is to add new provisions, much less rewrite a statute in its entirety. Whatever changes are desired, however, almost always will take longer and will require more effort than seems reasonable. Nevertheless, the legislative process, as slow and balky as it may be, is the only way to remove unnecessary constraints on the police executive's ability to bring about desirable change.

Union contracts are another matter. Most contracts have a specific term, at the end of which they must be renegotiated. Again, state laws and civil service regulations may govern some provisions of a police employment contract, but there also may be provisions that are freely negotiable. The police executive should decide well in advance which provisions need to be changed, and must be willing to offer something in exchange, such as a benefit that the police organization has sought for years but never has been granted.

The kinds of changes that are needed to implement community policing involve more than just organizational structures and technical systems. Police officers must fulfill new roles and functions, with new expectations about the way they will perform their duties. These fundamental changes imply other changes in the way police officers are recruited, selected, trained, and supervised. And these changes in turn imply other changes in the way police officers are hired, promoted, and disciplined. Many of these changes will be difficult; some of them will be impossible, at least until restrictions and constraints in state laws, civil service regulations, and union contracts have been removed.

Nevertheless, the changes are necessary if community policing is to fulfill its promise. In the rest of this chapter, we assume that somehow, with patience, persistence, and determination, the obstacles and roadblocks and brick walls have been eliminated, and the police administrator can devote full attention to the immediate task at hand: restructuring the very nature of municipal policing.

ROLES AND JOBS

The concept of social roles has been developed by sociologists and social psychologists to explain some aspects of the way people behave.[4] In a theatrical play, a role is a character's function in the story (hero, villain, and so on) and the character's relationship to the other characters. In much the same way, a person's role in a social group is the person's function and his or her relationship to the other members of the group.

We discuss the concept of social roles at considerable length in Chapter 2 and there is no need to repeat that discussion here. However, a brief recapitulation of the central points may be helpful.

Social roles are characteristics of social groups; they arise out of the various positions or functions that exist in the group. For example, in a school the most prominent positions are those of teacher, student, and staff member. Each of those positions or functions is associated with a set of expectations about how people in those positions will behave. This complex web of expectations and functions defines the several roles in such a group.

A law enforcement agency also is (among other things) a social group. Both formally, through its official organizational structure, and informally, through the personal interactions among its members (that is, the employees), the group contains a number of positions and functions, each of which is associated with a set of expected behaviors.

Many of these characteristics of a law enforcement agency are implicit and unconscious; the members of the group assume that lieutenants act differently from sergeants, who in turn behave differently from patrol officers. However, these sets of behaviors are *not* "facts of nature." They are learned, both consciously and unconsciously, as personnel are trained and as they become experienced in their day-to-day activities.

Now we are suggesting, and in fact urging, that attention be paid to these matters, that the roles associated with the various positions and functions in a law enforcement agency be consciously examined and, in many cases, redefined.

In any social group, the roles available to its members and the behaviors expected of them reflect the core values of the group: what it considers to be true, important, and valuable. In Chapter 4 we discuss the process by which the core values of a community policing agency should be articulated. Redefining the roles of the agency's personnel is therefore necessary as part of the process of implementing those core values. The redefinition is part of the process of aligning the agency's actions with its mission.

For example, if one of the agency's stated values is to form and maintain a partnership between the police and the community, there is a clear implication that police officers will treat their "partners," the citizens, with respect and will pay attention to their needs and interests. If officers in performing their daily work actually treat citizens brusquely and officiously, dismissing their concerns as irrelevant, there is a serious discrepancy between the agency's values and the way officers define their roles. Bringing the two into proper alignment is essential.

In a community policing agency as we have defined it (and this too is discussed at greater length in Chapter 2), the primary function of the patrol officers is to deliver a broad range of police services to the community. Those services include enforcing the law by identifying and apprehending offenders, assisting victims by gathering information about criminal incidents, maintaining social order by various means, and generally assisting the public in any sort of emergency. Performing these services efficiently and effectively requires a considerable range of skills and competencies, and also requires patrol officers to act in certain ways that are consistent with this role. If we expect patrol officers to do all of these things (and perhaps more besides), we might expect officers to behave in at least the following ways:

- Officers will treat all persons with respect and consideration, and will pay attention to their expressed concerns, needs, and desires.
- Officers will perform their assigned duties with initiative and diligence, particularly when responding to a situation that may involve a danger to life or property.
- Officers will solicit, recognize, and respect the concerns of the community with regard to matters of public safety and social order.
- Officers will act at all times in compliance with the law and the agency's rules, and in observance of the agency's values and standard procedures

We should note that the foregoing list is not intended as a complete description of the behaviors one might expect of patrol officers in a community-policing agency. For now, we merely wish to illustrate the kinds of issues that must be considered in redefining the patrol officers' role. A full definition of the patrol officers' role might require a longer list, and should include a more detailed description of the officers' duties.

Furthermore, it is clearly not sufficient to redefine just the role of the patrol force. *Every* position in the agency must be redefined in light of the agency's articulated mission and values.

Many, but not necessarily all, of the expected behaviors are likely to be very different from the roles in a traditional police agency. As we have said before, in a traditional agency the principal duty of supervisors (usually sergeants and lieutenants) is to enforce the agency's rules and policies, to ensure that operating-level personnel are in strict compliance. But if the operating-level personnel are expected to show initiative and to exercise a greater degree of autonomy and discretion in how they perform their work, they must be freed from an excessively detailed and restrictive set of policies. The role of the supervisor necessarily becomes that of a coach, guiding and assisting subordinates,[5] giving them information about their performance and the environment in which they are working (that is, both the agency itself and the community to which they are assigned),[6] and encouraging them to act according to the spirit of the agency's values, not just according to the letter of its rules.[7]

In fact, every person in a community-policing agency must adopt, as part of his or her basic set of skills and as part of his or her fundamental role, the dual roles of learner and mentor: learning to perform one's own job to the best of one's ability (and continually expanding one's capabilities in preparation for future advancement), and assisting one's peers and subordinates to do their jobs more effectively. This dual role becomes the primary function of the first-line supervisor. For second-level supervisors (generally lieutenants), the mentor role tends to become more dominant, alongside the broader role of facilitator: ensuring that subordinates have the information they need to do their jobs, securing the resources needed to successfully execute law enforcement strategies and tactics, assisting subordinates in identifying crime patterns that may be susceptible to specific problem-solving techniques, and removing impediments to success.

Upper-level managers in a community-policing agency (generally captains) have another crucial role: that of planner, anticipating developments in the community and needs within the agency over a period of a year or more. The accuracy and usefulness of their plans will depend to a great extent on the quality of information they receive from their subordinates.

Here again, there is a clear difference between community policing and conventional practices, in which mid-level managers collect information from subordinates only to document how much work is being performed and how well the personnel are complying with departmental regulations. When information is used only to compel compliance, there is a natural tendency for the information to become compromised and distorted: It is in the subordinates' personal interests not to let the bosses know everything. But when information is used to plan, to anticipate future needs, and to ensure that resources are allocated efficiently, there is a greater incentive for subordinates to provide the highest quality of information possible.

Even the highest levels of an agency are not exempt from a redefinition of roles. In a traditional police agency, the executive's role usually is defined in terms of "providing leadership," a term that is itself so vague and subject to myriad interpretations that it is almost meaningless. In practice, the traditional executive usually performs three roles: as the arbiter of disputes among subordinates, as the final policy and rule maker, and as the intermediary between the agency's personnel and the public (particularly the parent government).

We will address the issue of "leadership" shortly. For now, we suggest that the proper role of the executive in a community-policing agency is to provide the prevailing vision of what the agency should become, to articulate that vision in terms that both the public and the agency's personnel will understand and accept, and to provide guidance to the agency's managers as they align the organization and its members with that vision.

We do not suppose that anyone reading these role definitions would know precisely what each police officer is supposed to do on Monday morning, or at any other time. Those details make up the job description for each position in the agency. However, we are confident that any reasonably intelligent and imaginative police administrator, once the roles associated with each position have been defined, will be able to describe the specific tasks and procedures that are needed to carry out each role.

SOME IMPLICATIONS

Redefining the roles of an agency's personnel is much more than a matter of merely informing the employees that they are expected to perform new tasks and to behave in new ways, beginning Monday morning.

Performance Evaluation System

Unless there are also changes in the way performance is evaluated, employees justifiably will continue to do the things that they are required to do in order to be evaluated positively. If the performance evaluation system is based largely on quantitative measures, patrol officers will make every effort to answer as many calls as possible, issue as many tickets as they can, and in every other way "pad the numbers." They will not devote much time or energy to behaviors, such as soliciting the concerns and interests of the community, that are not reflected in the evaluation system.

The performance evaluation system in most traditional police agencies is geared toward measuring compliance and more or less arbitrary standards of effort. Officers are evaluated according to how well they observe the agency's rules and policies, and how much effort they are putting into their work, as indicated by the volume of work they accomplish. In many cases, there is no evidence that the rules and policies are actually necessary or that the effort is actually productive. Some police administrators candidly admit that they are merely measuring what is easily observed, not necessarily what is important.[8]

If quantitative performance measures are not very satisfactory—whether in a traditional agency or in community policing—qualitative measurement introduces a different host of problems. Qualitative performance evaluation usually consists of a list of personal characteristics or behaviors that employees are supposed to exhibit: "The officer is conscientious and diligent in performing assigned duties."[9] Such traits as "conscientiousness" or "diligence" are difficult to observe and subject to interpretation under the best of circumstances.

These problems are by no means unique to community policing. Fairly and objectively evaluating officers' performance always has been difficult. Many different systems have been developed; none has proven to be universally successful.

The changing roles of police personnel in community policing do not make these problems disappear. On the contrary, the difficulty is compounded when patrol officers are expected not just to perform a certain quantity of work, but to exercise discretion and initiative.[10] We cannot claim to have solved the problem in theory or in practice, but we can suggest a couple of directions that performance evaluation should take in a community-policing agency.

First of all, we believe that the philosophy of community policing requires operating-level personnel (which is to say, mostly patrol officers) to accept personal responsibility for the communities they serve. In other words, one basis for evaluating the performance of patrol officers is to consider the changes in levels of reported crime, the types of crimes reported, and the level of citizen satisfaction on each officer's assigned beat. Ultimately, a patrol officer should be held accountable for every known criminal incident or incident of social disorder that occurs on his or her beat. Patrol officers, after all, are hired, trained, equipped, and assigned for the specific purpose of deterring criminal activity and social disorder. Therefore, the continued presence of crime and disorder is a reflection of the officer's failure to perform. Conversely, positive changes—the reduction of crime and disorder, and the increase of citizens' perceptions of safety and tranquillity—reflect the success of the officer's efforts.

At first glance, the standard of performance we have just suggested seems harsh and perhaps unrealistic, and so it would be if we were proposing that officers should be penalized or rewarded for events that are clearly beyond the officer's control. No one could reasonably expect a patrol officer assigned to a low-income, high-crime neighborhood to "clean it up" overnight, or even over an extended period of time. Nor can one reasonably commend an officer on whose beat the crime rate has fallen—not because of the officer's performance but because of structural or demographic change (for example, the abandonment of an obsolete public housing complex). We are merely suggesting that an evaluation of each officer's performance should take into consideration the results that the officer achieves in the real world, in terms of the agency's stated mission and values.

At the same time, we suggest that the fundamental purpose of performance evaluation needs to be reconsidered. Most people, in and out of law enforcement, think of performance evaluation purely in terms of the distribution of rewards and punishments: Employees who are doing their job well are rewarded; those who are doing their job poorly are punished. We believe that the proper purpose of performance evaluation is to develop the individual capacities of all employees by identifying areas in which their performance can be improved, and by encouraging them to continue their efforts where improvement has been identified. In short, the goal of performance evaluation should be to design a "personal success strategy" for each employee.

Rewards and punishments are undoubtedly necessary and appropriate, but only in extreme cases. Too often, we think, rewards are offered for merely performing the minimum required quantity and quality of work. Whatever expectations or standards are established, they should serve as a benchmark against which to measure each employee's *minimum* performance. Rewards should be reserved for those whose work clearly *exceeds* the minimum.

On the other hand, the failure to meet the minimum expectations usually means only that an effort must be made to correct deficiencies. Employees should be encouraged and assisted to improve their performance, not penalized for failing to be perfect. Only in extreme cases, where the employee clearly has refused to make an effort to improve, where deficiencies have continued for long periods, or where the failure is attributable either to malice or to inherent incapacity, should an employee be penalized.

Performance evaluation in a community policing agency should be supportive, not punitive.[11] In addition, it should not be based solely on the observations of one supervisor. Each officer should be evaluated by several people who have an opportunity to observe his or her work: the immediate superior, peers, and other supervisory personnel. Thus a patrol officer might be evaluated by his or her sergeant, the sergeant's lieutenant, another sergeant who supervises patrol officers in an adjacent district, an investigator who works in the officer's district, and the two or three patrol officers assigned to adjacent beats on the same shift or to the same beat on different shifts. Each of these people have different opportunities to observe the patrol officer at work or the results of the officer's efforts; each brings a different perspective to the evaluation.

It is immediately apparent that performance evaluation can be time-consuming if it must be performed by six or seven different people for every employee. No police agency could afford the luxury of stopping all other activities for a day or two every six months so that employees can devote their attention to evaluating one another. Instead, a multiple-perspective evaluation system would require that evaluations be carried out continuously. If each employee is supposed to evaluate the performance of six or seven other people, then he or she should devote a reasonable amount of time once each month to one of the people to be evaluated. A few minutes spent in gathering one's recollections and impressions of an employee's recent performance should not be overly burdensome. Rather than an elaborate form to be filled out, the evaluation might consist of responding with specific comments to three or four specific questions.

Here again, we must point out that performance evaluation procedures are sometimes dictated by civil service laws and regulations or by police union contracts. Implementing the kind of performance evaluations we have described may not be possible until changes are made in the laws, regulations, or contracts.

Recruiting and Selection

The specific techniques and procedures used to recruit applicants for police employment, and to select from among the available applicants those who are to be hired, are not necessarily different in a community-policing agency from those used in a traditional agency. However, different kinds of people may be needed to make community policing successful.

By this we mean people with a somewhat different set of personal qualities and skills. In a traditional police agency, the requirements for new personnel usually have emphasized physical traits—strength, agility, endurance—and personal qualities such as assertiveness and self-confidence. There has been a widespread assumption that a successful police officer must be someone who has a "commanding presence" and a "take-charge attitude," terms that admittedly are not very clearly defined. These requirements stem from the traditional assumptions about the police officer's (and especially the patrol officer's) role and expected behaviors. The very phrase "patrol officer" evokes an image of a burly male chasing a bad guy through backyards and over fences, a kind of activity that real patrol officers perform only occasionally.

Patrol officers in a community-policing agency might still have to perform such physical feats. Much more often, the patrol officers are expected to perform a task that requires far less physical skill but considerably more intelligence: talking to people. Patrol officers talk to complainants and victims about crimes, to suspected offenders about their activities, and to other citizens about their concerns and interests. The ability to converse with a wide range of individuals, on diverse topics, demands a set of personal qualities and skills that previously have not been expected of police officers.

Articulateness may not be the only personal quality that recruiters should look for in a community-policing agency. It may not even be the most important, and certainly some of the physical qualities we mentioned should not be completely overlooked. Just as the performance evaluation system needs to be reconsidered, so does the system of recruitment and selection. Given an agency's mission and core values, the roles that personnel are expected to fill, and the behaviors that personnel are expected to perform, a specification of the desired personal qualities, demonstrated skills, and previous experiences should be drawn up.

Changes in the kinds of personnel that are wanted may imply changes in where recruiters look for them. For example, it may be that articulateness is a characteristic of individuals who have above-average intelligence (although not all bright people are necessarily articulate). Intelligent people can be found almost anywhere, but one place that generally contains a concentration of people who have above-average intelligence is a college or university.

Very few American law enforcement agencies require recruits to have a college degree (despite the urgings of August Vollmer as long ago as 1924). However, a growing number of agencies, including the more traditional ones, now require applicants to have at least one or two years of college, and preference may be given to applicants who have completed a two-year associate's degree. In effect, police administrators—much like personnel administrators in private businesses—are using colleges to screen out individuals who lack the intelligence or the initiative to seek higher education.

American law enforcement agencies conventionally use a "sweep-and-sift" approach to recruitment and selection. That is, they sweep up as many applicants as possible, then sift out the few who appear to best meet the agency's requirements for entry-level employment. Again, this is not especially different from the technique used by many private businesses to recruit and select employees, especially during an expansion phase or the start-up of a new business.

However, the various "filters" used to screen out unsuccessful applicants do not necessarily guarantee that the best-qualified applicants will be selected. All of the selection methods that are widely used—multiple hurdle, multiple assessment, assessment center, or some variation of these—have significant drawbacks. The multiple hurdle procedure, in which applicants must pass each of a series of tests before proceeding to the next step, is still widely used because of its relative economy (applicants who fail at any point are not tested any further), despite substantial evidence that it is the least reliable procedure in predicting the future success of personnel.[12]

One of the techniques used in screening ought to be far more useful than it is. Many police departments have required applicants to take a written psychological test, often the *Minnesota Multiphasic Personality Test* (MMPT), in order to screen out applicants who are temperamentally unsuited to police work. This test and others like it have been used for at least the past forty years and have been administered to tens of thousands of applicants. By now, there must be a large cohort of police officers who took the test when they first applied for a job, and who are now close to the end of their police careers. It might be extremely useful to compare the test results with the career records of these officers. Perhaps such a comparison would yield valuable clues about the kinds of personality traits and characteristics that are common among successful police officers.

The research to make such a comparison would not be easy. Most of the data, including test results, can be found only in each officer's permanent personnel file. These files generally are paper documents, not computerized databases. Furthermore, personnel files are understandably regarded as confidential, and a research design would have to protect the privacy of the individual officers. Nevertheless, even a limited study might be extremely interesting.

As far as we know, no such study has been done; or if it has, the results have not been published in the professional journals.

Affirmative Action and Minority Recruitment

In the past few years, affirmative action programs based on "quotas" or quantified goals have been under growing political attack. The basis for the opposition is that affirmative action, which simply means a specific effort to increase minority representation at all levels of society, discriminates against qualified majority citizens in favor of less-qualified minority individuals. If that accusation is true, it represents a serious violation not just of the rights of majority citizens, but of common sense. No public agency, and particularly a police agency, can afford the long-term consequences of giving preferential treatment in hiring, promotions, or any other way to people who are not qualified.

In most American police departments, minorities continue to be "underrepresented" at every level from the patrol force to the executive office. "Underrepresentation" means simply that the proportion of minority individuals in the agency is substantially less than the proportion in the general population of the community. If the community contains, say, 15 percent Hispanic citizens but the police department contains only 5 percent Hispanic officers, that is underrepresentation, and affirmative action programs are supposed to correct the imbalance by giving *qualified* Hispanic applicants preference over *equally qualified* majority applicants until the imbalance is corrected.

The problem faced by many police departments is that the most highly qualified minority citizens may not find a police career especially attractive. Those individuals often are sought avidly by private businesses and by other public agencies, and they often can attain higher salaries and better opportunities for advancement than a police department could offer. Some police administrators, under pressure from the community to reduce minority underrepresentation, may be tempted to change the rules: to use one yardstick to measure the qualifications of majority applicants, and a different yardstick for minorities. Such a tactic may well be unfair to the majority candidates; it is certainly unwise, and ultimately it is unfair to minority candidates who may be thrown into situations that they are not capable of handling.

A far better approach, we suggest, is to recognize that many of the personal qualities and skills required of successful police officers are not inherent and immutable. Of course there are some basic qualities, such as a certain level of intelligence and a reasonable degree of physical agility, that must be treated as minimum requirements. There are also a variety of traits that are highly desirable, that vary from one individual to the next, *and* that may be susceptible to development through training and experience.

For example, as we mentioned earlier, traditional police agencies usually seek recruits that are self-confident and assertive, and screen out applicants who appear to be deficient in those qualities. But self-confidence and assertiveness are both capable of being developed. In fact, merely being accepted for police employment is likely to boost an applicant's self-confidence to some degree, and every success in training should increase the cadet's sense of self-worth and competence.

In short, the solution to the affirmative action dilemma may be found in seeking applicants, regardless of their ethnicity, who possess a minimum set of irreducible qualifications *and* who demonstrate *potential* for the development of the full range of personal qualities and skills that are needed.

Thus the burden of staffing the community police agency with the best people shifts from the recruitment and selection process to the training process.

Training

Each of the fifty states has an administrative agency responsible for certifying or licensing police officers and for regulating their training. As is so often the case, the precise extent of those responsibilities varies from state to state, so that it is impossible to make valid generalizations about the kind or quantity of training that is required. For example, the Texas Commission on Law Enforcement Officer Standards and Education (TCLEOSE) prescribes a 560-hour "basic peace officer" course consisting of a specific number of hours devoted to each of nearly three dozen topics:

- Introduction and orientation (2 hours)
- Fitness and wellness (6 hours)
- History of policing (3 hours)
- Professionalism and ethics (8 hours)
- U.S. and Texas Constitutions and Bills of Rights (10 hours)
- The criminal justice system (2 hours)
- The Code of Criminal Procedure (16 hours)

- Arrest, search, and seizure (24 hours)
- Penal Code (40 hours)
- Traffic (72 hours)
- Civil process and liability (12 hours)
- Texas Alcoholic Beverage Code (4 hours)
- Drugs (8 hours)
- Juvenile issues; Texas Family Code (8 hours)
- Stress management for peace officers (8 hours)
- Field notetaking (4 hours)
- Interpersonal communications; report writing (24 hours)
- Use of force: The law (8 hours)
- Use of force: Concepts (16 hours)
- Strategies of defense: Mechanics of arrest (40 hours)
- Strategies of defense: Firearms (40 hours)
- Emergency medical assistance (16 hours)
- Emergency communications (12 hours)
- Problem solving and critical thinking (4 hours)
- Professional police driving (32 hours)
- Multiculturalism and human relations (12 hours)
- Professional policing approaches (6 hours)
- Patrol (40 hours)
- Victims of crime (8 hours)
- Family violence and related assaultive offenses (16 hours)
- Recognizing and interacting with persons with mental illness and mental retardation (6 hours)
- Crowd management (2 hours)
- Hazardous materials awareness (6 hours)
- Criminal investigation (45 hours)[13]

We present this outline not because the Texas course design is "typical"—there *is* no typical set of standards—nor because we intend to criticize it. We merely wish to illustrate the kind of training that this state licensing agency requires. Note also that the curriculum given here is a *minimum*, to which additional topics may be added, and the topics listed may be covered in longer units. The Austin Police Department's recruit academy, for example, is nearly twice as long and includes several topics not in the state curriculum.

Fully two-thirds of the state's required course is devoted to the technical and mechanical aspects of policing (381 hours); another 24 percent of the course is spent in studying the law and legal principles (and such related issues as police ethics).

We do not mean to imply that any of these technical, mechanical, and legal topics do not deserve to be included or that the number of hours devoted to this subject or that is inappropriate. Some subjects by their very nature take longer to cover than others. When the instruction necessarily involves practical experience to develop a skill, such as the use of firearms or emergency driving techniques, more time is required than might be needed for a straightforward lecture on, say, the alcoholic beverage laws.

However, the preponderance of technical, mechanical, and legal material in the basic peace officer course suggests that, at least in the view of the state agency that prescribes the course, police officers in entry-level positions (that is, patrol officers) are essentially technicians whose duties are primarily routine and mechanical in nature.

The role of the patrol officer in community policing is much broader than this, and the training of new personnel must reflect that role. It is not just that a unit on community policing should be added to the curriculum. Rather, the concepts and core values of community policing should be infused throughout the basic training course.

For example, such topics as professionalism and ethics, juvenile issues, interpersonal communications, problem solving and critical thinking, and several others, all lend themselves to a discussion of the role of the patrol officer in upholding social order in the community. The unit on criminal investigation should assume that, for many reported crimes, the principal investigator will be the patrol officer, supported by specialist detectives and criminalistics technicians.

Some topics that are vital to community policing are not included in the Texas basic course (or, probably, in most other states' comparable training). Units should be added to cover the role of the police in community development, tactical approaches to crime-specific problem solving, the police role in noncriminal order maintenance, and perhaps other subjects.

The basic peace officer course is taught in two-year and four-year colleges, in regional academies operated by regional Councils of Government, and in academies operated by the Texas Department of Public Safety and several metropolitan police departments. Understandably, the departmental academies concentrate on teaching their own organizational structure, policies, and procedures. The regional academies serve mostly small suburban and rural agencies, and that orientation is reflected in the course content. In both departmental and regional academies, the training must be geared to the roles and functions that entry-level officers actually will perform. Where the metropolitan department is being transformed into a community policing agency, major changes in the course content may be needed. Since most small suburban and rural law enforcement agencies already practice some form of community policing, out of sheer necessity, the regional academies (if they do not already) should present the course from that perspective.

Aside from incorporating community policing concepts throughout the curriculum, we suggest that more emphasis should be placed on the development of individual skills and personal qualities, not only in entry-level training but also in periodic training programs for all personnel. This kind of training should be designed to give police officers a deeper understanding of interpersonal relationships and the sources in society of disorder and crime; improved personal communications skills; and a range of self-development opportunities. It is not enough to teach the technical and mechanical aspects of enforcing the law without also teaching officers how those techniques and processes affect themselves and the people with whom they deal: victims, witnesses, offenders, and ordinary citizens.

We also believe that it is highly desirable for entry-level personnel to have ample opportunities to observe, and even to practice, the concepts and skills they are learning in the real world. The conventional system of training has been to immerse students in the classroom for weeks on end—fourteen weeks for the minimum entry-level training course in Texas. Only when the students have completed the basic course are they assigned to actually perform police work under the supervision of a field training officer.[14]

The Austin Police Department has introduced a series of "reality checks" into its recruit training by interspersing two to four weeks of academy instruction with one or two weeks of real-world experience. Cadets thus have an opportunity to observe the actual application of the concepts and skills they have just learned, through a series of specific learning experiences. The cadets do not merely ride with a patrol officer; they spend a week with the patrol officer, performing specific tasks related to their in-class training. The field training officer evaluates the cadet's performance on each of these prescribed tasks. After a week or two on patrol, the cadets return to the academy to discuss their experiences before going on to the next set of topics.

These excursions into reality should not involve just patrol. Cadets also should spend some time, in the midst of their recruit training, with detectives, 911 operators, criminalistics technicians, and various other technical specialists. In each case, the field training officers should be prepared with a list of specific training activities and objectives, to ensure that the cadets derive the maximum benefit from each experience and that there are no glaring discrepancies between the academy presentations and the field training.

This kind of training could be greatly expanded. One of the most valued steps in the training of medical doctors is the hospital internship or residency, during which newly graduated but not yet licensed physicians spend a certain amount of time in each of the various medical specialties. In principle, the new physician thus gains a better understanding of each of the specialties and how they are related to one another. Perhaps the same basic concept could be applied in law enforcement, with cadets assigned not only to patrol, but to officers in each of the other specialized elements of a police department before they are assigned to patrol.

Cadets also should be assigned, before they have completed their academy training, to the neighborhood in which they will be working. In this way, patrol officers on their first day already would be familiar with the community and with many of the people they are assigned to serve. The field training officer should introduce the cadet to community leaders and should share with the cadet much of what the senior officer has learned about the community.

Recruit training should be just the beginning of a career-long series of learning experiences for every police officer. In fact, most police academies offer a variety of courses on supervision (for sergeants and lieutenants) and management techniques (mostly for lieutenants, captains, and other mid-level managers). Some academies, especially those operated by state police agencies, also offer courses on advanced policing techniques and technical specialties, and "refresher" courses on basic law enforcement procedures. Again, the precepts of community policing should be incorporated into all of these courses, rather than being relegated to a separate class.

Formal instruction should not be the only mode of training for a police officer. Self-directed study and on-the-job learning also should play important roles in enabling every officer to do his or her present job more effectively and to prepare him or her for future career opportunities.

LEADERSHIP AND DISCIPLINE

The heading for this section is not a mistake. Leadership and discipline usually are regarded as two completely separate aspects of the management of human resources. In fact, they are two sides of the same coin. That coin is made of an alloy composed of equal parts of loyalty, trust, and integrity.

Conventional Concepts

The usual idea of leadership is that one person compels others to do what the leader wants done. Sometimes the concept of compulsion is softened by such terms as *persuades* or *motivates*, but in essence the idea is the same: that the leader imposes his or her will on a group of followers who, if left to themselves, would not know what to do or would not choose to do it. This concept of leadership, drawn from the military-corporate model of bureaucratic organization, rests on the assumption that most people are either unable or unwilling to perform their work with enthusiasm and initiative.

If that assumption is false, then the concept of leadership is invalid.

The conventional notion of discipline is that the members of a group must be required to conform to an explicit standard of behavior. The standard is specified in a set of rules, regulations, orders, and policies. Those who fail to comply with the standard are subject to punishment, varying in severity according to the seriousness of the offense, but imposed with equal justice and objectivity. This concept of discipline, also adapted from the military-corporate model, rests on the assumption that most people, left to themselves, are either unable or unwilling to obey the rules unless they are subjected to the fear of punishment.

Again, if the assumption is false, then the concept of discipline is invalid.

Three Personal Qualities

Loyalty, trust, and integrity are personal qualities that, to the extent that they are present, contribute to characteristic patterns of individual behavior. Together they produce both leadership and discipline.

Loyalty is a commitment to the success and well-being of one's group; for police officers, the group includes their colleagues, the agency as a whole, its mission and values, and ultimately the community they are sworn to serve. Police officers who are loyal to their community and to their department do not need to be told what to do, much less to be coerced into doing what is necessary. Because of their dedication to the community and the agency, they naturally do everything they can to contribute to the welfare of both.

Trust is a reasonable faith in the good will of others. Again, for police officers the others are colleagues, subordinates, and superiors within the agency, and the citizens with whom they come into contact. Trust rests on the assumption that most people, most of the time, speak and act honestly and with good intent, not necessarily out of virtue so much as out of rational self-interest.

Both loyalty and trust can be abused and corrupted. One of the tragic ironies of law enforcement, not only in the United States but throughout the world, is that those who are appointed to guard the public's safety and well-being are, by that very fact, exposed to a debilitating range of temptations and opportunities for illicit gain. In almost every instance of police scandal, one of the root causes has been the corruption of officers who previously were known as models of good character, but whose loyalties and trust were misplaced. When police officers are more loyal to their peers than to the community, they begin to overlook and excuse errors of judgment, petty infractions, and flaws of character in their colleagues. In time, they find themselves ignoring, rationalizing, and condoning flagrant misdeeds. When police officers withhold their trust from the public, and come to believe that only their immediate colleagues can be trusted to look out for their mutual interests, a "siege mentality" develops that further rationalizes and justifies corrupt behavior.

Integrity is the binding agent that, when present in sufficient proportion, prevents the corrosion of loyalty and trust.

Integrity means simply being true to oneself, being all of one piece. A steel bar has integrity if its crystalline structure is the same throughout, from end to end and from core to surface. If there are flaws in that structure, the bar will bend or break as soon as it is subjected to pressure.

A person who has integrity is honest in all matters, large and small, whether to his or her advantage or disadvantage. A police officer who has integrity is loyal not only when it is in his or her personal interest, but also when it is in the interest of the agency and the community. He or she is dedicated not to the camaraderie of his or her peers, but to the stated goals of the agency and to the values that those goals are intended to serve.

That is why the mission and values statements we discuss so laboriously in Chapter 4 are not merely platitudinous expressions of pious sentiments. They are the foundation on which the integrity of the agency and its personnel must rest.

People who are loyal to a higher set of values than self-interest, who trust in the good will and support of others, and whose actions are guided by their own integrity do not need to be coerced by the fear of punishment. They discipline themselves.

True Leadership

True leadership is expressed through such actions as identifying a need, articulating a goal, sharing information that is useful to others, and joining in a group effort to accomplish the group's purpose. We can illustrate this concept through a hypothetical scenario.

Lieutenant Adams has received a memo from the Crime Analysis Unit (CAU) concerning a sharp rise in the number of daytime residential burglaries reported in the Woodland Park neighborhood. Adams brings the memo to the attention of the three sergeants in whose district the burglaries have occurred.

Sergeant Baker, the day watch platoon leader, points out that most of the burglaries have been "hit-and-run" attacks on first-floor apartments in several blocks of multi-story tenements. The pattern suggests either juveniles or drug addicts, rather than "professional" burglars.

Sergeant Charles, the evening watch platoon leader, agrees and adds that her officers have reported an unusual amount of activity in and around an abandoned storefront. They suspect that the building might be used as a crack house. She observes that the possible crack house apparently was established at about the same time that the rise in the number of burglaries began. Based on this limited information, Lieutenant Adams and Sergeants Baker, Charles, and Davis (the night watch platoon leader) decide that action should be taken to determine whether the abandoned storefront is being used as a crack house and whether that is related to the incidence of burglaries.

Lieutenant Adams contacts Detective Edwards, a drug abuse investigator, and asks for assistance. Edwards, meeting with the lieutenant and sergeants, says that their suspicions may be justified but are not sufficient to warrant a raid on the possible crack house. Furthermore, a raid is inherently a hazardous event, and much more information is needed.

The three sergeants present the situation to their patrol officers at roll call and ask the officers to gather as much information as they can.

Officer Frank, on the day watch, makes a point of parking her patrol car and walking through the neighborhood around the crack house. She talks to residents and shopkeepers, casually inquiring about who is using the abandoned store, when they are there, and what they seem to be doing. The people in the community know and trust Officer Frank, and readily tell her what little they know.

Meanwhile, Officer George, also on the day watch, makes a special effort to patrol the blocks of tenements, particularly checking the alleys behind the buildings. He does not apprehend any burglars, but there are fewer reported burglaries in the neighborhood that week.

On the evening watch, Officer Henry drives past the suspected crack house several times, observing the presence of lights inside the building. He does not see any people going in or out, but the pattern of lights being turned on and off gives him some idea of the pattern, and especially the timing, of activity in the building.

Officer Henry passes along his observations to the night watch officer on his beat, Officer John. She also drives past the suspected crack house at varying times, and is able to note the license plates of several cars that come and go during the night. She runs the plates and finds that three of the cars belong to individuals with prior arrests and convictions for distribution of cocaine and other drugs, among other offenses.

The officers report their information to their sergeants, who meet again with Lieutenant Adams and Detective Edwards. Meanwhile, the detective has contacted the owner of the abandoned building, who expresses surprise that anyone is using the place. He provides Detective Edwards with a detailed description of the building, including the location of entrances and the interior floor plan. He also gives Detective Edwards written consent to search the premises.

Detective Edwards then obtains an arrest warrant for the known individuals who have been present at the building (on probable cause for trespassing) and a search warrant based on the owner's consent. Edwards meets again with Lieutenant Adams and with the evening and night watch sergeants and patrol officers, to plan a raid on the suspected crack house. The raid is carried out; drugs are indeed found on the premises and in the possession of the people there. Several arrests are made, the building is secured against further intrusions, and, over the succeeding weeks, the number of residential burglaries in the area declines markedly.

The point of this fictional scenario is not to present a model of effective problem-oriented policing, but to illustrate a concept of leadership. Every one of the officers described in this scenario demonstrated leadership by identifying a need, articulating a goal, sharing information that was useful to others, and joining in a group effort to achieve a common objective.

In short, leadership has little to do with the idea of one person imposing his or her will on others. Rather, leadership involves engaging in a partnership with others to achieve common goals. Loyalty, trust, and integrity are indispensable to this partnership.

True Discipline

The word *discipline* is derived from the Latin word for instruction; it is, of course, closely related to the word *disciple*, which originally meant a student. The association of discipline with punishment actually can be traced back to the Middle Ages when religious doctrine was taught by the use of harsh methods, including tongue-lashings and, sometimes, whippings to correct errors.

Police officers are neither more nor less human than other people, and human beings make mistakes. They sometimes are careless or inattentive, or in a foul mood, or preoccupied with their personal concerns, or momentarily lacking in energy. They sometimes misapply policies, misinterpret a factual situation, or make errors in judgment.

When a person is genuinely loyal to his or her group, such lapses are obviously uncharacteristic and unlikely to be repeated. The person's colleagues and immediate superiors, when they become aware of the mistake, usually have to do nothing more than determine that the person is aware that the action he or she took was wrong. In most cases, when a person acknowledges a mistake, he or she also recognizes the cause of the mistake and what, if anything, should be done to prevent a recurrence.

When someone makes a mistake and does not recognize it, then the person's peers and immediate superior have a responsibility—out of their loyalty to the group and its goals, and toward their colleague—to instruct, advise, coach, or use whatever technique is appropriate and effective in making the person aware of the mistake and how to avoid repeating it.

The vast majority of errors in judgment or mistakes in performing expected behaviors have no serious, irreversible consequences. However, mistakes do sometimes cause harm, and the nature of policing creates the possibility of extensive harm to innocent citizens—and to police officers themselves—when proper procedures are ignored or incorrectly followed. The first responsibility of a supervisor or other superior is to mitigate the damage caused by a mistake. After that has been done to the extent possible, the supervisor or manager must see that anyone wrongly harmed by an officer's error receives full restitution. Finally, the supervisor is responsible for using the appropriate instructional technique to ensure that the officer will not repeat the mistake.

Some errors in judgment or performance go beyond the ability of the police organization to repair. No police officer can be permitted to violate the law, or to flout certain rules and regulations that are indispensable to the proper functioning of the agency. Such actions can only be understood as a lack of loyalty to the agency and its mission, and a flaw in the offender's integrity. A rare and uncharacteristic error of this magnitude, if there are extenuating circumstances, might be redressed with an appropriate punishment, such as a brief suspension from duty accompanied by mandatory retraining. More than one such incident, or a continuing pattern of minor offenses that the person seems unwilling to correct, can only be corrected by removing the person from the agency altogether.

We have suggested that discipline should not necessarily be associated with punishment, but now we seem to be saying that if an officer makes a sufficiently serious mistake, or a number of minor mistakes, he or she should receive the severe punishment of being fired. In fact, we do not regard termination of employment, under these circumstances, as a form of punishment. An officer who is unable or unwilling to display loyalty and integrity is poorly suited to the demands of policing and is more likely to be successful in some other field of endeavor. Furthermore, the police department has an obligation to its community to remove from its membership an individual who poses a danger to citizens, fellow officers, and to himself or herself.

Such extreme measures should be, and in most police departments are, rare. Most of the time, discipline should not even be an issue. Personnel at every rank, out of their dedication to the common enterprise, should be alert not only to their own mistakes but also to those of their peers and subordinates, and should freely offer corrective advice, coaching, or instruction.[15]

When people are cooperatively engaged in an enterprise that is personally meaningful to each individual, that expresses the core values they share, and that contributes to the achievement of mutually accepted goals, the overriding importance of both leadership and discipline tends to fade away. People lead themselves: Every member of the group, at least sometimes and in some ways, becomes a leader. And people discipline themselves and each other, correcting their own mistakes and helping colleagues to correct theirs. When people act out of loyalty, trust in one another, and integrity, there is very little that any manager or executive needs to do.

FOOTNOTES

1. Lee P. Brown, "Community Policing: A Practical Guide for Police Officials," in *Perspectives on Policing*, no. 12 (September 1989) (Washington, D.C.: National Institute of Justice, U.S. Department of Justice, 1989), p. 4.

2. Robert Fogelson, *Big City Police* (Cambridge, Mass.: Harvard University Press, 1977), p. 15.

3. For a discussion of police unions and union-like organizations, see Alfred R. Stone and Stuart M. DeLuca, *Police Administration: An Introduction,* 2nd ed., (Englewood Cliffs, N.J.: Prentice Hall, 1994), pp. 457-459.

4. Elisha Y. Babad, Max Birnbaum, and Kenneth D. Benne, *The Social Self* (Beverly Hills, Calif.: Sage, 1983), pp. 211-228.

5. Kendall Murphy, "Generative Coaching: A Surprising Learning Odyssey," in Sarita Charola and John Renesch, eds., *Learning Organizations* (Portland, Ore.: Productivity Press, 1995), pp. 192-214.

6. Tom Peters, *Liberation Management* (New York: Alfred A. Knopf, 1992), pp. 235-236.

7. James Champy, *Reengineering Management* (New York: Harper Business, 1995), p. 29.

8. George L. Kelling and Elizabeth M. Watson, "Creativity with Accountability," in Larry T. Hoover, *Police Management Issues and Perspectives* (Washington, D.C.: Police Executive Research Forum, 1992), pp. 148-149. See also the discussion in Mary Ann Wyckoff and Timothy Oettmeier, *Evaluating Patrol Officer Performance under Community Policing: The Houston Experience* (Washington, D.C.: U.S. Department of Justice, National Institute of Justice, 1994).

9. Stone and DeLuca, *Police Administration*, p. 305.

10. Bureau of Justice Assistance, *Understanding Community Policing* (Washington, D.C.: U.S. Department of Justice, 1994), p. 22.

11. Champy, *Reengineering Management*, p. 143.

12. Stone and DeLuca, *Police Administration*, pp. 279-290.

13. *Basic Peace Officer Course* (Austin, Tex.: Texas Commission on Law Enforcement Officer Standards and Education, 1995), p. 1.

14. Field training practices have been extensively discussed and criticized. See, for example, Michael S. McCampbell, "Field Training for Police Officers: State of the Art," in Roger C. Dunham and Geoffrey P. Alpert, eds., *Critical Issues in Policing* (Prospect Heights, Ill.: Waveland Press, 1989), pp. 111-120; also, Philip Bonifacio, *The Psychological Effects of Police Work* (New York: Plenum Press, 1991), pp. 30-32. Despite the criticisms and apparent need for improvement, we consider field training to be an indispensable part of recruit training.

15. Champy, *Reengineering Management*, p. 105.

CHAPTER 7

ADDRESSING THE ISSUES: THE QUALITY OF COMMUNITY LIFE

In Chapters 4, 5, and 6 we describe the steps that we consider necessary in order to transform a traditional law enforcement agency into an agency that is committed to community policing. In this chapter, we offer some examples of the kinds of activities and behaviors that we regard as hallmarks of community policing.

We must acknowledge that this chapter represents, in some respects, our idealized vision of community policing and how neighborhood police officers should act. It is fair to say that no law enforcement agency in the country (or in the world, for that matter) completely fulfills this vision. As we pointed out earlier, community policing is by its very nature a "work in progress," continually evolving and expanding as police administrators discover from experience what works best in their particular communities.

In Chapter 2, we present a definition of the assumptions that underlie the philosophy. The first proposition is that "the primary purpose of the police is to assist the public in establishing and maintaining a safe, orderly social environment."

We also say that identifying and apprehending criminals is one, but not the only one, of the services performed by the police to attain that purpose.

Putting this issue into broader terms, we can say that the primary function of the police, in partnership with the community, is to develop and maintain a desirable *quality of life*.

THE QUALITY OF LIFE

The quality of life in any community has a number of components, most of which are clearly far beyond the control, or even the responsibility, of the police. While there is no universally accepted definition of "quality of life," some of the factors that are often cited include the community's economic status, the physical condition of the buildings and public spaces in it, the natural environment, and the presence of cultural and leisure amenities. None of the factors just mentioned are the direct concern of the police. However, underlying all of them is one fundamental requirement: an orderly, peaceful, and secure social environment.

Crime and disorder sap even the most vigorous economy, diverting capital from productive activities into protection and the replacement of stolen or destroyed property, discouraging investment, and imposing the burden of medical expenses on those who, in many cases, can least afford them. The constant fear of crime and the sense of insecurity prevents members of the community from enjoying leisure activities and discourages artists, performers, and entrepreneurs from coming into the community.

According to the well-regarded theory of universal human needs, first developed by the American psychologist Abraham Maslow, the need for security—freedom from threats to one's person and property—is second in importance only to the need for food, shelter, and other material necessities of life.[1]

In short, the quality of life in a community begins with the establishment and maintenance of a secure and peaceful social environment and that is the first responsibility of the police.

MANAGING NEIGHBORHOODS

Some of the critics of the community policing movement have argued that the police, out of practical necessity, must play only a *limited* role in maintaining the community's quality of life. While the police may provide some useful services to prevent crime, to engage residents in self-protection, and to promote social order, those activities must remain secondary to the one function that is exclusive to the police: responding to complaints of specific, verifiable crimes, and identifying and apprehending the perpetrators. According to the critics, if the police try to do too much, they run the risk of doing nothing very well, including that essential crime-busting duty.

Criminologist Larry T. Hoover, in the introductory chapter to his anthology on community policing, argues that the full implementation of community policing would require the police to become, in effect, *managers* of the neighborhoods in which they serve. He feels that this represents a major change from their previous responsibilities, and that it may go too far, particularly since most police agencies are already strained to meet the demands on their time and resources.[2] Since it is unlikely that the resources available to the police will be greatly enlarged anytime soon, Hoover warns that it may be impractical and illogical for the police to accept such a huge expansion of their responsibilities.

It is certainly true that community policing, as we have discussed it in previous chapters, involves a substantial change in the role of the police. It is also true that an increase, or at least a redeployment, of resources may be necessary in order for police officers to fulfill that enlarged role. However, we do not agree that community polic-ing requires police officers to become permanent *neighborhood managers*.

Most neighborhoods do not need managers, in any reasonable sense, if the term means someone who oversees the physical and social environment. The concept of the neighborhood manager strikes us as assuming that people cannot manage their own affairs without some outside paternalistic agent.

No one could sensibly argue that a stable, upper-income neighborhood of attractive homes and vital businesses would need, or would welcome, the imposition of neighborhood managers. Even in middle-class suburbs, for all their growing pains and mobility, usually there is no shortage of long-time residents who look out for their own neighborhoods and, to some extent, for their own neighbors. Most people would insist that the people in these neighborhoods are perfectly capable of provid-ing whatever management might be needed and desired.

The problem, of course, is that not all neighborhoods are middle-class or better. There are neighborhoods in which poverty, physical deterioration, and social disorder appear to be endemic, and no one seems to be able or willing to do much about it. Perhaps these neighborhoods truly do need managers, and perhaps, for whatever rea-sons, capable managers do not arise of their own accord.

Police officers are the only government employees who are present in the com-munity twenty-four hours a day, seven days a week, throughout the year. They are the only government employees who are responsible for observing the activities of resi-dents and the condition of the physical environment. They are the only government employees who have any authority, albeit limited, to go wherever they wish, speak to anyone, and act on their own initiative to correct any condition that they regard as dangerous or threatening. If anyone must serve as a neighborhood manager, that role seems to fall, by default, to the police.

However, the role of neighborhood manager need not be held permanently by the police even in the most disintegrating neighborhood. We do not envision patrol officers assuming a permanent role as neighborhood managers. At worst, we see patrol officers and their immediate supervisors taking responsibility for finding, developing, and cultivating natural leadership within the community. As that leader-ship emerges, and as the social and physical deterioration of the neighborhood itself is ameliorated, the police management role should gradually decline. The goal is not merely to make the quality of life in the neighborhood better, but to install the social mechanisms to ensure that it *stays* better.

Achieving that goal requires a commitment of personnel and resources, not only to solve crimes and catch bad guys, but to develop a secure and orderly com-munity. One of the essential resources for this purpose is information.

ESTABLISHING COMMUNITY KNOWLEDGE

Before the police can begin to address the manifold, and often interrelated, problems of a community, they must know a great deal about the community, its physical and social conditions, and the people who live and work there. Getting the information is not particularly difficult: Police officers on the street collect most of the information that is needed as a corollary of their routine work, even in a traditional agency. In community policing, patrol officers must recognize that collecting information is in fact a significant part of their role. They must be trained to know what kinds of information are needed, where it is to be found, and how it can be used.

However, it is not enough for patrol officers merely to collect information if they keep it all to themselves. Information is a perishable commodity: It must be kept fresh, and it must be readily accessible to those who need it.

The advent of relatively inexpensive computers, beginning in the early 1970s, enabled at least some police departments to establish better control over the acquisition and recording of information. The early computers, because of their limited capabilities, imposed a degree of order on the way information was recorded. As computers became progressively more capable and less expensive, information that previously would have been stored away in filing cabinets became more readily accessible to detectives and, eventually, patrol officers.

But even with the most efficient desktop and laptop computers available today, there are still problems in handling information that no police agency, to our knowledge, has completely solved.

This is not the place for a detailed examination of the problems and possible solutions. In broad terms, there are two basic issues: whether information is accurate and complete, and whether it is accessible to the people who need it.

Review Processes

Field officers' reports, whether written on paper, submitted on computer disks, or transmitted by radio signals from mobile terminals or laptops equipped with wireless modems, always should be reviewed to ensure that a high quality of information is maintained.

For crime-specific reports, the information should be recorded in a standard form that elicits all of the significant details. The source of each item of information—whether a victim's statement, a witness's statement, or an officer's observation—should be clearly indicated. Information from two or more sources should be consistent, or the inconsistencies should be flagged for corroboration.

Few agencies require field officers to submit non-crime-specific information in written form. Usually, if the information is collected at all, it consists only of officers' oral comments to their colleagues and supervisors. A few agencies have attempted to develop comprehensive and rather elaborate systems for collecting and analyzing this kind of information, but the burden on field officers can quickly become overwhelming.[3]

Accessibility

Accessibility is an even more difficult problem. Written reports tend to become buried in file cabinets and on cluttered desks. Indexing systems are helpful but require a very large investment of personnel time; often the indexing staff cannot keep up with the flow of incoming information, so the indexes become useful mostly for statistical and historical purposes. Computerized database systems are supposed to make large volumes of information immediately accessible to everyone who needs it, but again the task of re-recording the information in computerized form from written reports tends to fall farther and farther behind the contemporaneous flow of information, and some database systems require considerable expertise to locate and recapture needed information.

For the more informal non-crime-specific information, there is one solution that we believe to be effective. The solution is simply to make one person responsible for collecting, analyzing, and maintaining this kind of information, for each area of the agency's jurisdiction. That one person then becomes a *single point of contact (SPOC)* for every kind of information about his or her area of responsibility.

The SPOC's main function is to acquire and analyze *non*-crime-specific information. The sources of information should include written and oral reports from field officers (patrol officers, street detectives, and sergeants), and from as many other sources as possible. Newspaper articles (especially in community-oriented newspapers), radio and television reports, and even conversations on radio "talk shows" may contain useful information. The SPOC also should talk to community leaders and residents on a regular basis, both formally in community meetings and informally in telephone or personal conversations. In short, the SPOC should know *everything there is to know* about his or her assigned area that might have some bearing on the community's safety and security.

By the same token, the SPOC should be the primary *source* of information about the community for superior officers and for his or her subordinates. Anyone who wants to know about patterns of crime, gang activity, the presence of "crime magnets" (such as bars, strip clubs, massage parlors, "modeling" studios, "adult" bookstores and video shops, and so on), or other matters related to crime and social disorder should be able to obtain ample information from the SPOC.

The SPOC should be in an appropriate position to collect, analyze, and disseminate this information. We believe that the SPOC should be a command officer, not a staff officer, with authority to direct subordinates to collect needed information. In the Austin Police Department, for example, the sector lieutenants have been designated as SPOCs. Each of the six lieutenants is the commander of all patrol forces in his or her sector, an area that varies in size and population: The smallest sector has a population of about fifty thousand, while the largest sector has a population of more than one hundred thousand.

We also suggest that the number of SPOCs in an agency should be relatively small. For a medium-sized agency, there might be only one or two SPOCs, whose rank could be anywhere from sergeant to captain. For a very large agency, there should be no more than one or two SPOCs for each major section of the jurisdiction. One of the duties of the SPOCs should be to share information with one another; if there are too many SPOCs, that duty is likely to be slighted.

Each SPOC should have exclusive responsibility within his or her area. If there were two or more SPOCs with the same territory, inevitably there would be conflicts and inconsistencies between them.

The sector lieutenants in Austin not only act as SPOCs, but actively command their patrol force. The sector lieutenants also have the authority to call for additional resources, through a support lieutenant assigned to each sector who coordinates requests for assistance from specialist investigators or technical specialists, and through the street detectives assigned to each patrol district.

Regardless of the rank they hold or which box they occupy in the agency's organization chart, SPOCs are key figures in community policing. They are the interface between the community as a whole and the agency, just as the patrol officers are the interface between the residents of their beats and the criminal justice system.

NEIGHBORHOOD-ORIENTED PATROL

Throughout this book, we have repeatedly emphasized the crucial role of the patrol force in community policing.

Patrol officers are expected to accept *personal responsibility* for the safety of the neighborhood to which they are assigned. In a sense, this is a restoration of the concept of patrol that existed in the earliest days of organized law enforcement. The difference is that today's patrol officers are far better trained and equipped, and have many more resources to draw upon, than did the neighborhood patrol officers of a century ago.

In order to gain intimate knowledge of the neighborhood, patrol officers must interact both formally and informally with the people of the community: residents, business operators, workers, even people who are just passing through the area. The purpose of this kind of interaction is to obtain information about the social conditions in the neighborhood, and to determine the community's perceptions of crime and social disorder.

Neighborhood-oriented patrol officers are not expected to solve every problem in the community, but to engage the community itself in solving the problems. They are expected to observe physical conditions in their neighborhoods, and to know when and how to inform building inspectors of apparent violations of the building code, how to track down absentee landlords through tax and deed records, and how to inform the appropriate agencies about vacant lots choked with weeds, trash, and vermin.

Patrol officers should be sufficiently familiar with zoning laws and state statutes to recognize when legal businesses that are often "crime-magnets," such as sexually oriented businesses, pawn shops, liquor stores and bars, and (in some states) off-track betting parlors, are improperly located or operated. Patrol officers should know when, how, and where to report tenants who are being victimized by inadequate maintenance, improper eviction or the threat of it, and (in states that enforce rent controls) rent gouging. Likewise, patrol officers should know when and how to assist rental managers and landlords in dealing with unruly or irresponsible tenants.

Patrol officers cannot be expected to solve every problem nor to intervene in every dispute. Often their role is to see that the problem is addressed by the appropriate governmental agency or social service organization. Many problems can be handled by advising a resident or business operator, giving information about the proper agency to contact or how to make a complaint. Especially in low-income neighborhoods, residents often need nothing more than practical advice and encouragement to approach official agencies without being intimidated.

Neighborhood Organization

In neighborhoods where some degree of community organization already exists— active church groups, parent-teacher organizations, service clubs, and so forth—patrol officers are expected to work closely with those organizations to identify and correct problems. Where there are no such organizations or they are ineffectual, the long-term goal of the patrol force should be to help establish or strengthen them.

Neighborhood development at this level often requires the guidance and active participation of superior officers, such as a sector lieutenant or captain, as well as other resources from the larger community. Patrol officers should know when and how to call upon those resources for assistance. Some law enforcement agencies, especially in major metropolitan areas, may find it useful to establish a technical support unit specifically for the purpose of assisting patrol officers in neighborhood development. It is only in this area, neighborhood development, that the police may sometimes be called upon to act as "neighborhood managers." Their success is measured by the rate at which their "management" responsibilities decline, as the community becomes increasingly self-reliant. The goal is for the police to be partners with the community, not its managers.

The Chicago Police Department has adopted the Chicago Alternative Policing Strategy (CAPS), a major element of which is a neighborhood management program. In ten of the city's twenty five precincts (chosen on the basis of diverse socioeconomic factors), patrol officers are assigned in teams of eight or nine officers to each beat. The beat officers, as a group, are responsible for organizing and conducting community meetings in which citizens and the officers jointly identify crime-related problems, develop strategies to attack the problems, and evaluate the results after the strategies have been implemented. In many cases, the problem-solving strategy, or "beat plan," involves not only police activity but also the participation of other citizens, social service organizations, and other city agencies. The beat officers have the authority to submit, through their precinct commanders, City Service Request Forms to enlist the help of other city agencies.[4]

Community Involvement

Citizens often are not aware that they have any responsibility for maintaining a safe and orderly neighborhood. Under the traditional system of law enforcement, the only responsibility of citizens has been to report specific incidents of crime and, in such cases, to provide whatever information they have as victims or witnesses. The police typically have shown little interest in information about general social conditions or citizens' perceptions and concerns (except as they may be transmitted through the political system).

In community policing, citizens are expected to do much more: to provide the police with information about actual and potential criminal activity, to inform the police about social conditions in the community and the citizens' perceptions of problems, and to participate with the police in solving problems.

Leadership must be exercised by the police themselves to build a partnership with citizens, to establish the community's role in that partnership, and to encourage citizens to become involved in protecting themselves and maintaining a secure community. The primary role of the police still is, and always will be, to suppress crime by enforcing the law. By attacking crime-generating social conditions and by building self-reliant, self-managing communities, the police ultimately reduce crime at its source.

CRIME-REDUCTION STRATEGIES

Neighborhood development is a long-term process; it should not be expected to yield immediate, dramatic results. Meanwhile, the police still must respond to calls for service, many of which involve ordinary, everyday criminal acts. Community policing, however enthusiastic its advocates may be, does not promise to stop burglars from burgling, thieves from stealing, or abusive individuals from beating their spouses.

Identifying "Hot Spots"

Some criminal activity is essentially random and therefore unpredictable. However, a large part of the crime problem in every community consists of activities that are habitual and repetitive, or that are concentrated at identifiable locations. Police officials have long realized that such patterns of criminal activity can be recognized and can provide a basis for effective law enforcement techniques.

Criminologists Ron Clarke and Marcus Felson have developed a "criminology of place" theory that, in essence, defines every criminal act as an intersection of the offender, the victim, and the location. When criminal acts occur repetitively, the pattern can be disrupted by identifying and removing any one of those three factors. Conventionally, the police always seek to catch the offender. However, experience shows that removing only the offender does not necessarily solve the problem: if the victim and the location remain unchanged, new offenders soon appear and the criminality continues. By removing the victim (such as by encouraging people to use simple, commonsense methods to protect themselves and to avoid dangerous habits), or by removing or altering the location (such as by demolishing an abandoned building that is used by prostitutes or drug dealers), a more lasting solution can be found.[5]

Identifying "hot spots," specific locations that seem to attract criminal activity, is not difficult. Computerized dispatching systems usually have call analysis features that enable the police to identify the locations to which officers are called frequently; the same information can be produced by analysis of noncomputerized dispatch records, although the task is much more tedious.

Once the hot spots have been identified, the next step—and sometimes the hardest step—is to determine the most effective technique to "cool them off." Depending on the character of the crime-generating site and the nature of the crimes being committed, the solution may require nothing more than a period of intensive tactical patrol and zero-tolerance enforcement. In other cases, specialized techniques such as covert surveillance or a "sting" operation may be more effective.

Sometimes the solution does not require intensive enforcement at all, but merely rearranging the social landscape. An example from the Austin Police Department will illustrate what we mean.

The example involved a privately owned apartment complex consisting of two buildings, both two stories high. One building was more or less square in plan; the other building was L-shaped, with a parking lot separating the two buildings.

The complex had gained an unwelcome reputation as a haven for drug dealers, who used the parking lot as a drive-through marketplace, shielded from the street by the square building. Repeated raids had little effect; after a few days, the buyers and sellers would be back in business.

The owners of the apartment complex, at the urging of the police, put up wire mesh fencing and gates across the entrances to the parking lot, in an effort to restrict access to legitimate residents, the majority of whom were not involved in the drug trade. The "drive-through" traffic was reduced, but not the market. Buyers simply parked along the curb outside of the complex and walked through to meet the dealers.

When it was clear that the problem had not been solved, the patrol officers went to the city's public works department and suggested a few improvements to the traffic flow pattern at the busy intersection where the complex was located. In a few days, city crews erected "no parking" signs along the curbs on both of the intersecting streets. Now the drug buyers, if they wanted to do business at the complex, had to park several blocks away and risk getting caught carrying the merchandise back to their cars, or they had to risk having their cars towed away. Within a few days, the marketplace evaporated.

We do not claim that putting up a few no parking signs eliminated drug trafficking. Presumably, neither the buyers nor the sellers decided to "go straight"; they just decided to go elsewhere. However, breaking up the drive-through market greatly increased the security of the residents of the apartment complex, and discouraged the myriad other forms of criminal behavior that are associated with drug trafficking.

A second example, also from the Austin Police Department, illustrates a greater degree of citizen involvement.

For many years, a two- or three-block stretch of South Congress Avenue, about two miles south of the state capitol, had become a "marketplace" not for drugs but for prostitution. The legitimate businesspeople whose small shops line the street, and the residents of the quiet, working-class neighborhoods just east and west of the avenue, frequently complained to the police about the streetwalkers who congregated in the area, soliciting passing motorists and harrassing pedestrians. The police conducted periodic raids and undercover operations, but, again, removing one set of offenders from the street merely created vacancies that were quickly filled by others.

At a community meeting held to discuss the problem, and other crime problems in the neighborhood, a citizen offered an inspired suggestion. He asked the patrol officers whether he could use his video camcorder to tape the activity on the avenue, possibly to make a presentation to the city council about the problems faced by the neighborhood. After the meeting, the patrol officers checked with their supervisors and were told that they could neither participate in nor prohibit the videotaping, but that they should be present to prevent any violent confrontation.

With the tacit encouragement of the police, citizens set up a schedule for their video "production." Several residents met on the avenue, "armed" with their video cameras, while patrol officers stood nearby.

The results were immediate and dramatic. As soon as the video cameras' lights went on, the ladies and their prospective customers suddenly remembered that they had urgent business elsewhere. Unfortunately, not enough improper activity remained on the street to make a compelling presentation for the city council.

The videotaping was repeated several evenings in succession, and then on an irregular basis over several weeks. Again, it is not likely that all of the prostitutes abandoned their criminal behavior. But they did abandon the neighborhood that found their presence objectionable.*

Problem-Solving Approaches to Crime

The two examples just cited involved relatively short-term efforts to solve specific problems of crime and social disorder, and required nothing more than a cooperative effort of citizens, the patrol force, and other public agencies. Sometimes more is needed.

The general usefulness of a problem-oriented approach to policing has been accepted in American law enforcement at least since Wilson and Kelling's "Broken Windows" article in 1982 and their follow-up article, "Making Neighborhoods Safe," in 1989.[6] The basic concept of problem-oriented policing was explored in detail in Herman Goldstein's 1990 text, *Problem-Oriented Policing*.[7] Examples of specific problem-oriented approaches to solving crime problems, with varying degrees of success, have been widely reported.

Another example from the Austin police indicates what can be accomplished when police officers show initiative and creativity.

The success of the efforts to eliminate the drive-through drug market in a private apartment complex attracted considerable attention, not least from the owners of rental properties in all parts of town. Many of the apartment complexes were owned by nonresident investors and real estate companies, some of which were located in distant cities. They relied on hired managers to screen tenants, collect rent, and maintain the property. However, apartment management is a relatively low-paying occupation, especially in low-income neighborhoods. The turnover rate among managers was very high. Many of the managers had no training and knew very little about how to screen prospective tenants to keep out potential troublemakers.

The police helped the apartment owners' association develop a training program for managers. One session, taught by police officers, was devoted specifically to tenant screening. At first, some owners were skeptical about the program and reluctant to pay for their managers' training. However, these attitudes changed dramatically after the program had been offered for less than a year. A follow-up study showed that not only were there fewer police calls and tenant problems at the apartments whose managers had been trained, but rent collections were up and the percentage of delinquent renters was substantially reduced. Now most of the larger apartment complexes and many of the smaller ones in Austin require new managers to complete the training program, and refresher courses have been developed for more experienced managers.

A second example is even farther removed from conventional law enforcement techniques. A patrol sergeant in a working-class area grew increasingly frustrated over the amount of time his officers were spending on an endless series of minor public disturbance calls, shoplifting complaints, fights, and so forth. He knew that many of these calls involved teenagers—both dropouts and recent high school graduates— who simply had nothing better to do than to "hang out" on street corners and at local

---

*It is worth noting that the tapes not only were never shown to the city council, but that no other use ever was made of the tapes. In fact, often the camcorders did not contain any tape at all.

shopping centers. Many of them expressed a desire to find a job, but they lacked even the most basic job-finding skills.

The sergeant developed his own long-range problem-solving strategy. He began by approaching the principal of the area's high school, inviting him to co-sponsor a job fair. The principal agreed to make the school cafeteria available one evening. Next, the sergeant contacted employers in the area: large factories and small businesses of every kind. The response was generally very positive. The area was just beginning to recover from a decade-long economic slump, and many employers were in need of entry-level personnel.

The third step in organizing the job fair was publicity. The patrol sergeant made up a flyer, persuaded a print shop to make several hundred copies free of charge, and put the flyers up on bulletin boards in grocery stores, a neighborhood recreation center, a branch library, and everywhere else he could. An article in the weekly community newspaper and announcements on a neighborhood-oriented radio station also promoted the job fair.

The event was a considerable success; hundreds of young people (and some of their elders) attended, meeting with prospective employers and learning what they needed to do to get a job. More than a hundred teenagers were hired on the spot or in the following few days. Many others made contacts that eventually led to their being hired. Perhaps most significantly, the employers and school authorities agreed to repeat the job fair periodically.

We have described these two examples because they involved the use of a problem-solving approach that went beyond merely enforcing the law or suppressing criminal activity; they attempted to address the underlying social conditions that lead to crime and disorder. Whether apartment manager training programs or job fairs would be successful in other communities is not the point. In every city and in every neighborhood, the police must look beyond workload analysis, call volume, and crime pattern analysis, to discover and attack the fundamental causes of crime.

Wherever a specific pattern of criminal activity can be identified, the problem-oriented approach may be successful. In the past four years, Austin police in close collaboration with federal agents, the county sheriff's office, and the police in adjacent communities have carried out five major projects to attack the drug trade. Each project involved extensive undercover surveillance and a coordinated approach to identification, arrest, and prosecution. Special projects also have been used to target school truancy and associated juvenile crime, crimes (mainly burglary and theft) involving high technology industry, and other problems that go beyond the boundaries of a single neighborhood or that require specialized expertise.

We see problem-oriented policing not as an alternative, but rather as a major aspect of neighborhood policing. Identifying problems of crime and disorder, often in conjunction with the community itself, and determining the most effective way to solve the problems should be one of the responsibilities of the patrol force. Patrol officers and their superiors are in the best position to identify the problems and to consult with community leaders and residents about possible solutions. When necessary, they should be able to draw on other resources: additional personnel for short-term intensive patrol, investigators for wide-area projects, and specialists for technically sophisticated operations.

Furthermore, the neighborhood patrol force should look beyond the police agency for supportive partners within the community.

DEVELOPING POLICE-COMMUNITY PARTNERSHIPS

We have mentioned repeatedly throughout this text that police officers should make every effort to develop a working relationship with members of the community through existing organizations, such as school groups, churches, and so on. The primary responsibility for developing these partnerships rests with the neighborhood patrol officers. However, not all problems of crime and social disorder are confined to a single neighborhood, and not all of the police-community partnership should be limited to the patrol officer and neighborhood organizations.

Partnerships Beyond Neighborhoods

Just as beat officers should develop a working relationship with the citizens on their beats, patrol sergeants and lieutenants should develop a relationship with organizations that reflect citizens' concerns over a larger territory. In many cities there are associations that represent residents of a wide area. These organizations may be formally structured as neighborhood associations with a broad agenda for improving and maintaining the community, or they may be single-issue groups concerned specifically with environmental preservation, economic development, and so forth. Even purely social or hobby organizations may provide the basis for developing a police-community partnership beyond the neighborhood level.

Police specialized units and technical support units should not be left out. Their role in community policing is to support the neighborhood patrol force, but their focus should be on the whole community. They too should seek out community organizations that are devoted to solving crime-related problems. Some examples are fairly obvious: the unit responsible for investigating sex crimes should develop a partnership with a rape prevention group; the unit responsible for investigating domestic abuse cases should seek partnerships with organizations that provide shelters for battered wives, or that counsel abusive parents; property crimes investigators should work cooperatively with the owners and managers of pawnshops to close off a common method of disposing of stolen goods.

In general, the philosophy of community policing discourages the use of highly specialized police units. Both research and practical experience have demonstrated conclusively that specialization has been carried to excess in conventional police agencies, with poor results.[8] However, there are circumstances when the establishment of a specialized unit may be appropriate in response to a particular crime problem.

For example, in recent years Austin and other cities with a concentration of high-technology industries have experienced growing problems of extremely sophisticated crimes involving computers and computer components. Some of the components, such as microprocessors, are very small and very valuable, making them attractive targets for thieves. A handful of prototype computer chips can be more valuable than a truckful of consumer goods.

In cooperation with the managers of several high-tech factories and their trade association, the Austin police established a high-tech crimes unit. Officers assigned to the unit receive special training, provided by personnel from private industry. The high-tech companies also provide samples of the sophisticated—and expensive—equipment that is both used and targeted by criminals. Through this cooperative arrangement, the police have been able to identify, investigate, and stop thefts and burglaries from chip fabrication plants, and have begun to attack even more sophisticated crimes involving the infiltration of computer networks and databases.[9]

Getting the Big Picture

Historically, American local governments have evolved on a piecemeal basis with an emphasis on independent agencies, each with its own funding source or taxing authority and its own, independently elected or appointed governing body. Many agencies have been established by legislation on an *ad hoc* basis, to deal with the "crisis du jour." Little if any attention is given to providing linkages among agencies with similar or related areas of responsibility.

Major problems of crime and social disorder cannot be attacked effectively on a piecemeal basis; they demand a coordinated, comprehensive approach. Such an approach can be attained only by cooperation among a variety of public agencies, of which the police department is pivotal.

In Austin as in most other American cities, attention has been drawn to an increasingly critical issue: the rising rate of serious juvenile crime. This issue has become the focal point of an effort to overcome the institutional barriers and jealousies among the various agencies and entities responsible for one aspect or another of the juvenile justice "system."

The need for a more coordinated approach has been recognized for years. For that matter, American police agencies historically have regarded juvenile crime prevention as a crucial aspect of protecting the community from crime. Up to the late 1960s, in many municipal police departments the only crime prevention unit was the juvenile division, and most police officials subscribed to the theory that diverting young people from criminal activity was the best way to reduce future crime.

Over the past four decades, a different approach to crime prevention evolved, placing more emphasis on education, self-protection, and citizen-police collaborations such as Neighborhood Crime Watch. Direct involvement in the juvenile justice system became merely a routine part of enforcing the law.

By 1985, the Austin Police Department's juvenile unit was reduced to the single function of compiling statistics on juvenile encounters with the police (which, under Texas law, technically are not arrests).

Responsibility for dealing with juvenile crime in Austin and Travis County was divided among the Travis County Juvenile Court (TCJC, which is not a "court" in the usual sense, but is the state-established agency formerly known as the Juvenile Probation Department), the six public school districts that serve various portions of the county,** the county's criminal district courts, the district attorney, the sheriff, and the police department. The city's health and human services department and its county-level counterpart also were responsible for providing various social services to juveniles and their families, and therefore had some stake in the juvenile crime problem.

To further illustrate the organizational complexities, the Juvenile Court, district courts, county social services agencies, district attorney, and sheriff all are funded by the county commissioners. The district court judges, district attorney, and sheriff are elected directly by the public, as are the commissioners. The county attorney, also funded by the county but elected independently, also has limited jurisdiction over some criminal offenses. The city's social services agency and the police department are, of course, funded by the City Council and governed by the council and city manager. The independent school districts each have their own exclusive territory, none of which cover all of the city of Austin, and two of which include portions of the adjacent county.

During the late 1980s, several attempts were made to bring together representatives of all these entities, to establish a comprehensive effort to combat juvenile crime. In 1988, the federal Office of Juvenile Delinquency Prevention (part of the Department of Justice) offered to fund a special Serious Habitual Offender Comprehensive Action Program (SHOCAP) targeted at juvenile repeat offenders. SHOCAP was supposed to be implemented in 1990, but as of 1995 had accomplished very little.

In 1992, the Austin City Council established a program called "Opportunities for Youth" (OFY) whose specific task was to determine what resources were available and what might be needed to address a wide range of concerns, such as teenage pregnancy, drug and alcohol abuse, victimization of young people, and juvenile crime. The OFY program began by asking the city auditor to conduct research into each of these areas of concern. The auditor's office produced reports on teen pregnancy and youth unemployment in 1992, and the following year conducted performance audits of three social service agencies with responsibility for some aspects of juvenile social problems.

In 1994, the city auditor, at the request of OFY, began a comprehensive performance audit of the county's juvenile justice system. A performance audit, unlike a conventional financial audit, involves more than merely examining records and internal procedures. The performance audit included an intensive review of agency documents and procedures; interviews with agency personnel, clients, and other interested parties; and research of social science literature to determine what "best practices" have been identified in the field. The goal of the performance audit was to answer three questions:

- *Are the agencies doing what they are supposed to be doing?* Each of the agencies covered by the audit is subject to the state statute or local ordinance that created the agency, and that specifies its purposes or goals. In some cases, notably the police department, the agency is subject to myriad laws and parent-government policies, not all of which apply directly to juvenile crime.

**In Texas as in some other states, public schools are organized into independent school districts, governed by an elected Board of Trustees with its own taxing authority; they are not controlled by the city or county government.

- *Are the agencies' activities having the intended or desired effect?* In principle, an agency might be (and in this case generally was) performing precisely the tasks and duties assigned to it, but having little or no positive effect.
- *What could be done to improve the agencies' effectiveness?* Comparison of the local agencies' performance to the "best practices" reported in the literature presumably would give some guidance to answering this question.

The city auditor released its report in March 1995. Space does not permit us to reproduce all of its findings here, but a tiny sample will convey the general impression:

> The current response is ineffective with serious repeat offenders in the juvenile population. . . .[T]he Austin/Travis County policy making process is not designed to support collaboration. . . .At the agency level, neither system design nor program development reflects a systemwide focus.[10]

The auditor's report is noteworthy for the candor, bluntness, and thoroughness of its findings. Again, because of limited space, we can offer only a couple of illustrative examples of those findings:

> The Austin/Travis County juvenile justice system does not provide an effective response to a subpopulation of juvenile offenders who recidivate with increasing frequency and violence . . . Currently the components of our system are still carrying out their various roles independent[ly] of each other's activities.[11]

> Lack of coordination among the various system components has created a situation in which the adoption of policies and procedures in one component can adversely impact one or more of the others. More importantly, the relations between the component parts has often been characterized by distrust, competition, and blaming. As a result, coordination of basic management elements essential to effective control of the juvenile crime problem is not occurring consistently.[12]

> . . . [N]o one agency acting alone can improve the response of the entire system. As each agency feels itself under intensifying public scrutiny and pressure, each tends to react by blaming one or more of the others for the problem. This has increased tension among the system's participants and created an environment in which shifting the responsibility from one agency to another becomes an even more attractive alternative.[13]

It seems to us very likely that a comparable performance audit of the juvenile justice system in almost any large American city would result in similar findings. However, the purpose of the audit was not merely to discover what was wrong, but to propose ways to fix the problem. The Austin city auditor's report concluded with no fewer than thirteen recommendations for specific actions.

The first recommendation was that the Community Justice Council (CJC) establish a separate entity specifically to address the need for coordination in the juvenile justice system. The CJC was created by state law to provide public input to, and oversight of, the adult criminal justice system, but there was no provision for the juvenile system. The auditors recommended that the proposed Juvenile Agency Coordinating Committee (JACC) be comprised of representatives of the district courts (a district judge who hears juvenile cases), the Austin City Council, the County Commissioners, the Austin Independent School District, and the district attorney: in short, representatives of all of the elected officials who are directly involved in the juvenile justice system.

The auditors further recommended the creation of a separate entity, the Management Coordination Team (MCT), consisting of the chief executives of the various juvenile justice agencies: the city Health and Human Services Department, the Police Department, Travis County Juvenile Court, the Family Justice Division of the District Attorney's Office, and the public school system.

The other recommendations involve specific steps that were proposed to improve the juvenile justice system, but clearly the most important of the recommendations were those just described. As envisioned by the auditors, JACC would be responsible for developing policies to remove institutional barriers and to implement the interagency collaboration that was perceived as essential to a more effective juvenile justice system. The MCT would be responsible for implementing those policies within the various agencies, and to recommend to JACC further steps to attack juvenile recidivism.

The auditors also recommended that the Community Action Network, a cooperative planning committee that includes representatives of virtually all of the public and private social service agencies in Travis County, add a representative of the juvenile justice system to its governing board.

These three recommendations all had the same core purpose: to provide a forum for all of the agencies concerned with juvenile crime to plan and implement a comprehensive attack on the problem, particularly the problem of serious repeat offenders who are culpable for a disproportionate number of crimes.

Each of the agencies was asked to respond to the auditors' recommendations. Without exception, every agency agreed with every one of the recommendations; in several instances, the agencies described their own efforts to initiate and carry out the recommendations, or added further suggestions.

The two coordinating bodies, JACC and MCT, were formed in the fall of 1995. At this writing, slightly more than a year later, the new system already is bearing fruit. Soon after MCT was established, the members spent several hours "brainstorming" areas of need in the juvenile justice system. The long list of possible needs then was pared down and items on the list were assigned priorities according to the responsibilities of the various MCT members, the resources that were available, and the concerns that had been expressed by JACC.

Out of this process came a determination that there was an urgent need for a unified, comprehensive juvenile intake facility (JIF): a place to which every juvenile could be taken, after an arrest or involvement in a possible criminal incident. As envisioned by the task force, the JIF would be located near, but apart from, the city-county juvenile detention center and juvenile probation offices. The JIF would be staffed by personnel from each of the juvenile justice agencies.

The essential mission of the JIF is to examine each case that is brought to it—a juvenile arrested as a suspect in a crime, or for possible involvement in criminal activity—and determine the most appropriate disposition. The JIF staff could refer the juvenile to the detention center (formal arrest), divert the juvenile to a treatment program, or release the juvenile to his or her parents or guardian, with or without further requirements. By treating each case intensively and comprehensively, the JIF would simply eliminate the "cracks" through which too many juveniles had fallen in the past.

Partners at Every Level

The primary duty of mid- and upper-level police managers is to look beyond their office walls, to identify and analyze broad patterns of criminal activity on a citywide basis, and to plan the resource acquisitions and deployments that will be needed in the future.

Here, too, partnerships with the community must be cultivated. Captains, majors, and assistant chiefs with broad departmental responsibilities should develop relationships with community organizations and individual community leaders who can provide information about social and economic trends, public perceptions of crime-related conditions, and the availability of community resources.

At the upper-management and executive levels, police officials must be particularly concerned with developing working relationships and cooperative arrangements with their counterparts in other governmental entities.

Table 7.1 presents a summary of the kinds of community partnerships that we envision in a fully developed community policing environment. We do not mean to suggest that all of these partnerships presently exist in Austin or any other city, and of course the actual form of the various partnerships will depend on many local factors, but the philosophy of community policing should lead to something along the lines illustrated here.

Table 7.1 Police-Community Partnerships at Every Level

Police Personnel . . .	. . . Address These Issues with . . .	. . . These Community Partners
Police Executive (Chief, Sheriff)	Major citywide crime and social problems, especially those that are long-standing and contribute to public concern	Elected officials; executives of other public and private agencies, major industries, citywide community organizations; school superintendents
Upper-level Management (Deputy Chief, Assistant Chief)	Citywide crime and social problems, mostly those with a specific focus; trends and patterns of criminal activity	Divisional managers of public and private social service agencies, businesses; leaders of major civic and service organizations; school district assistant superintendents
Mid-level Management (Major or Captain) (Commanders of specialized units)	Trends and patterns of criminal activity	Community activists and leaders of community organizations; representatives of private agencies and business associations in related fields; school district central administrators
Patrol Commanders and Supervisors (Sector or Precinct Level) (Captains, Lieutenants, Sergeants)	Crime and social problems beyond neighborhood level	Operating-level personnel of public and private agencies; leaders in area-wide community organizations; middle and high school faculty and administrators

Table 7.1 (*Con't*)

Police Personnel . . .	. . . Address These Issues with . . .	. . . These Community Partners
Neighborhood Patrol Officers	Crime and social conditions at the neighborhood level	Neighborhood residents; business owners and employees; religious, social, and service organizations; elementary and middle school faculty and administrators

Partisanship

Table 7.1 suggests that community policing personnel at several levels should develop partnerships with community leaders, some of whom are likely to be identified with political organizations. The potential dangers of partisanship cannot be avoided.

At the national level, the American political system is dominated by two major political parties, both of which strive to maintain the largest possible membership by appealing to the broad middle of the spectrum of political ideologies. Both parties are highly competitive and together account for virtually the entire political system.

At the local level, historically the political system has been dominated by one party or the other for long periods of time. Entrenched political majorities have tended to see social issues primarily in terms of maintaining their political power, sometimes at the expense of the public as a whole.

There are some indications that these local political fiefdoms are less potent than they were even a few decades ago. In most major American cities, the two national parties have reached rough parity and the ability to compete vigorously for public favor. Whether the same condition exists in smaller cities depends on local history and the prevailing political culture.

The partnerships that we advocate between the police and the community cannot ignore political reality, but also must be thoroughly nonpartisan. Any hint that the police are controlled by one political faction, or that the police favor one political party or ideology over another, could be fatal to the very idea of community policing. The police, by law and by the nature of their mission, must be independent of the political system, and must be perceived by the public as thoroughly nonpartisan.

Achieving both the appearance and the reality of nonpartisanship requires that the police adopt and maintain two policies: First, the police-community partnership must be open to all members of the community without favor, and must be conducted publicly and openly; second, the decisions made by police officials must be based solely on the application of sound principles of law enforcement, backed up by objective evidence of effectiveness and impartiality.

SHARING INFORMATION

In a very broad sense, almost everything we have described and suggested in this chapter involves the collection, dissemination, and application of information. One could say that the essential difference between traditional policing and community policing comes down to three issues: (1) What kinds of information do the police need, (2) Who is responsible for collecting that information, and (3) How is that information used?

In traditional policing based on the "professional" model, the only kind of information needed by the police is information about specific instances of the violation of a law, including the identity of the violator and the types of evidence needed to prove the violation in court.

In community policing, information about specific violations is still important, but it is not the only kind of information needed to make communities safe and secure. The police also need information about general social conditions and about the community's perceptions of crime and safety. At the neighborhood level, the police need a great deal of information about the people in the community and their social relationships and behaviors that may influence the presence of crime and social disorder. At higher levels, police personnel need information about broader patterns of criminal activity and social disorder, and about the resources available within the community to solve these problems. At the highest level, the police need to cultivate partnerships with every major element of the community, to design and carry out long-range efforts to reduce crime and to alleviate crime-generating social conditions.

In traditional policing, most crimes are initially investigated by patrol officers, but only to provide a minimum of information to initiate an investigation by specialist detectives. The specialists have the primary responsibility of collecting the information needed to prove a crime and convict the perpetrator.

In community policing, the patrol officer has the primary responsibility of collecting as much information as possible about specific incidents of crime and, when there is sufficient information, acting to identify and arrest the perpetrator. Specialist investigators serve as a resource to the patrol force, assisting in complex cases, providing technical expertise when needed, and assuming primary responsibility for the investigation of crimes that extend beyond the neighborhood level.

In traditional policing, information about crimes is restricted to a few individuals, generally the patrol officer who initiates an investigation and the detectives who carry it to completion, if possible. Information about general trends and patterns in criminal activity may be collected by a specialized analysis unit, and some information is widely distributed to patrol and investigative units in order to alert them to possible criminal activity, suspects whose whereabouts are unknown, and so forth.

In community policing, information about specific crimes and about social conditions should be shared among all of the people, in the police force and in the community, who may be affected. The role of the "single point of contact" is not only to collect information but, just as important, to make it available to everyone who needs it.

Information systems that rely entirely on written documents simply cannot accommodate the many kinds of information that a community policing system requires. In fact, community policing in its fullest expression would be extremely difficult, perhaps impossible, if it were not for the extraordinary advances in information processing and communications technologies that have occurred in the past two or three decades.

We have already mentioned the increasing reliance of modern police departments on computers, particularly the relatively inexpensive but powerful desktop and laptop computers that are now available. Computer technology now makes it possible for all kinds of information to be collected, analyzed, and stored, almost instantaneously, in centralized data bases, and made accessible through wired networks and over radio systems.

Advanced two-way radio systems, using digital technology, are more adaptable to different communications needs and intrinsically more secure than conventional police radios. Such features as "panic buttons," message storing, and data communication can be implemented in digital radio systems that would be difficult or impractical with conventional analog technology.

Cellular telephones and digital pagers can make every field officer directly accessible to the public, reinforcing the bonds of partnership between neighborhood patrol officers and the people in their communities. In the near future, an even more advanced technology, generically known as "personal communications systems," may replace both cellular phones and pagers, combining and expanding upon the features of both.

Computer-based voice-mail recording systems also increase the public's access to individual police officers, again supporting the concept of the police-community partnership.

Mobile data terminals in police vehicles give field officers nearly instantaneous access to computer-based information, as well as improving the efficiency of police dispatching and call assignment. Laptop computers allow for the rapid and efficient collection and storage of information by field officers, reducing the time spent on both investigative and administrative report-writing. When laptop computers are equipped with wireless modems for radio communication, the best features of both technologies can be combined.

The global positioning satellite (GPS) system that has been developed in the past few years now makes it possible, with a relatively inexpensive device, to determine a person's or vehicle's precise location. Some GPS receivers are combined with computer-based mapping systems; they can tell the user not only where he or she is, but how to reach a destination. The GPS system also can be combined with radio transmitters to inform the police communications center of the precise location of a vehicle or person.

With the exception of the personal communications systems, which are just now being introduced, all of the technologies described in this section are currently and widely available, and generally far less expensive than comparable older technologies.

But the point is not to adopt the latest "gee-whiz" gadgets. The point is that the police today, more than ever before, have the opportunity to be accessible to the public, and to collect, store, and disseminate vast quantities of information. Both of these capabilities are essential to the implementation of community policing.

FOOTNOTES

1. Abraham H. Maslow, *Motivation and Personality* (New York: Harper and Row, 1954).
2. Larry T. Hoover, "The Police Mission," in Larry T. Hoover, ed., *Police Management Issues and Perspectives* (Washington, D.C.: Police Executive Research Forum, 1992), pp. 2-18.

3. John E. Boydstun and Michael E. Sherry, *San Diego Community Profile: A Final Report* (Washington, D.C.: The Police Foundation, 1975). The San Diego Police Department required patrol officers to develop an extensive "inventory" of information about their beats, to be recorded on standardized forms. Other agencies, including Houston, have attempted to implement similar systems, generally with poor results due to the inability or unwillingness of patrol officers to collect, report, and update the information.

4. *Joint Community Police Training* (brochure) (Chicago: Chicago Police Department, 1996).

5. Clarke and Felson's theory is discussed in Christopher R. Braiden, *Policing: From the Belly of the Whale*, unpublished monograph dated September 1992, p. 51. Braiden was at the time a superintendent in the Edmonton, Alberta, Police Service (a position roughly equivalent to an assistant chief in a U.S. agency). The "criminology of place" theory also is described in the Chicago Police Department's *Joint Community Police Training* brochure.

6. James Q. Wilson and George L. Kelling, "Broken Windows," in *Atlantic Monthly*, March 1982; and "Making Neighborhoods Safe," in *Atlantic Monthly*, February 1989.

7. Herman Goldstein, *Problem-Oriented Policing* (New York: McGraw-Hill, 1990). Also see Goldstein, *The New Policing: Confronting Complexity* (Washington, D.C.: National Institute of Justice, 1993) (monograph adapted from a speech given by Goldstein).

8. David H. Bayley, *Police for the Future* (New York: Oxford University Press, 1994), pp. 5-9; also see John J. Broderick, *Police in a Time of Change* (Prospect Heights, Ill.: Waveland Press, 1987), pp. 198-200.

9. Sue Barton, *Self-Reliant Neighborhoods: A Bridge to the Future* (Austin, Tex.: Austin Police Department, 1996), p. 5.

10. Office of the City Auditor, *Opportunities for Youth Partnered Audit: Austin/Travis County Juvenile Justice System* (Austin, Tex.: City of Austin, March 1995), p. S-1.

11. City Auditor, *Partnered Audit*, p. 10.

12. City Auditor, *Partnered Audit*, p. 16.

13. City Auditor, *Partnered Audit*, p. 26.

CHAPTER 8

EVALUATING COMMUNITY POLICING IMPLEMENTATIONS

Historically, American law enforcement agencies have never been known for their eagerness to embrace the most progressive and sophisticated management practices. Even the most enthusiastic advocates of "scientific" reform, at the end of the nineteenth century, failed to persuade America's police chiefs that such practices as planning, training personnel, and evaluating results were essential.

Eventually, most large-city police departments established some sort of planning unit and began requiring recruits to undergo some sort of training. Over the years, the extent of both police planning and recruit training have slowly increased. But to this day, few municipal police agencies make more than a token effort to evaluate the results of their activities.

EVALUATING COMMUNITY POLICING

When a police department begins to implement the philosophy of community policing, there can be no question that the public has a legitimate interest in, and right to know, how effectively the new methods of policing are working. For decades, the public has been told repeatedly that there is only one way for a police department to be organized and managed. Now the advocates of community policing are claiming that there is a better way, and citizens—whose very lives, not to mention tax bills, depend to some degree on the effectiveness of the police—naturally want to see those claims verified.

Furthermore, the philosophy of community policing is based on a partnership between the police and the citizenry. The police therefore owe their partners, the public, as much information as possible about how well the partnership is working. It is unreasonable to expect citizens to contribute much to the partnership if they are kept in the dark about the agency's mission, goals, and operations—and the results of all three.[1]

Informing the public thus becomes a central concern in a community policing organization. It is no longer enough to give the news media an annual statistical summary of the "crime rate" and let them come to their own conclusions. The police executive has a responsibility to provide timely, accurate, and significant information to the public. The information must be appropriate; that is, it must fairly indicate whether the agency is doing its job well. It also should reflect the real problems of crime and social disorder that the community must face.[2]

Changing the Criteria for Evaluation

The criteria for evaluation also change. For a traditional police department, it may be sufficient to judge the agency's performance in reducing reported crime incidence and improving clearance rates. For a community-policing agency, those statistical measures are just the beginning.

No single measure of an agency's performance can meet all of these criteria, especially in a police department whose goals and operations are as diverse as they are in a community-policing agency. The key is to develop a system of evaluation based on the agency's explicitly stated mission and goals.

Not only must the agency as a whole be evaluated, but each element of the agency should be expected to serve the overall mission through the attainment of its own specific goals. At every level, goals must be specified and related to the agency's overall mission. The goals then must be translated into measurable objectives, and a systematic means must be established to determine whether, or to what degree, each objective is being attained.

Missions, Goals, and Actions

Before it is feasible to evaluate what the police *are* doing, there needs to be a general statement of what the police are *supposed* to be doing. That is the essential purpose of the mission statement discussed at length in Chapter 4. In effect, the mission statement represents the agency's institutional pledge to the community.[3]

The mission statement, in turn, forms the basis for the department's goals and objectives. The process of goal setting has been thoroughly explored in police management literature and does not need to be recapitulated here.[4]

Most management authorities agree that all elements of the organization should participate in goal setting. For a community policing agency, this means that every employee of the agency should have at least the opportunity to contribute, and representatives of the community must be deeply involved. No matter how short or long the list of goals may be, it is important for the agency to establish a genuine institutional commitment to the achievement of all of them. Participation at every level is essential in obtaining that commitment: street-level officers, supervisors, managers, executives, and indeed the whole community should feel that the goal statements represent what they want their police department to be and to do.

The goal statements represent an ongoing commitment that may take many years to accomplish, or, in some cases, may never be finally accomplished. Just as a football team measures its progress toward the goal line in successive first downs, the police agency needs a way to measure its progress toward the accomplishment of its goals.

The "measuring stick" consists of a set of objectives that the agency intends to achieve within a stated period of time. Long-range objectives usually are stated for a three- to five-year period; short-range objectives usually are stated for a one-year period. Just as the goal statements reflect the agency's mission statement, each stated objective should reflect one of the agency's goals.

Goals and objectives should be reviewed periodically, and objectives should be adjusted each year to reflect the previous year's experience and expectations for the coming year. Furthermore, this exercise ought to be a routine part of a law enforcement agency's planning and budgeting system, regardless of the agency's operating philosophy or organization. After the entire process has been completed once, repeating it is much less burdensome.

Finally, the process of developing goals and objectives requires every member of the department to think through his or her job, career aspirations, and responsibilities to the community. Establishing an explicit set of goals and objectives can have a highly beneficial effect on departmental morale, and this alone can justify the time and effort required.

Converting Objectives into Actions

Football coaches, after their team has just lost a game, sometimes say, "We had a great game plan, we just couldn't execute it." In much the same way, merely having a comprehensive set of goals and objectives accomplishes nothing unless the agency's day-to-day operations achieve the objectives.

The mission statement, goal statements, sets of measurable objectives, and all the rest are merely words on paper. If they are stuffed into a file cabinet and forgotten, the time and effort spent on developing them will have been largely wasted. The ultimate purpose of the exercise is to provide a superior service to the community, which means that changes in the agency's operations must be put into effect. The goals and objectives serve to define how those changes should be made.

For now, we will assume that the goals and objectives have been converted into actions, that changes have been made in the agency's policies and operations. Now we are ready to return to the main subject of this chapter: evaluating whether, or to what degree, those policies and operations have had the intended and desired effect.

CRITERIA FOR EVALUATING A COMMUNITY-POLICING AGENCY

If, as we maintain throughout this text, a community-policing agency is different in philosophy, in policies, and in operation from a traditional agency, the criteria for evaluating the agency ought to be different from those that apply to a traditional department. Whatever evaluation methods may be used, they should reflect those different criteria.

Because there is no single, universally accepted definition of "community policing," there are no universally accepted criteria for evaluation. However, we suggest that the answers to the following questions will serve as indicators of an agency's progress in implementing the community-policing philosophy:

I. Organizational Structure

1. *What proportion of the department is involved in the direct delivery of police services?* In a community-policing agency, every effort should be made to increase the presence of uniformed police officers "on the street" not only for enforcement purposes but for direct police-citizen contact. The allocation of personnel to off-street duties, whether supportive services or the management bureaucracy, should be limited as far as practical without sacrificing the quality of service.

2. *How are resources allocated in comparison to stated priorities?* For example, if the agency's goal is to involve officers in the community, the officers must have time freed from other duties, such as responding to calls for service. Are there enough officers available to respond appropriately to calls for service without absorbing all of the officers' time and energies? Are there mechanisms to reduce the number of calls that require the dispatch of a patrol officer, such as "teleserve" and call intervention systems?

3. *To what extent has responsibility for decision making been decentralized, or "pushed down"?* Responsiveness to the community requires decisions about operational matters to be made at the lowest levels possible, consistent with the agency's overall philosophy and goals. Are patrol officers and investigators, and their immediate superiors, allowed—and even required—to make significant decisions about the allocation of time and other resources, the enforcement tactics to be applied to specific situations, and other matters, or are most policy decisions still being made by upper-level managers? Do employees at every level understand what kinds of decisions they are expected to make, and what the limits of their authority are? Do they feel comfortable in exercising this authority, or are they confused or uncertain about what is expected of them?

4. *How, and how well, does management discharge its functions?* Reducing layers of bureaucracy and pushing decision-making authority down to lower levels do not eliminate the need for agency management. Managers still must plan for ongoing change in the agency, must define goals and objectives, and must articulate policies that establish the framework and the parameters within which lower-level personnel are expected to operate. Do managers understand and carry out their role effectively? Is responsibility for strategic, long-range planning distributed appropriately among managers, with provision for coordination among the agency's elements?

5. *Do first-line supervisors and managers discharge their roles effectively?* Do they understand their role as "coaches"? Do they coordinate activities among

units and shifts to achieve consistency and effective police services? Do they encourage subordinates to show initiative? Are officers and noncommissioned personnel consistently, promptly, and publicly rewarded by their immediate supervisors for their efforts and effectiveness?

6. *How well are departmental components integrated?* Is there a single, department-wide understanding of the agency's purposes, and are all elements of the department committed to that purpose? Do personnel from different districts, divisions, and bureaus share information freely, and have appropriate opportunities to do so? Is there a general "team spirit" and lack of factionalism?

II. Community Involvement

1. *Is the community involved in all aspects of the agency?* Are community members involved in recruiting, training (perhaps as volunteer instructors in such areas as ethnic/cultural sensitivity), and policy development? Are citizens used as volunteers in as many areas as possible? What mechanisms for community involvement have been established, and how well are they working? Do officers "on the street" understand their role in promoting community involvement through direct police-citizen contacts? Is the community involved in upper-level management as well as street-level operations?

2. *Are all elements of the community involved?* Are established neighborhood organizations part of the community-involvement process? Is attention given to developing neighborhood organizations where none already exist? Are all ethnic/cultural elements of the community represented? Is the business community involved, perhaps through "loaned executives" or policy-development "think tanks," or through the assignment of employees with specialized skills as police interns? How is the agency linked to community resources, such as other governmental agencies or institutions, colleges, public schools, and major voluntary organizations?

3. *Are there connections between the police and the other elements of the criminal justice system?* Is information shared among the police, prosecutors, and community corrections personnel (aside from routine exchanges of information about specific cases)? Is there a coordinated, planned effort on the part of each element to contribute to the community's safety and well-being?

III. Quality of Service

1. *Is there a shared vision and sense of mission?* Do all personnel understand the agency's commitment to excellence in serving and protecting the public? Is there a department-wide focus on improving neighborhood safety? Do all elements of the department, especially patrol and investigations, have the same understanding of their respective contributions to the department's mission and goals?

2. *Does each element of the agency have a strategy to reduce crime?* Are patrol units and investigators encouraged to "see the forest as well as count the trees," to look at the overall crime problems in the community, to analyze

trends in the types of crimes being committed and so forth? Is there a consistent emphasis on reducing the need for enforcement services by reducing the incidence of crime without sacrificing citizens' confidence and satisfaction?

3. *Are police services "customer-friendly"?* How do personnel, especially 9-1-1 operators, answer the phone? Are they courteous and concerned, or brusque and indifferent? Is it easy to reach the most appropriate element or officer? Are all operating units listed in the telephone directory? If the agency has a "teleserve" unit (to take crime reports by telephone when there is no real need to dispatch an officer), is it readily accessible to complainants? Do people understand what the teleserve unit is intended to do?

4. *Are nonenforcement activities also "customer-friendly"?* Is the recruiting process accessible to all parts of the community? Is the process fair and considerate of applicants? If the agency is responsible for inspection services, are the inspections conducted in a manner that is considerate of business owners and other citizens? Are safety and crime prevention educational programs available to all citizens and designed to meet the differing needs of the neighborhoods?

IV. Measures of Citizen Satisfaction

1. *Is there specific evidence of citizen satisfaction?* Do citizens voluntarily express appreciation for effective police work? Do people *act* as if they consider their neighborhoods safe, such as by their presence on the streets or in public places in the evening?

2. *What do citizens expect from contacts with police officers?* Are community involvement sessions bogged down by a litany of complaints? Do citizens come forward on their own with complaints of excessive use of force or other improper police acts? How often do citizens complain of rudeness on the part of a police officer, and how are such complaints handled?

3. *Does the agency have "success stories" that reflect problem-solving achievements?* Have significant neighborhood crime problems been resolved through an effective police-citizen partnership? Is the public aware of these "success stories"? Do the local news media report them prominently? Are personnel commendations also reported?

4. *Do the police and the community agree on the role of the police as community builders?* Are the police seen as more than just enforcers of the law, but as facilitators or catalysts in developing each neighborhood as a safe, high-quality environment?

V. Measures of Employee Satisfaction

1. Do employees feel that they have been trained and educated appropriately to perform their assigned duties? Do they continuously seek training and educational opportunities to enhance their performance and to prepare for their future responsibilities?

2. Do employees feel that they receive sufficient information from their superi-

ors and from the agency's management? Is the information timely, accurate, and appropriate to their needs? Are rumors and gossip dealt with promptly and decisively, to ensure that all matters of concern to personnel are addressed accurately?

3. Are employees supported in maintaining a healthy, positive attitude toward their duties, with assistance available during or following crises or traumatic incidents? Do supervisors know how to coach and counsel their subordinates?

4. Are employees aware of opportunities for their personal and career development? Do they feel that the opportunities are appropriate and beneficial? Are employees supported by their supervisors and managers in their efforts to advance their careers?

5. Do employees feel empowered to make important decisions about their duties? Do employees feel that their decisions and judgments, made honestly and within the parameters established by departmental policy, are supported by their supervisors and managers? Do employees at every level understand who is responsible for the various kinds of decisions that are made on a daily basis?

Few agencies will completely satisfy all of these criteria, and no police agency meets all of them perfectly. The purpose of evaluation is not to justify complacency, but to document areas of success and to identify room for improvement. Community policing is not a game to be won; it is a goal to be sought, through systematic, continual change.

EVALUATING AGENCY PERFORMANCE

The criteria just listed are intended only as a guide to the kinds of questions that should be asked in evaluating a community-policing agency's performance. The specific criteria that should be applied to an agency must be derived from its goals and objectives, as we discussed earlier.

Once the criteria have been determined, a variety of methods of evaluating the agency's success can be adopted. Some of them may be implied by the objectives themselves.

For example, if one of the agency's objectives is to reduce the incidence of reported residential burglaries by 10 percent, it is a simple matter to compare the number of reported burglaries this year with the figure for last year, and calculate whether the 10 percent objective has been reached.

The same principle applies to many other objectives that are stated in terms of measurable activities. If one of an agency's objectives is to reduce the patrol response time to, say, an average of three minutes, the calculation of average response time can be performed automatically by most computer-assisted dispatching systems.

These evaluations, however, necessarily apply only to the *quantitative* aspects of the agency's performance: how many, how big, how often, and so forth. Objective quantitative measures are important, but they tell only part of the story. Some of the criteria we have listed do not lend themselves to quantitative measurement; they concern the *qualitative* performance of the agency: how well it is doing its job. Later we will discuss some of the methods that can be used to assess the quality of an agency's performance, but we must acknowledge that qualitative measurement is always difficult and always involves, to some extent, subjective judgments. One of the unfinished tasks of the community policing movement is to develop more and better methods of assessing the qualitative performance of police agencies.

Measuring Crime

The one form of evaluation that is practiced by most—but not all—American law enforcement agencies is the collection of statistics on crime incidence through the Uniform Crime Reporting System (UCRS). The system was first proposed by the nascent International Association of Chiefs of Police about 1909, but was not fully implemented until 1930.[5] Not all police agencies participate in the voluntary system, and some of those that do participate do not adhere strictly to the UCRS guidelines and definitions of various categories of crime.

For all its faults, the UCRS is the *only* source* of statistical information about the extent of lawlessness and the effects of police activities in America. When the news media proclaim that "crime rates" are rising or falling, they are almost always talking about the UCRS statistics. For most citizens, those "crime rate" figures are the only presumably objective criteria by which the effectiveness and efficiency of local law enforcement may be judged.

The Uniform Crime Reports are supposed to be an index of the number of crimes reported to the police and the portion of those reported crimes that are "cleared" by the arrest of the alleged perpetrator. If the number of reported crimes falls, and if the percentage of cases cleared rises, presumably the police are doing a good job.

However, the usefulness of the UCRS to evaluate a police department depends partly on the assumption that the statistics are accurate and reliable in themselves, and doubts on this score have been raised by critics of the system. In particular, numerous surveys of the general public have shown that many crimes are never reported to the police at all, and therefore are overlooked in the UCRS.[6]

Of course, no one could reasonably expect the police to "solve" unreported crimes. At most, the clearance rate for reported crime ought to be of some use as an indicator of the agency's effectiveness in dealing with the crimes that come to its attention. Unfortunately, "clearance rates" do not always tell the whole story, either. A crime may be considered "cleared" when an arrest is made, even though ultimately the alleged perpetrator is not charged with any crime, or is charged with a different offense (usually as a result of a plea bargain), or is charged and tried but acquitted. Or a suspect may be arrested for one crime, which is then considered "cleared," when in fact he or she is the perpetrator of several other crimes for which, because of insufficient evidence, no charges can be brought. The latter situation is especially common

*The FBI has introduced a new crime reporting system, the National Incident-Based Reporting System (NIBRS), essentially a more sophisticated system than the UCRS with elaborate checks on the accuracy and validity of crime reports. The Austin Police Department was the first major city police agency to adopt the NIBRS.

with property crimes such as burglary and shoplifting, and may partly account for the dismally low clearance rates for these crimes.

The FBI, the IACP, and several other law enforcement professional organizations, all of which share responsibility for maintaining the UCRS, are well aware of the criticisms and flaws, and have made improvements in the system periodically. But the underreporting of crimes and the difficulty in correlating known crimes with clearances are inherent problems for which there probably is no perfect solution.

But even if the statistics generated by the UCRS were perfectly accurate, they still would represent only one aspect of the evaluation of a police agency. The fact remains that the law enforcement practices of any police agency are only one factor in the incidence of crime in a community and in the reduction of social disorder.

Performance Auditing

In Chapter 7, we discuss a performance audit conducted by the city of Austin in which the juvenile justice system in the city and surrounding county was examined. The audit was performed by the city auditor under an agreement with the county government.

Most people are familiar with the concept of financial auditing, but the term *performance auditing* may be unfamiliar. Financial auditing has been a common practice in governmental management, in one form or another, for more than a century. Performance auditing is a relatively new concept, although it has existed for more than thirty years.

A financial audit is an examination of an organization's financial records by an independent agent, usually by people trained in accounting. The purpose of the audit is to verify that the records accurately reflect the receipt and disbursement of the organization's funds and property. In addition, the audit may result in recommendations for improvements in the organization's handling and accounting of its funds and property.

A performance audit is an examination of an organization's overall performance, to determine whether the organization is achieving its intended purposes and whether its methods of operation are as efficient and effective as they might be. The results of a performance audit may include recommendations for changes in the organization's structure or operating procedures and practices to achieve its purposes and goals more efficiently or effectively.[7]

The idea that the performance of governmental agencies should be independently audited, as well as their financial records, developed during the 1960s. In 1972, the Comptroller General of the United States issued the first set of standards for performance auditing of federal agencies. The standards—the set of rules and procedures by which an audit is conducted—have been revised several times since, and are published periodically in a volume known to governmental auditors as "the Yellow Book."[8]

A performance audit usually is conducted by auditors who have been especially trained in these procedures. The starting point for any performance audit is a review of the mission and goals of the agency to be audited, usually based on the law and the regulations by which the agency was established as well as any documentation produced by the agency describing its purposes. The auditor then seeks to determine, by examining the agency's records and by interviewing agency personnel, clients, and other interested and qualified observers, whether the agency is achieving its intended goals, to what degree or extent the goals are being achieved, and what, if anything, could be done to enable the agency to perform more efficiently or more effectively. The auditor produces a report of these findings, usually including a set of specific recommendations.

Even though performance auditing has a relatively brief history, it has undergone several changes in its aims and methods. Originally, the primary purpose of a performance audit of a governmental agency was to determine whether the agency was in compliance with the law and whatever rules or regulations were applicable. Beginning in the late 1980s, the emphasis began to shift from compliance (which has an obvious similarity to the "command-and-control" management traditionally practiced by police agencies) toward efficiency: whether the agency being audited is using its available resources economically, to produce the most benefit for the lowest cost. In the past few years, the emphasis on efficiency has been expanded to include a greater emphasis on effectiveness: whether the agency is accomplishing its intended purpose, and whether the results are beneficial to society.[9]

The performance audit of the juvenile justice system in Austin and Travis County began with a study of the Travis County Juvenile Court, which by law is the primary agency responsible for dealing with juvenile offenders. However, the study quickly expanded to include all of the agencies that directly or indirectly have an impact on the juvenile justice system. One of the audit's most significant findings was that there was virtually no coordination or even communication among the several agencies. In this case, what began as a performance audit of one agency grew to be a study of the interrelationships among all of the agencies concerned with, or to some degree responsible for, a major issue of concern to the community. Naturally, the Austin Police Department was among those agencies, and the audit's findings included several recommendations for changes in the way the department deals with juveniles.

All aspects of a police agency could be audited for similar purposes: to determine whether the agency is performing its stated mission as efficiently and as effectively as possible. The methods for conducting such an audit are available from the sources listed in the endnotes.

The results of a performance audit often include recommendations for changes in an agency's structure and practices. The value of these recommendations, of course, depends greatly on the competence of the auditors. If the auditors are insufficiently trained, or if they approach their task with some political or ideological bias, the results may be not just worthless but potentially damaging to the agency or institution being examined. For this reason, it is essential that the auditors' preliminary report be made available to the agency's executive, who should have an opportunity to provide additional information, to refute inaccurate or misleading statements, and to either accept or reject, with an explanation, the auditors' recommendations.

One of the most useful functions of a performance audit is the opportunity for the auditors to make agency managers aware of the successful techniques or procedures being used by other, similar agencies to achieve the desired results. When an audit's recommendations are based on these "known best practices," an agency manager has little excuse to ignore them.

Because a performance audit always begins by reviewing an agency's stated purposes and goals, the value of the audit's findings will depend to a great degree on the validity of those objectives. If the agency's mission is vague and its goals are trivial or inappropriate, the performance audit is doomed from the very beginning. Once again, we see the importance of the mission statement and goals statements discussed in Chapter 4, and the significance of the effort expended in developing those statements is manifest.

Recidivism and the Police

The ultimate purpose of the criminal justice system as an institution of society is not just to catch and punish bad people, but to discourage criminal behavior altogether. If the criminal justice system works the way it is intended, people who are proven to have committed an offense against society will, through a combination of punishment and rehabilitation, choose in the future to remain law-abiding. At least, that is the theory on which the system is based. Clearly, the police play an important role in this system, but it is also a limited role.

Nevertheless, the true test of the system as a whole is the rate of recidivism: the percentage of those who, having once been convicted of an offense and presumably reformed, subsequently commit new crimes.

Since the police have no control over what happens to offenders after they are presented in court, it would be unreasonable to hold the police responsible for offenders' behavior after they are returned to society. But recidivism still may tell us something useful about the effectiveness of the police.

A high rate of recidivism means that a relatively small number of individuals are responsible for a disproportionately large volume of crime. In fact, some studies have shown this to be the case: Repeat offenders account for more than their "share" of criminal activity, especially for such crimes as drug trafficking and property crimes.[10]

In some states, the local police are notified every time an offender is released on probation or parole, or upon completion of a sentence. The notification laws, unfortunately, vary widely: Some states have none, and some states provide notification only for certain categories of offenders.

Where adequate notification laws do exist, there should be policies and procedures to track those offenders who are statistically most likely to recidivate.[11] The patrol officers who are responsible for the neighborhoods in which ex-offenders are living should be aware of their presence and should be alert for any indications of renewed criminal activity. While the police cannot be held directly accountable for recidivism, they should be expected to address the problem effectively.

Calls-for-Service Profiles

By far the largest part of any police agency's work consists of responding to calls for service. An analysis of the calls and how they are handled should be part of the evaluation of the agency's effectiveness and efficiency.

Calls-for-service (CFS) profiles usually include, at a minimum, an analysis of the chronological and geographical patterns of the calls received by the agency, which results in an analysis of the service workload assigned to each patrol unit. This information is useful mostly for allocating patrol units, but it also can produce insights into patterns of criminal activity in the community. If the analysis also includes a breakdown by the various types of call (crime in progress, crime not in progress by type, other emergency, nonemergency, and so on) and shows the amount of time spent on each type of call, much can be learned about how patrol officers are spending their time. These analyses may indicate a need to beef up the teleserve and call intervention procedures, as we discuss in Chapter 6, or to make other adjustments in patrol call assignment practices.

Virtually all large police departments and many medium-sized and smaller ones use computer-assisted dispatching (CAD) systems, most of which are designed to produce at least some CFS profiles automatically. However, the systems are not being used to best advantage unless someone takes the time to study the analyses and recommend appropriate changes in personnel allocations and operating procedures.

Problem-Oriented Policing

One of the uses of CFS profiles and other types of incident analysis is the development of problem-oriented policing (POP) projects. This is not at all a new idea in American law enforcement, but it has been given increased emphasis in recent years through the efforts of criminologists James Q. Wilson and Herman Goldstein and through the positive results of POP projects in Newport News, Virginia, and several other cities.[12]

The question we raise here, with regard to the evaluation of a community-policing agency, is whether the agency uses its CFS profiles and other sources of information to generate effective POP projects, whether the projects are successfully implemented, and whether the projects have the intended effect of reducing both criminal activity and fear of crime in the community.

INDIRECT METHODS OF EVALUATION

All of the approaches to evaluation that we have described so far are objective in nature: They are intended to determine whether in fact the agency is doing what it is supposed to do, and whether its activities are in fact having the intended effects.

Limitations of Objective Measurement

There are several dangers to this sort of objective evaluation. First of all, as we have pointed out, variations in the volume of reported crime can be caused by many different factors; the effectiveness of the police is only one factor, and may not be the most important one.[13] Not only is there an unknown volume of unreported crime, but it is not always clear that reported incidents are recorded consistently.

The definitions of various types of crimes in the UCRS may differ from the definitions used in state criminal statutes, and local police departments may classify similar incidents in different ways. Even within a single department, a particular crime could be regarded as a "theft" by one investigator and as a "burglary" by another, depending on their understanding of the circumstances of the crime. In short, the numbers that seem to represent factual incidents may obscure differences of opinion and interpretation.

Secondly, while measurable objectives are important and should be used to evaluate some aspects of an agency's performance, they are not the only indicators of an agency's effectiveness. In some respects, objective measures can be extremely misleading.

It is generally accepted, whether or not it should be, that patrol response time is a significant measure of police efficiency. It is probably universally true that citizens want the police to respond instantaneously when they call for help. However, the fact is that the vast majority of calls for police assistance do not involve an emergency and do not require an immediate response by a uniformed patrol officer. In many cases, a complainant's need for immediate attention can be satisfied if a report is taken by telephone—*provided* the citizen is reassured that the purpose of the telephone report is to enable the police to make an appropriate and timely investigation.

Some studies have shown that, on average, the length of time between a citizen's discovery of a crime and the initial report to the police (almost always by telephone) is much greater than the average patrol response time.[14] If it takes the victim half an hour to get around to calling the police, does it really matter whether the police respond in three minutes, five minutes, or ten minutes?[15]

What really matters to the citizen is the *quality* of the police response. Automatically dispatching a patrol officer to "investigate" every complaint is neither efficient nor effective; there needs to be a range of responses that are appropriate for the many different types of calls for assistance that a police agency receives. Implementing such a range of responses (which may include taking reports by telephone, referring the caller to another agency altogether, or sending a specialist investigator, in addition to the standard dispatching of a patrol officer) requires training the dispatcher or telephone operator not only to use the most appropriate response but also to explain to each caller the purpose and appropriateness of each response.

Finally, an excessive reliance on easily quantifiable measures may lead to what is often called "the activity trap."[16] If a person's or an agency's performance is evaluated solely on the basis of the number of activities reported, or some equally quantifiable measure, there is a natural inclination for the person or agency to perform as many such activities as possible, whether or not they are doing any good for anyone. If patrol officers are evaluated on the number of traffic tickets they issue, then naturally they will go out of their way to issue as many tickets as they can—even if it means neglecting other important duties. In extreme cases, the activity trap can lead to such disasters as fraudulent reporting.

We are not suggesting that measures of activity should be ignored. Changes in crime rates, clearance rates, response time, and other relatively straightforward performance measures are important and should be recorded, with proper attention to the flaws and dangers we have mentioned. However, these measures should not be misinterpreted as the sole indicator of an agency's effectiveness and success in achieving its objectives.[17] As we noted earlier, the qualitative performance of an agency also must be assessed, usually by less direct means than its quantitative performance.

Indirect Measures

Some aspects of a police agency's performance cannot be measured directly merely by collecting statistics on police activities.

For example, one of an agency's goals might be to reduce citizens' fear of crime and to increase the public's sense of security in their homes and neighborhoods. One might suppose that a reduction in the crime rate or an increase in the clearance rate would satisfy this goal, but the assumption may be false. Public *perceptions* of criminal activity (and other social conditions) do not always correspond to reality.

Unreported crime is another issue that requires indirect methods of measurement. It should be obvious that there is no direct method of measuring what is unknown. It is impossible to be certain whether changes in reported crime rates reflect actual increases or decreases in the volume of crimes committed, or merely a change in the proportion of unreported to reported incidents.

The very existence of a large volume of unreported crime was not even suspected until surveys were conducted by the National Opinion Research Center (NORC) in the mid-1960s. The surveys were funded in part by the Law Enforcement Assistance Administration and were intended to measure the public's general attitudes about crime and their local law enforcement agency. The discovery that many crimes are simply not reported to the police at all came as a shock to most police authorities.[18]

Surveys

Few police executives ever considered the use of public opinion surveys before the NORC studies. Since then, there has been growing interest in the use of this technique to measure agency performance.[19] Unfortunately, many police administrators still believe that opinion surveys are unreliable, unreasonably expensive, and irrelevant to their concerns.

We suggest that a well-designed, properly conducted survey can be immensely valuable as an indirect method of measuring an agency's performance.

Social scientists have refined the techniques of surveying to a high level of sophistication. All surveys are based on a simple principle: that it is possible to determine the public's attitudes or ideas about a given subject by sampling a small number of individuals.

There are three aspects of surveying that must be borne in mind:

- Surveys are most useful in determining attitudes, ideas, and beliefs, rather than specific facts.
- The wording of the questions in a survey is of critical importance in establishing the survey's validity and reliability.
- The selection of the individuals to be surveyed (the sample) is of critical importance in determining the overall reliability of the survey.

Many different methods of conducting surveys have been developed. Questionnaires can be sent by mail or other means to selected individuals, who are asked to fill out the form and return it. Questions also can be asked over the telephone or by person-to-person interview. Each method has advantages and disadvantages. Regardless of the survey method used, the wording of the questions is extremely important. A question is *valid* if it accurately provides the information that is being sought. A question is *reliable* if all respondents understand it clearly and answer it accurately. Validity and reliability together determine whether the answers accurately reflect the respondents' attitudes, beliefs, or ideas. In order to be both valid and reliable, a question must not influence the respondent to answer in any particular way.

The business of designing, conducting, analyzing, and interpreting a survey should not be performed by amateurs. As in most endeavors, the experience, integrity, and talent of the people who perform the survey will determine whether the results are reliable and useful. Very few police departments have staff members with the necessary training and experience to design, conduct, and interpret the kind of survey we have been discussing, nor do very many police departments need to have such people on their staff.

Besides commercial polling companies, there are nonprofit organizations that exist primarily to design and conduct opinion surveys on issues of general public interest or scientific interest. These organizations usually are associated with colleges and research institutions. There also are individuals in the academic community who have experience in performing surveys and who might be interested in working with a local police agency, either free of charge or at nominal cost.

The design and validation of the survey instrument (the list of questions) needs to be done only once. In subsequent years, the same questions and procedure should be used, with only minor modifications or corrections to improve the reliability of the results. By using the same questions and procedures every year, the results can be compared from year to year, and the cost of the survey design can be amortized over several years.

A police department can use surveys to learn what its clientele, the people in its community, want their law enforcement agency to do, how the people perceive crime and social conditions in the community, and whether the people are satisfied with the quality and quantity of police service that is being rendered. These and many other similar questions should serve as part of the evaluation of the agency's effectiveness, along with the objective performance measures we discussed earlier.

Unsolicited Compliments and Complaints

Letters to the police executive and other personnel, complaints filed by citizens against individual officers, letters to the editor of the local newspaper, and various other media of expression provide significant clues about the public's opinions. Someone in the police agency should be assigned the responsibility of collecting, summarizing, and analyzing this kind of material.

Of course, complaints against officers also must be investigated and, if the complaint proves to be valid, disciplinary procedures must be followed. Our point here is that the complaint also contains information about the citizen's expectations and perceptions of police performance. For example, a complainant might write something like, "This officer treated me rudely. I have never been treated so rudely by one of your officers before." While the complaint is an accusation against an individual officer, it is also indirectly a compliment to the agency as a whole: Apparently the citizen expects police officers, based on the citizen's past experience, to act courteously and professionally.

If many complaints all concern the same issues—such as rudeness of officers in their citizen contacts—there is a strong indication that something is wrong and needs to be addressed quickly, through changes in training, closer supervision, or, depending on the nature of the problem, adjustments in departmental policies.

Victimization Surveys

Surveys of the public are conducted periodically under the auspices of the U.S. Department of Justice to determine the extent of unreported crime, the effects of crime on victims, and the public's perceptions of crime problems. These surveys are generally national in scope, but some of the statistical information is analyzed for regional or metropolitan areas. This kind of information serves as a "quality check" for the local police.

Public Involvement in Evaluation

Finally, just as police agencies should involve the community in identifying law enforcement needs and problems, the police also should look to the community for participation in the evaluation of agency performance. A chief's forum or other citizen participation organization should be given a definite role in the evaluation process.

Ultimately, it is the citizens who pay the bills, through higher taxes and insurance premiums, for inadequate, inefficient, or ineffective police protection. They are the police department's customers, and it is the proper business of a community-policing agency to make sure that its customers are satisfied.

FOOTNOTES

1. George L. Kelling, Robert Wasserman, and Hubert Williams, "Police Accountability and Community Policing," in *Perspectives on Policing*, no. 7 (November 1988), 3.

2. George L. Kelling and Elizabeth M. Watson, "Creativity with Accountability," in Larry T. Hoover, ed., *Police Management Issues and Perspectives* (Washington, D.C.: Police Executive Research Forum, 1992), pp. 148-149.

3. David L. Carter, "Community Alliance," in Hoover, ed., *Police Management*, p. 80.

4. Alfred R. Stone and Stuart M. DeLuca, *Police Administration: An Introduction* 2nd ed. (Englewood Cliffs, N.J.: Prentice Hall, 1994), pp. 103-109. For more detail, see William H. Newman, E. Kirby Warren, and Jerome E. Schnee, *The Process of Management*, 5th ed. (Englewood Cliffs, N.J.: Prentice Hall, 1982), pp. 40-80.

5. V. A. Leonard, *The Police Records System* (Springfield, Ill.: Charles C. Thomas, 1970), pp. 56-57.

6. One of the first studies of unreported crime was reported by the National Opinion Research Council in 1966. See James Q. Wilson, *Thinking About Crime*, rev. ed. (New York: Basic Books, 1983), p. 66. See also Dennis Banas and Robert C. Trojanowicz, *Uniform Crime Reporting and Community Policing: An Historical Perspective* (East Lansing, Mich.: Michigan State University Press, 1985).

7. Commonwealth of Pennsylvania Department of the Auditor General, *Citizen's Guide to the Department of the Auditor General*, at http://www.auditorgen.state.pa.us/citguide/Performance.html (1997). Also, North Carolina Office of the State Auditor, *Performance Audits*, at http://www.sips.state.nc.us/OSA/perform/pasoup.htm (1997).

8. Comptroller General of the United States, *Government Auditing Standards, 1994 Revision* (Washington, D.C.: Comptroller General, 1995). This document is available at http://www.sips.state.nc.us/OSA/yellow/ybtoc.htm (1997).

9. Stephen A. Trodden, Inspector General, U.S. Dept. of Veterans Affairs, *Performance Auditing: The Perspective of a United States Inspector General*, address to the Organization for Economic Cooperation and Development Symposium on Performance Auditing and Performance Improvement in the Public Sector, Paris, France, June 6-7, 1995. This document is available at http://www.sbaonline.sba.gov/gopher/ignet/invent/innov/dvapaper.txt (1997).

10. Anthony V. Bouza, *The Police Mystique* (New York: Plenum Press, 1990), pp. 100-108.

11. The Austin Police Department, for example, has established computer-based tracking systems for parolees, gang members, and juvenile repeat offenders; see Sue Barton, *Self-Reliant Neighborhoods: A Bridge to the Future* (Austin, TX: Austin Police Department, 1996), p. 10.

12. For examples, see Bureau of Justice Assistance, *Understanding Community Policing: A Framework for Action* (Washington, D.C.: U.S. Department of Justice, 1994), pp. 18-21.

13. David H. Bayley, *Police for the Future* (New York: Oxford University Press, 1994), p. 10.

14. Wilson, *Thinking About Crime*, p. 71.

15. Bayley, *Police for the Future*, pp. 17-20.

16. Dennis R. Longmire, "The Activity Trap," in Hoover, ed., *Police Management*, pp. 117-132.

17. Kelling and Watson, "Creativity with Accountability," pp. 148-149.

18. Parviz Saney, *Crime and Culture in America* (Westport, Conn.: Greenwood Press, 1986), pp. 19-20.

19. R. M. Patterson and Nancy K. Grant, "Community Mapping: Rationale and Considerations for Implementation," in *Journal of Police Science and Administration*, 6, no. 2 (June 1988), 136-143.

SELECTED BIBLIOGRAPHY

The endnotes to each chapter include nearly all of the sources we have used in the preparation of this text. This annotated bibliography includes those that we have found most useful and that should be most widely available.

History of American Law Enforcement

Lawrence Friedman's *Crime and Punishment in American History* (New York: Basic Books, 1993) is a recent, scholarly, and highly readable overview of the history of American criminal justice, from pre-colonial days to the present. It should be considered an indispensable companion to the several histories of policing, including **Samuel Walker's** classic, *A Critical History of Police Reform* (Lexington, Mass.: Lexington Books, 1977); **James F. Richardson's** *Urban Police in the United States* (Port Washington, N.Y.: Kennikat Press, 1974); and **Robert Fogelson's** *Big City Police* (Cambridge, Mass.: Harvard University, 1977). **Arno Press** of New York has performed an exceptional service by reprinting some documents from the past, including the *Report of the Select Committee of the New York City Board of Aldermen on the New York City Police Department* (orig. 1844) and **August Vollmer's** report to the Los Angeles Board of Supervisors (orig. 1924).

Sociology of Crime

It would be hard to imagine a more comprehensive and profound study of the social aspects of crime and law enforcement than *Thinking About Crime*, by **James Q. Wilson** (New York: Basic Books, 1983, rev. ed.), which contains an expanded version of the article, "Broken Windows," co-written by **George Kelling**, which originally appeared in **Atlantic Monthly**. *Criminology and Justice*, by **Lydia Voigt, William E. Thornton Jr., Leo Barrile,** and **Jerrol M. Seaman** (New York: McGraw-Hill, 1994), offers a more recent and less philosophical overview. **Parviz Saney's** *Crime and Culture in America* (Westport, Conn.: Greenwood Press, 1986) presents an explicitly sociological approach to the subject.

Civil Rights and Law Enforcement

The history of the civil rights movement through the American legal system is outlined in *Crusaders in the Courts*, by **Jack Greenberg** (New York: Basic Books, 1994). For a more detailed look at the decisions of the U.S. Supreme Court under Chief Justice Earl Warren, see **G. Edward White**, *Earl Warren: A Public Life* (New York: Oxford University, 1982); Friedman also covers these matters thoroughly.

Community Policing, Problem-Oriented Policing, and Other Recent Reforms

If nothing else, the theorists and advocates of police reform have produced an impressive pile of literature. The general texts on community policing, problem-oriented policing, and variations on these themes that we have found most useful include (in no particular order):

Geoffrey P. Alpert and **Roger C. Dunham**, *Policing Urban America*, 2nd ed. (Prospect Heights, Ill.: Waveland Press, 1992).

Frank Schmalleger, *Criminal Justice Today* (Englewood Cliffs, N.J.: Prentice Hall, 1991)

Larry T. Hoover, ed., *Police Management: Issues and Perspectives* (Washington, D.C.: Police Executive Research Forum, 1992).

Bureau of Justice Assistance, *Understanding Community Policing* (Washington, D.C.: U.S. Department of Justice, 1994).

Herman Goldstein, *Problem-Oriented Policing* (New York: McGraw-Hill, 1990).

David H. Bayley, *Police for the Future* (New York: Oxford University, 1994)

Robert C. Trojanowicz and **Samuel L. Dixon**, *Criminal Justice and the Community* (Englewood Cliffs, N.J.: Prentice Hall, 1974).

In addition, the **U.S. Department of Justice** has published a series of monographs under the general title, *Perspectives on Policing.* Many of the issues concern community policing and its variants. **George L. Kelling, Herman Goldstein, Lee P. Brown,** and other leaders of the community policing movement have been frequent contributors.

Organizational Development and Change Management

The sheer volume of works on these subjects is overwhelming; we cannot claim to have examined more than a small sample, and may have overlooked some valuable works. However, we found these books, although not specifically concerned with law enforcement or police agencies, to be especially lucid and useful:

Leon Martel, *Mastering Change: The Key to Business Success* (New York: Simon & Schuster, 1986).

James Champy, *Reengineering Management* (New York: Harper Business, 1995).

James O'Toole, *Leading Change* (San Francisco: Jossey-Bass, 1995).

INDEX

A

Accessibility, 143–45
Activity trap, 173
Administrative Services, 101
Adolescents, 39–40
  and street crime, 69
Affirmative action, 129–30
African-Americans:
  and law enforcement, 22–25
  migration of, 22
Anticommunist hysteria, 18–21
Antidrug laws, 17–18
Anti-Saloon League, 7
Arrest vs. ignore concept, 65
Arthur, Chester A., 14
Articulateness, as candidate quality, 128
Assessment of the community, 76–77
  allies/resources, identifying, 88
  analyzing and interpreting, 85–88
  city manager/county supervisor, interviewing, 75
  common themes, identifying, 85–86
  constraints, identifying, 86
  draft of plan, circulating, 98–99
  goals/objectives, setting, 95–97
  mission statement, 88, 89
    example of, 91
  potential resistance, identifying, 86–87
  priorities, establishing, 91–95
  purpose of, 77
  sharing the results, 97–99
  stratified group meetings, 75–77
  values statement, 88, 90
    example of, 92
  vision statement, 88–89
    example of, 91
  what to ask, 77–79
Atomistism, of communities, 37
Austin Police Department, 105, 110–12
9-1-1 system, 116–17
Organizational Design Team (ODT), 110–11

Organizational Design Team (con't.)
  sector lieutenants, 111–12
  specialized programs, reorganization of, 112
  support lieutenants, 112
Automobile, and crime prevention, 18
Autonomous identity, 39

B

Bayley, David, 47–48
Beat profiling, 29
Beats, 44, 101
  assignments, 108
  redesigning, 107–8
Blizzard of Trivial Offenses, 65fn
"Broken Windows" article (Wilson/Kelling),
    27, 65
Brown, Lee P., 29, 48
Brown v. Board of Education, 5, 23
Bureau of Alcohol, Tobacco, and Firearms
    (ATF), 30
Burger Court, 22
Burger, Warren, 22

C

Call intervention, 115
Calls-for-service (CFS) profiles, 171–72
Carter, David L., 49
Carter, Jimmy, 25–26
"Cells," 20
Cellular telephones, 159
Central business district (CBD), 44–45
Chain of command, 103–4
Change:
  and crisis, 84–85
  dealing with, 82–85
  managing:
    human resources, 119–38
    structures and systems, 100–118
  See also Managing change
Chicago Alternative Policing Strategy
    (CAPS), 146
Cities:
  central business district (CBD), 44–45
  city planning, 45–46
  extraterritorial jurisdiction (ETJ), 45–46

gentrified neighborhoods, 45
  subdivision development, 45
  transition zone, 45
  zones, 45–46
Citizen-Oriented Police Enforcement (COPE)
    program (Baltimore, Md.), 29
Citizen satisfaction, measures of, 166
Civil disobedience, 23–24
Civilianization, 106
Civil Rights Act (1964), 25
Civil Service Reform Act (1883), 14
Civil War era, law enforcement in, 12, 13
Class, 67
Colonial period, law enforcement in, 9–10
Command and control system, 101–4
Common Council of New York City, 2, 10–11
Communist Manifesto, 18–19
Communities:
  adolescent groups, 39–40
  behavior patterns in, 38–39
  characteristics of, 66–73
  and geography, 36
  groups, 38–39
  social roles in, 38–39
  social science concepts, 38–43
  types of, 37
  See also Community characteristics
Community:
  assessing, 76–77
  and crime, 43–44, 63
  family as, 39
  as a place, 35–36
  sense of, 36–37
    neighborhoods lacking, 70
    Community characteristics, 66–73
  crime/poverty, 67–68
  degree of homogeneity/heterogeneity, 70–72
  mobility, 69–70
  precincts/neighborhoods, 67
  sociology/demography, 67
  stability, 69
Community involvement, 146, 165
Community knowledge, establishing, 142–45
Community life, quality of, 141
Community policing, 27–28, 29
  basic concept of, 94

components of, 48
conventional practices compared to, 124
and crime statistics, 55
defined, 47
development of, 74
evaluating, 161–63
  changing the criteria for, 162
  converting objectives to actions, 163
  criteria for, 163–67
  indirect methods of, 172–76
  missions/goals/actions, 162–63
implementation of, 122
myths/misconceptions about, 54–56
new models/assumptions, 52–53
and officer workload, 54–55
patrol officer, primary responsibility of, 158
and patrol officers as "social workers, 55–56
as a philosophy of policing, 31
police personnel roles, changes in, 126
primary function of patrol officers, 123
traditional law enforcement practices
  compared to, 54
Company towns, 46
Complaints:
  against officers, 175
  response to, and initial investigation, 62
Consolidation of programs, 107
Constables, 2, 9–12
Constitution of the United States, 3, 30
Continuing investigation, 62
Corruption, 15
Cressey, Donald, 51
Crime:
  and community, 43–44, 63
  defined, 3
  and globalization, 83–84
  measuring, 168–69
  and poverty, 67–68
  problem-solving approaches to, 149–51
  and technology, 83
  unreported, 174
Crime-magnets, legal businesses as, 145
CrimeNET, 112
Crime prevention, 63
Crime Prevention Bureau, 107
Crime-reduction strategies, 147–51

  hot spots, identifying, 147–49
  problem-solving approaches to crime, 149–51
Crime targeting, 28
Criminal behavior, causal factors, 68
Criminal Justice and the Community (Tro-
  janowicz/Dixon), 36
Cyclical change, 82–83

D

Debs, Eugene V., 19
Declaration of Independence, 3, 4
De facto ghettos, 71–72
Democratic National Convention antiwar
  demonstrations, 25
Demographic communities, 37, 41
Department of Labor, establishment of, 7
Digital pagers, 159
Directed-Area Response Team (DART)
  (Houston, Texas), 29
Directed patrol, 62–63
Discipline, 134–38
  conventional concepts of, 134
  true, expression of, 137–38
Dissent of the governed, 5–6
Districts, 44, 67, 101
Dixon, Samuel L., 36
Draft of plan, circulating, 98–99
Drug Enforcement Agency (DEA), 30

E

Eighteenth Amendment, 17
Eisenhower, Dwight D., 21, 23
Employee satisfaction, measures of, 166–67
Engels, Friedrich, 18–19
Ethnicity, use of term, 37fn
Executive-level personnel, and assessment of
  community needs, 75
Experimental district, identifying, 94
External authority, 75
Extraterritorial jurisdiction (ETJ), 45–46

F

Family:
  as a community, 39, 41

Family *(con't.)*
  surrogate, 40
Federal Bureau of Investigation (FBI), 17, 30
Field officers' reports, 143
First Amendment, 24
First-line supervisors, and assessment of community needs, 75
Foot patrol, 27–28
Fourteenth Amendment, 23

G

Gandhi, Mahatma, 24
Gentrified neighborhoods, 45
Geographical communities, 37, 41
  territories, 43–44
Geography, and community, 36
Ghettos, 70
  de facto, 71–72
  and heterogeneity, 72–73
Gideon v. Wainwright, 21
Globalization, and crime, 83–84
Global positioning satellite (GPS), 159
Goals:
  aligning organization and, 100–104
  setting, 95–97
Goldstein, Herman, 28
Great Depression, and drug abuse, 18
Griffin v. California, 21
Group meetings, 75–77

H

Hammurabi of Babylon, 2, 4
Heterogeneity:
  degree of, 70–72
  and ghettos, 72–73
Heterogeneous social groups, 4
Hierarchical relationships, 39
Hiss, Alger, 20
Homogeneity, degree of, 70–72
Homogeneous social groups, 4
Hoover, J. Edgar, 20
Hoover, Larry T., 65, 141
Houston, lack of zoning laws in, 46
Houston Police Department, 73
Hypotheses, 49

I

I Led Three Lives, 20
Indirect evaluation methods, 172–76
  objective measurement, limitations of, 172–73
  public involvement in evaluation, 176
  surveys, 174–75
  unsolicited comments/complaints, 175
  victimization surveys, 176
Information, sharing, 157–59
Integrity, 134–35, 137
Interest communities, 41
Internal authority, 75
International Association of Chiefs of Police (IACP), 15, 17, 18, 168
Investigations, 101
Investigator, change in role of, 109

J

Jim Crow laws, 5, 22
Johnson, Lyndon B., 24
Juries, 10
Jurisdiction, 43–44
  extraterritorial, 45–46

K

Kansas City preventive patrol experiment, 51, 62, 63
Kelling, George L., 27, 36, 65–66
Kennedy, John F., 24
Kent State University antiwar demonstration, 25
King, Martin Luther Jr., 23–24
Ku Klux Klan, 22

L

Larson, John A., 16
Law enforcement, 1, 8–18
  current state of, 29–31
Law enforcement agencies:
  and antiwar protests, 24
  as social group, 122–23
Law Enforcement Assistance Administration (LEAA), 25–26, 30, 174

funding of, 26–27
Law enforcement services, 62–63
Laws, 1–3
    creation of, 4–8
    and law enforcement, 1
Leadership, 134–38, 146
    true, expression of, 135–37
Lenin, V. I., 19
Locke, John, 3–5
London Metropolitan Police, 2, 11
Lower-level personnel, and assessment of
    community needs, 75
Loyalty, 134–35, 137
Lynch mobs, 22

M

McCarthy, Joseph, 20–21
McLaren, Roy C., 49
Magistrates, 9–10
Managing change, 100–118
    beats/shifts, redesigning, 107–8
    commanding and controlling, 101–4
    police organization-community partnership,
        104–10
Mapp v. Ohio, 21
Marijuana Tax Act (1937), 17
Marshals, 2, 10
Martel, Leon, 82–83
Marx, Karl, 18–19
Membership, and reference groups, 40–41
Minnesota Multiphasic Personality Test
    MMPT), 129
Minority recruitment, 129–30
Miranda v. Arizona, 21
Mission statement, 88, 89
    example of, 91
Mobile data terminals, 159
Mobility, 69–70
Montague, Ashley, 38
Montgomery bus boycott, 23
Mores, 4
Muir, William Ker, Jr., 38
Murphy, Patrick V., 36, 47
Murrow, Edward R., 20

N

National Association for the Advancing of
    Colored People (NAACP), 25
National Incident-Based Reporting System
    (NIBRS), 168fn
National Opinion Research Center (NORC),
    174
National Police Chiefs Union, 15
Neighborhood Crime Watch, 152
Neighborhood-oriented patrol, 145–46
    community involvement, 146
    neighborhood organization, 145–46
Neighborhood-oriented policing, 29
Neighborhoods, 37, 44, 46–47
    boundaries, recognition of, 107–8
    characteristics of, 66–73
    cities as collection of, 46
    managing, 141–42
    transitional, 66–67, 70
Newport News (Virginia) problem-oriented
    approach, 28–29
Nicholas, Czar of Russia, 19
Night watch, 10
9-1-1 system, 113–16
    nonemergency calls to, 113–15
    priority system, 115
    teleserve unit, establishing, 114–15
Nixon, Richard M., 22, 24–25
Nonautomotive patrol, 64
Nonenforcement services, 63–64
Nuclear family, 39

O

Objectives, setting, 95–97
Omnibus Safe Streets and Crime Control Act
    (1968), 25
Order maintenance, 64–66
    community definitions of order, 64–65
    seeking an alternative to, 65–66
    traditional views of, 64
Organization, aligning with its goals,
    100–104, 108
Organizational Design Team (ODT), Austin
    Police Department, 110–11
Organizational structure, 164–65

P

Parent authority, 75

Parks, Rosa, 23

Patrol, 2–3, 101, 103
  as backbone of police force, 105–6
  directed, 62–63
  foot, 27–28
  neighborhood-oriented, 145–46
  officers' workload, managing, 116
  random automotive, 64
  watches, 2, 101

Peel, Robert, 2, 61

Peers, 39

Pendleton Act, 14

Performance auditing, 169–71
  in Austin/Travis County, TX, 170
  standards for, 169

Performance evaluation system, 125–27
  in community policing agency, 127

Plessy v. Ferguson, 5

Police, and the community, 27–28

POLICE acronym, 91

Police agencies:
  aligning structure of, 91–95
  evaluating performance of, 167–72
    by indirect methods, 172–76
  performance auditing, 169–71
  primary purpose of, 120
  as social groups, 122–23
  specialized programs, accumulation of, 107

Police brutality, 25

Police-community partnerships, 104–10
  Austin Police Department, 152–56
  beyond neighborhoods, 151–52
  developing, 151–57
  levels of, 156–57
  partisanship, 157

Police executive, 101–2
  and assessment of community needs, 75
  role of, in traditional agency, 124–25

Police Executive Research Forum (PERF), 28

Police Foundation, 26–27

Police reports, 109

Police services, 62–64
  law enforcement services, 62–63

nonenforcement services, 63–64
  regulatory enforcement services, 63

Policies, 103

Policing:
  concept of, 47–49
  philosophy of, defining, 49
  reinvention of, 25–29
  team, 27

Poverty, and crime, 67–68

Precincts, 44, 67, 101

Priorities, establishing, 91–95

Problem-oriented policing, 28, 149–51, 172

Problem-Oriented Policing (Goldstein), 29

Procedures, 103

Professional model of policing, 49–51
  failure of, 51

Prohibition, 7–8, 17

Prohibition Party, 7

Punishment, for performance, 126–27

Q

Quality of life, 141

Quality of service, 165–66

R

RAND Corporation, 26
  criminal investigation study, 51

Random automotive patrol, 64

Rebellion, adolescent, 40–41

Recidivism, 171

Recruitment/selection, 127–29
  affirmative action, 129–30
  minority recruitment, 129–30
  screening, 128–29
  training, 130–34

Red Scare, 18–21

Reference groups, 41–43

Regulatory enforcement services, 63

Resistance to change, identifying, 86–87

Resources:
  freeing, 106–7
  inefficient use of, 103

Review processes, 143

Rewards, for performance, 126–27

Roll-out, scheduling, 94

Roosevelt, Theodore, 22
Rosenberg, Julius and Ethel, 19–20
Rousseau, Jean Jacques, 3, 5
Rules, 103

S

Seattle Crime Prevention Council (SSCPC), 74
Second Treatise of Civil Government, The
    Locke), 3
Secret Service, 30
Sectors, 101
Segregation, 24–25
Sheriffs, 9–10, 12
Shifts, redesigning, 107–8
Single point of contact (SPOC), 144–45, 158
Skolnick, Jerome, 47–48
Slavery, 13
Social Contract, The (Rousseau), 3
Social disorder, 67–68
Social roles, 122
Socioeconomic status, 67
Spoils system, 12
Stalin, Josef, 19
Street crime, defined, 69
Street detectives, 112
Structural change, 83
Support Services, 101
Supreme Court, 18, 21–23
Surreptitious investigation, 62
Surrogate-family group, 40
Surveys, 174–75
    victimization, 176
Sutherland, Edwin, 51
Sweep-and-sift approach, to
    recruitment/selection, 128–29
Sykes, Gary, 36

T

Team policing, 27
Technical Services, 101
Technology, 83, 158–59
    and handling of information, 143
    use of, 116–18
Territories, 43–44
Test bed, identifying, 94

Texas Commission on Law Enforcement Offi-
    cer Standards and Education
    (TCLEOSE), 130–31
Texas Criminal Code, 3
Trade unions, 6–7
Training, 130–34
Transitional neighborhoods, 66–67, 70
Transition zone, 45
Trojanowicz, Robert J., 27–28, 36
Truman, Harry S., 21, 23
Trust, 134–35, 137
Twenty-first Amendment, 8
Two-way radio systems, 159

U

Un-American Activities Committee, 21
Uniform Crime Reporting System (UCRS), 168
Unions, 6–7
Unreported crime, 174
Upper-level managers:
    and assessment of community needs, 75
    in community-policing agencies, 124
U.S. Department of Justice, 48–49, 65

V

Values statement, 88, 90
    example of, 92
Victimization surveys, 176
Vietnam War protests, 24
Vision statement, 88–89
    example of, 91
Vollmer, August, 15–17, 49, 51, 61, 105, 128
Volstead Act, 17
Voting Rights Act (1965), 25

W

Wards, 44
War protests, 24
Warren Court, 21–23
Warren, Earl, 21
Watches, 2, 101
Watson, Elizabeth M., 29, 73–74
Weber, Max, 102
White Citizens' Councils, 23
Whitmire, Kathy, 29

Wilson, James Q., 27, 36, 65–66
Wilson, Orlando W., 49, 51
Women's Christian Temperance Union, 7
Workload, managing, 113–16

Y

Yellow Book, 169

Z

Zones, 45–46
Zoning authority, 45